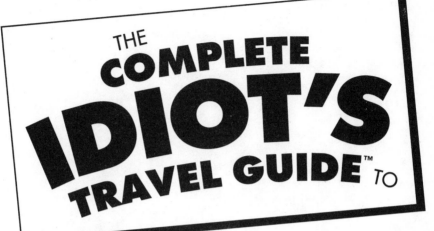

New Orleans

by Big Ray Jones

Macmillan Travel   Alpha Books
Divisions of Macmillan Reference USA
A Simon & Schuster Macmillan Company
1633 Broadway, New York NY 10019-6785

MACMILLAN is a registered trademark of Macmillan, Inc.
FROMMER'S is a registered trademark of Arthur Frommer. Used under license.
THE COMPLETE IDIOT'S GUIDE name and design are trademarks of Macmillan, Inc.

ISBN 0-02-862303-7
ISSN 1096-7621

Editors: Matt Hannafin and Vanessa Rosen
Special thanks to Mary Herczog
Production Editor: Christy Wagner
Page Layout: Angela Calvert & Daniela Raderstorf
Proofreaders: Kim Cofer & Megan Wade
Design by designLab
Digital Cartography by Peter Bogaty & Ortelius Design
Illustrations by Kevin Spear

Special Sales

Bulk purchases (10+ copies) of Frommer's and selected Macmillan travel guides are available to corporations, organizations, mail-order catalogs, institutions, and charities at special discounts and can be customized to suit individual needs. For more information, write to: Special Sales, Macmillan General Reference, 1633 Broadway, New York, NY 10019.

Manufactured in the United States of America

Contents

Maps

About the Author

"Big Ray" Jones has been living in New Orleans for all of his adult life. He is licensed by the city of New Orleans as a tour guide and currently works as a taxi driver, where he uses his extensive knowledge of the city to entertain his passengers. Before taking up the life of a cabby, "Big Ray" used to give historical, romantic, and fun tours on mule-drawn carriages through the French Quarter.

When he's not behind the wheel, "Big Ray" is behind a computer, writing about the city he knows and loves. He writes a column for a small French Quarter newsletter called *Vieux Carre Verite*. You can also find him on the Internet either hosting a discussion group called the New Orleans Mailing List or at his Web page (www.neosoft.com/~rayjones/welcome.html), which is chock-full of information about New Orleans as well as the state of Louisiana.

Acknowledgments

I'd like to dedicate this book to the members of my New Orleans Internet mailing list who love New Orleans so much they can hardly let a day go by without talking to someone about their city. I'd also like to thank members of the Greater New Orleans Freenet, my friends, members of my family, and espe-cially my wife, without whose help this book would not have been possible.

An Invitation to the Reader

In researching this book, we discovered many wonderful places—hotels, restaurants, shops, and more. We're sure you'll find others. Please tell us about them, so we can share the information with your fellow travelers in upcoming editions. If you were disappointed with a recommendation, we'd love to know that, too. Please write to:

The Complete Idiot's Travel Guide to New Orleans
Macmillan Travel
1633 Broadway
New York, NY 10019

An Additional Note

Please be advised that travel information is subject to change at any time—and this is especially true of prices. We therefore suggest that you write or call ahead for confirmation when making your travel plans. The author, edi-tors, and publisher cannot be held responsible for the experiences of readers while traveling. Your safety is important to us, however, so we encourage you to stay alert and be aware of your surroundings. Keep a close eye on cameras, purses, and wallets, all favorite targets of thieves and pickpockets.

The following abbreviations are used for credit cards:

AE	American Express		EURO	Eurocard
CB	Carte Blanche		JCB	Japan Credit Bank
DC	Diners Club		MC	MasterCard
DISC	Discover		V	Visa
ER	enRoute			

Introduction

If New Orleans is the Big Easy, shouldn't it be easy to find your way around and have fun here? The answer is yes—up to a point. After that point, you need a good local friend to show you his favorite haunts. And that's where I come in. I'll walk you through every step involved in creating the perfect vacation from start to finish, describing everything from exploring the birthplace of jazz to enjoying some of the best gourmet food in the world and strolling with you through the picturesque and historic streets of the French Quarter—the "old city" of New Orleans.

The Complete Idiot's Travel Guide to New Orleans is divided into six parts, and from necessities such as deciding when to go, finding the best hotel in your price range, and learning the lowdown on the French Quarter to hedonistic pleasures such as satisfying your craving for authentic Cajun cuisine and hearing some jazz greats, it'll steer you in the right direction.

Part One explains all you need to know before you go. When it comes to vacations, a little advance planning can make a big difference. You may be asking yourself about the best time to go to New Orleans, how to get there, whether to join a tour, and how much it's all going to cost. Maybe you're wondering if Mardi Gras is the right time to come. You'll find the answers in this section, as well as the scoop on all the goings-on in New Orleans from Jazz Fest to the Tennessee Williams Festival. You'll also find useful addresses, phone numbers, and Web sites where you can get more information and budget tips and worksheets that will help you manage your finances and compare airfares and schedules.

Part Two is all about hotels. I give you the skinny on which are the best New Orleans neighborhoods to stay in and share some ideas on how to find the bargains. A special feature of this book is the use of indexes, which divide up listings into special categories, so that before you read through all my reviews, you'll already have an idea of which places are in the best neighborhoods and in your price range.

Part Three gets you from the airport, train station, or highway to your local hotel, with specific instructions on locating a shuttle or taxi. Once you settle in, you'll want to know where to go. I describe where things are, explain how to get around in the city, and detail each neighborhood.

Part Four feeds you information about the New Orleans dining scene from casual Cajun to some of the most elegant gourmet restaurants in the world. Once again, indexes are provided to help you narrow down your choices.

Part Five describes the sights, from the French Quarter to the best parks and most interesting historic buildings. Because planning your sightseeing can be tiring work, I've provided some sample itineraries to get you started and created a chapter that will lead you through the process of planning an itinerary of your own.

Part Six belongs to the night. It covers the major night spots, from the best places to hear jazz and zydeco to unique nighttime cruises around the city. It also explains where to find out what's happening, where to buy tickets, and how to avoid the French Quarter crowds.

Extras

This book has several special features that you won't find in other guidebooks and that will help you use the information efficiently. As mentioned previously, **indexes** cross-reference the information in ways that let you see at a glance what your options are in a particular subcategory—Creole restaurants, French Quarter hotels, kid-oriented sights, and so on. I've also sectioned off little tidbits of useful information in **sidebars,** which come in five different packages.

Dollars & Sense

Here you'll find tips on saving money and cutting corners to make your enjoyable trip affordable.

Bet You Didn't Know

These boxes offer you interesting historical facts or trivia about the city.

Extra! Extra!

These boxes provide handy facts, hints, and insider advice.

Tourist Traps

These boxes steer you away from rip-offs, activities that aren't worth it, shady dealings, and pitfalls to be avoided.

Time-Savers

Here you'll find ways to cut down on downtime, avoid lines and hassles, and streamline the business of traveling.

Sometimes the best way to fix something in your mind is to write it down, and with that in mind, I've provided **worksheets** to help organize your thoughts. (Underlining or highlighting as you read along isn't a bad idea, either.)

A **kid-friendly icon** is used throughout the book to identify those activities, attractions, and establishments that are especially suited to people traveling with children.

Appendixes at the back of the book list important numbers and addresses covering every aspect of your trip, from reservations to emergencies.

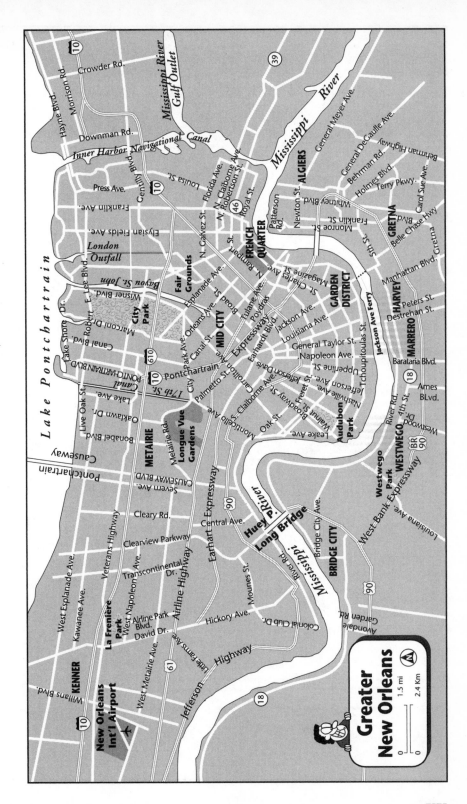

Greater New Orleans

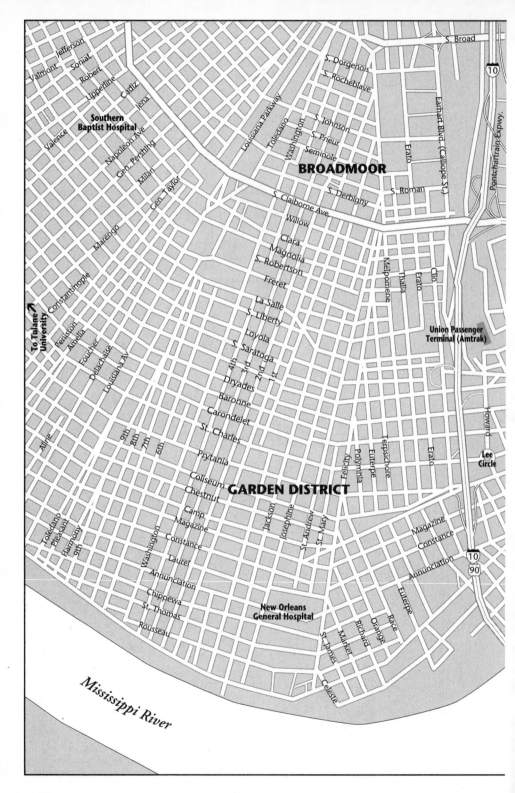

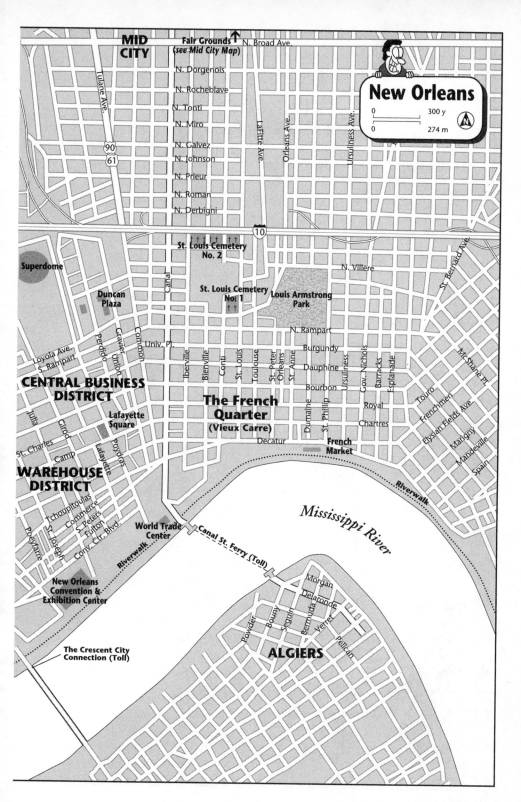

City Park
and Mid City Area

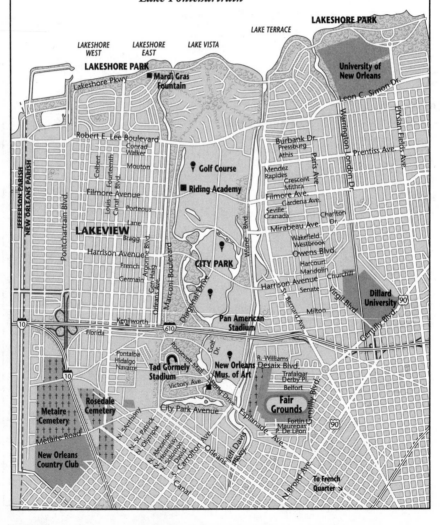

Part 1

Be Prepared: What You Need to Do Before You Go

Welcome to Europe! Now, in case you're scratching your head over that, let me clue you in to this: When you make a trip to New Orleans, you get a dose of French culture and a smattering of Spanish, plus a healthy helping of West African and Native American cultures. All these ingredients are mixed up into one of the richest cultural stews around. With New Orleans' rich history and diverse population, a vacation there is almost like taking a trip around the world.

You won't have to cross the Atlantic, but you will have to get there from wherever you are, and that's where this section of the book comes in. I'll share everything you'll need to know to plan your trip, including how to decide when to go, how to find the cheapest tickets, when to book your room, and what to bring. I'll also let you in on what you'll need to know if you're planning to visit during Mardi Gras or one of the other million festivals celebrated here. Remember, knowledge is power, and this section will make you knowledgeable enough to get your trip arranged the way you want it.

How to Get Started

Information, Please

Your visit begins long before you set foot in a plane, train, or car. The first step in any trip is to accumulate travel facts. If you have a phone, a computer, or just a pen and some stamps, you can assemble a wealth of information about the city from the privacy of your own home by inquiring with local tourist offices, the Chamber of Commerce, and travel sites on the Internet—your mailbox will be full of tourist brochures in no time. Just remember, though, that almost every one of them will have been produced by someone with a vested interest in luring you in, so they're not going to be what you'd call unbiased. Take everything they promise with a grain of salt, and compare your data with information in this book (or if you want to augment our info, with the listings in one of those super mondo complete, explore-every-nook-and-cranny guidebooks, such as *Frommer's*).

Direct from the Horse's Mouth: Information Resources

You may find these sources useful when you start to plan your visit. Many other more specific sources will be mentioned throughout the guide.

➤ The **New Orleans Metropolitan Convention and Visitors Bureau** (1520 Sugar Bowl Drive, New Orleans, LA 70112; ☎ 800/672-6124 or 504/566-5003; Web site **www.nawlins.com**) is an old hand at helping visitors plan trips to New Orleans.

➤ For information on all the festivals in the area, contact the **Louisiana Association of Fairs and Festivals** at ☎ 504/446-1462 or write to them at 601 Oak Lane, Thibodaux, LA 70301.

➤ Check out the New Orleans section of the *Frommer's* Web site at **www.frommers.com**.

➤ If you're interested in going beyond New Orleans and exploring Louisiana, call the **Louisiana Office of Tourism** (☎ 800/261-9144); write to them at PO Box 94291, Baton Rouge, LA 70804; or check out their Web site at **www.louisianatravel.com**.

➤ You can reach **The Greater New Orleans Black Tourism Network** by phone at ☎ 800/725-5652 or 504/523-5652 or on the Web at **www.gnobtn.com**.

➤ A great source of New Orleans festival information is on the Internet at **neworleans.net/festpages/festhome.html**.

Bet You Didn't Know

During the 18th century, French colonists in Acadia, Nova Scotia, who were displaced by British rule, moved to the new French territory of Louisiana and formed an outpost in the countryside some 100 miles west of New Orleans. Over 200 years later, and a little to the west of New Orleans, you'll find the descendants of these Acadians, some still involved in farming and trapping, still holding on to their unique brand of French, and proudly calling themselves "Cajuns."

Crawling the Web

If you're hooked up to the Internet, it's a good idea to visit New Orleans on the information superhighway before visiting in the flesh. The following list of Internet resources will get you started. From any one site you can usually find links to hundreds of related sites.

➤ **www.neosoft.com/~rayjones/welcome.html** is my home page. Check it out.

➤ **www.frenchquarter.com** is an information source for all things related to the French Quarter.

➤ **www.usacitylink.com/citylink/mardigr** is the official Mardi Gras Web site, with parade schedules, scenes from last year's celebration, 50 Mardi Gras and Cajun food recipes, and more.

➤ **www.neworleans.net** is the official site of the *Times-Picayune* newspaper and is loaded with info on festivals, sightseeing, weather, and more.

➤ **www4.linknet.net/dixiepixie/fqrats.htm** is the home page of the New Orleans French Quarter Rats, a group of locals who share inside info on the city.

➤ **www.amberle.com/mgt/** is Amberle's Mardi Gras Tidbits page, with Mardi Gras stories, images, information, and route maps.

➤ **www.lhin.lsu.edu/** is the home of Louisiana Heritage Internet, a guide to resources on the natural and cultural heritage of Louisiana and the Lower Mississippi Delta.

➤ **www.planet9.com/vrnewo.htm** presents virtual 3-D images of New Orleans, with scale models of the Superdome, the World Trade Center, Jackson Square and the French Quarter, and more. Touch one of the images with your cursor to display the name and address of the building.

➤ **www.gayneworleans.com** is just what it sounds like: an Internet resource for gay locals and travelers to New Orleans.

When Should I Go?

Your trip will be a lot more enjoyable if you travel to New Orleans at the right time of year. But when *is* the right time? If you're trying to get away from crowds, forget about Mardi Gras and Jazz Fest, when the city is overrun by visitors and hotel rooms are booked up ages in advance. On the other hand, you could easily *be* one of that horde, if you plan way ahead.

Another crowd-control measure is to call the **New Orleans Metropolitan Convention and Visitors Bureau** (☎ **800/672-6124** or 504/566-5005) to see whether there are any conventions scheduled for the time you hope to visit. New Orleans has become a mecca for conventions in recent years, and depending on the size of the event, a convention could affect your ability to find a room.

It's the Heat: And *also* the Humidity

If you're really looking to have the city to yourself, come to New Orleans in the summer, when tourism is down and temperatures are up—and I mean *way* up. It can get up into the 90's or 100's and stay there for days or weeks at a time, and it isn't any of that Arizona dry heat, either; it's wet, sticky, and heavy. New Orleans heat settles in like a sleazy uncle and won't go away.

Some people like that, though. You've been warned. The period between Thanksgiving and Christmas is also traditionally slow.

Singin' in the Rain

New Orleans normally gets more than 60 inches of rain each year. Statistically speaking, the rain in any one month is pretty much the same as in any other; however, May is when most of the record-breaking downpours have been recorded. July is the wettest month, and October is the driest. On average, it rains one day out of every three during the year, but New Orleans also has been drenched with as much as 18 inches of rain in 24 hours. Basically, it could rain most anytime. Come prepared.

The following is a simple chart listing the average high and low temperatures in Fahrenheit and centigrade, as well as the average rainfall in inches and the average number of rainy days each month. (Information was compiled from National Weather Service records, 1870 through 1996.)

Time-Savers

If there are two or more in your party, take a cab from the airport instead of the Airport Shuttle. The price is nearly the same, and it's a lot faster, more private, and much more convenient.

	JAN	FEB	MAR	APR	MAY	JUN	JUL	AUG	SEP	OCT	NOV	DEC
AVERAGE HI °F	62°	65°	71°	78°	84°	90°	91°	90°	87°	80°	70°	65°
AVERAGE HI °C	17°	18°	22°	26°	29°	32°	33°	32°	31°	27°	21°	18°
AVERAGE LOW °F	45°	48°	54°	61°	68°	73°	75°	75°	73°	62°	53°	48°
AVERAGE LOW °C	7°	9°	12°	16°	20°	23°	24°	24°	23°	17°	12°	9°
INCHES RAIN	5	5	5	5	5	5	7	7	6	3	4	5
RAINY DAYS	10	9	9	7	8	10	15	13	10	5	7	10

Don't Get Left Out in the Cold: Bringing the Right Clothes for the Season

As you can see from the chart, New Orleans doesn't have much of a winter. December, January, and February are the coldest months, but the term "cold" is pretty relative: average highs are in the 60's and 70's and average lows are in the mid 40's. Occasionally, the temperature dips into the 20's or 30's, but these cold snaps don't last very long. The temperature, however, can change very quickly. The temperature may drop as much as 20 or 30 degrees from morning to evening. It can be in the mid 70's or even 80's one day and in the 40's or 50's the next.

During the **winter months,** come expecting mild weather, but be prepared for chilly or even cold weather. Most of the time, you'll be fine in short-sleeved garments, but bring a light jacket or sweater for those cool evenings and for air-conditioned restaurants. If you have the room, consider bringing a medium-weight jacket as well.

March, April, and **May** are very pleasant, weather-wise, with average highs in the 70's and 80's and lows in the 50's and 60's. It gets chilly in early March and hot near the end of May, but for the most part, it's clear sailing. Bring a light sweater or jacket along, just to be on the safe side.

From **June through September** the average highs are in the 80's to mid 90's and often soar into the 100's, with humidity near 100% as well. During this time of year, New Orleans meteorologists can go on vacation because the forecast is pretty much the same day after day: hot with a chance of afternoon showers. Take my advice: In midsummer, wear lightweight and light-colored clothing. Limit your outdoor excursions to the morning and evening or nighttime hours. If you venture out in the middle of the day, use sunscreen and drink plenty of fluids.

The weather in **October** and **November** is similar to what you can expect in March, April, and May, but the nights are sometimes a little cooler. These two months are the driest of the year, but that doesn't mean it won't rain.

Extra! Extra!

The first two to three weeks of December are usually slow. In order to attract customers, hotels and restaurants often offer bargain rates. This is a great time to experience New Orleans without the crowds or the high prices.

Bet You Didn't Know

Even mules, who are genetically programmed to live in warm climates, are taken off the streets if it gets too hot. Use this fact as a weather indicator; if you don't see any mules around, it might be best to stay inside.

Gone with the Wind: Hurricanes in New Orleans

In addition to heat, summer in New Orleans also means tropical storms and hurricanes. Our hurricane season begins June 1 and ends November 30, with most storms taking place in August, September, and October. They're not common, though: Only 17 major hurricanes have struck anywhere along the Gulf Coast in the past 97 years, and the last one to hit New Orleans came through more than 30 years ago. Of course, there have been a few close calls.

Bet You Didn't Know

The first statue in the United States dedicated to a woman can be found in New Orleans at the corner of Camp and Prytania streets. Margaret Haughery was an Irish immigrant who devoted her life and the profits from her business to taking care of orphans. When she died, her fortune was left to charity. The statue was erected in 1884.

Hitting the Big Events & Festivals

If you're coming to town to see a big festival such as Mardi Gras or Jazz Fest, then this whole discussion of weather may be academic: You'll be gearing your trip to take advantage of the event, and weather be damned. Of course, if you are coming for one of these big festivals, you need to do more advance planning than you'd otherwise have to do. The city gets unnaturally crowded and expensive, and finding places to stay and eat becomes a Herculean task.

What follows is a seasonal list of the big events. For a more detailed discussion of the festivals, see chapter 4.

January/February/March

➤ The **USF&G Sugar Bowl Football Classic** is played on January 1st, and the crowds start pouring in around late December. If you like football and you have lots of money to spend, this is the perfect time to visit. Call ☎ **504/525-8573** for more information.

➤ **Carnival** begins January 6 and ends on Mardi Gras day. Most of Carnival is local and doesn't affect tourism, except for the two weeks leading up to Mardi Gras. At this time, good luck finding a vacant hotel room within 100 miles of the city (if you haven't reserved ahead). Call ☎ **800/672-6124** or 504/566-5055 for specific dates.

➤ **Mardi Gras** day always falls on the Tuesday 46 days before Easter. It can

Time-Savers

Few events in New Orleans are held on the same date each year. For exact dates, check with the **Louisiana Association of Fairs and Festivals** (☎ **504/446-1462**) or the **Louisiana Office of Tourism** (☎ **800/261-9144**). Another great source of information on every festival in the state is the *Times-Picayune* festivals listing, on the Web at **neworleans.net/festpages/festhome.html**.

be as early as February 3 or as late as March 9. On this day and most of the two weeks preceding it, life is hectic in the Big Easy, to put it mildly. Call ☎ **800/672-6124** or 504/566-5055 for more information.

➤ **The Black Heritage Festival** is a two-day celebration with craft exhibits, soul food (such as jambalaya, fried chicken, and gumbo), and live music. It's usually held in late February or early March along the Riverwalk, in Audubon Park, and at the various Louisiana State Museum buildings. Call ☎ **800/774-7394** or 504/581-4629 for more information.

April/May/June

➤ **St. Patrick's Day** is always March 17, and parades and celebrations take over the city. Call ☎ **504/525-5169** for more info. The Downtown Irish Club always sponsors a parade the Friday before St. Patrick's Day.

➤ **St. Joseph's Day** falls on March 19, and the Italians often celebrate in conjunction with the Irish St. Patrick's Day, with parades and sumptuous food offerings. Call ☎ **800/672-6124** for more information.

➤ Held over four days in March, the **Tennessee Williams New Orleans Literary Festival** celebrates the life of this famous playwright with performances, lectures, and walking tours. Call ☎ **504/286-6680** or check out the Web site at **www.gnofn.org/~twfest**. You can contact the box office at ☎ **800/479-8222.**

➤ During the **Spring Fiesta,** visitors can take tours of historic private homes and gardens that are usually not open to visitors. It's held in late March or early April. Call ☎ **504/581-1367** for more information.

➤ The **French Quarter Festival** is held on the second weekend in April (unless it conflicts with Easter). It's meant to be a local event, but it's getting bigger and more popular every year and may soon rival the Jazz and Heritage Festival as a tourist attraction. There's plenty of free entertainment (unlike Jazz Fest, which is by ticket only) and inexpensive food, making it a great time to come. Check room availability first—like I said, this festival is getting more popular every year. Call ☎ **800/673-5725** or 504/522-5730. The Web site is located at fqfestivals.org.

➤ The **New Orleans Jazz and Heritage Festival** is held the last weekend in April (Friday through Sunday) and the first weekend in May (Thursday through Sunday). After Mardi Gras, this is the biggest festival, and if you like great music and fantastic food, this is the time to come. It's crowded, prices are higher, and hotel and restaurant reservations are hard to come by—so plan ahead. When Jazz Fest ends, some people start counting the days until the next one. Call ☎ **504/522-4786** or check out the Web site at **www.nojazzfest.com.**

➤ The **Greek Festival,** celebrated over the last weekend in May, features Greek food, dancing, crafts, and music. Call ☎ **504/282-0259** for more information.

➤ The **Reggae Riddums Festival** will transport you to a Caribbean island with calypso, reggae, and regional food. It's held over the second weekend in June. Call ☎ **888/767-1317** or 504/367-1313 for more information.

July/August/September

➤ The relatively new **Essence Festival** will be held here for the fourth consecutive year over Fourth of July weekend in 1998, but it could leave town after that. An estimated 40,000 to 50,000 people come together to hear performers such as Gladys Knight, Patti LaBelle, The Isley Brothers, Kenny G., Maya Angelou, Clarence Carter, and Irma Thomas. Call ☎ **800/725-5652** or 504/523-5652 or check the Web site at **www.gnobtn.com**.

➤ If it's the weekend before Labor Day, it must be **Southern Decadence.** During this festival, thousands of gay men and lesbians converge upon the city and, on Sunday, assemble in the 1200 block of Royal Street to follow a secret parade route known only to the grand marshal. There are drag queens galore; there's lots of drinking—it's wild. Call ☎ **800/876-1484** or 504/522-4087, or check out the Web site at **www.southerndecadence.com**.

October/November/December

➤ The conventioneers are coming! Fall is prime convention season. Conventions of 10,000 or even 20,000 people are commonplace. To find out when they'll be here (and thus avoid them), you can call the **New Orleans Metropolitan Convention and Visitors Bureau** at ☎ **800/672-6124** or 504/566-5005, or check its Web site at **www.neworleanscvb.com**. You can also call the Convention Center directly at ☎ **504/582-3000.**

➤ Fall is also **football season.** An average of 38,000 (out of a capacity of 77,000) attended New Orleans Saints games at the Superdome in 1996, but with Mike Ditka as the Saints new coach, you can expect that number to increase. Although most fans live locally, restaurants fill up quickly and taxis become harder to find. Check with the **Saints** office at ☎ **504/731-1700** for scheduled home games.

➤ **Louisiana Jazz Awareness Month** takes place in October. There are nightly concerts, lectures, and special radio programs, all sponsored by the **Louisiana Jazz Federation.** Call ☎ **504/522-3154** for more information.

➤ Generally held during the second weekend in October, the **Gumbo Festival** is a feast for sore stomachs, with every type of gumbo you can imagine—and lots that you can't—plus carnival rides, games, and jazz, blues, and Cajun music to help you get your appetite up. Call ☎ **504/436-4712** for more information.

➤ **Halloween** in New Orleans is ghoulish. For children, there's the Boo-at-the-Zoo (October 30 and 31) and a yearly program at the **Louisiana**

Children's Museum (☎ **504/523-1357**; Web site: **www.lcm.org**). For adults, events include the Anne Rice Vampire Lestat Extravaganza, the Moonlight Witches Run, and the French Market Pumpkin Carving and Decorating Contest (☎ **800/460-0865** or 504/522-0865). For information on all these events, call the New Orleans Metropolitan Convention and Visitors Bureau (☎ **800/672-6124** or 504/566-5055).

➤ Thanksgiving weekend is the annual **Bayou Classic,** a college football rivalry between Grambling University and Southern University at Baton Rouge. Approximately 75,000 people turn out to witness this clash, so make your hotel and restaurant reservations early. ☎ **504/ 771-3170.**

➤ During the **Celebration in the Oaks,** running from late November to early January, sections of City Park are draped with lights and light- ed figures in holiday themes. The display is open for walking tours, dri- ving tours, and carriage tours. Call ☎ **504/483-9366** or 504/483-9415 for info.

➤ The Jackson Square **New Year's** celebration is beginning to look a little like New York's, with a lighted ball dropping from the top of Jackson Brewery.

We Are Family: Traveling with Your Kids

When it comes to satisfying the kids at a hotel, a rooftop swimming pool, a cool elevator, or even a friendly staff can make all the difference in the world. In chapter 7, I'll identify places I think your kids might like with an easy-to-spot icon. I've also used the same symbol to highlight restaurants and attractions that children usually enjoy.

Preparation

To help make your trip fun for your kids as well as yourself, let them partici- pate in the planning process. Encourage them to read through this book and through any tourist brochures you get and allow them input in organizing your sightseeing schedule. If they feel like it's their vacation too, they'll be more likely to have fun when they get there.

Tourist Traps

If you're bringing your car to New Orleans, be sure to ask beforehand how much your hotel or motel charges for parking. If the rate is high—some places charge more than $20 a day—you can save a bundle by spending a few minutes driving around and finding one of the many $5 or $10 parking lots in the Central Business District and French Quarter.

Keeping the Kids Entertained

No matter how much planning you do, your kids may get bored and cranky. Be sure to take along some toys or activities that will keep them occupied. You know your kids better than I do. If they like to color, bring along some coloring books and crayons. If they like music, bring along a radio or a portable CD player. If they like to read, let them pick some books to bring.

Throughout chapters 14 and 15, I've highlighted attractions that kids particularly enjoy. Here are some of my picks:

➤ Mimes, clowns, and other street performers in the French Quarter

➤ Canal Street Ferry ride across the river

➤ Beignets at Café du Monde

➤ Louisiana Children's Museum

➤ City Park

Dollars & Sense

Take a ride over to Algiers on the Canal Street Ferry. It's a great way to see the Mississippi River up close, kids enjoy it as much as adults, it can even be romantic, and best of all, it's free!

You can also call **Accents on Arrangements** at ☎ **504/524-1227** to learn about their special New Orleans children's tours.

Sitting Services for Kids

If you want to leave the kids and go out on your own, some hotels provide baby-sitting services; just ask the hotel's concierge. If your hotel doesn't provide such a service, you should call the following agencies. They'll sit with your kids, take them on organized outings, or create a personalized itinerary:

➤ **Accents on Children's Arrangements** (☎ **504/524-1227**); licensed, bonded, insured

➤ **Dependable Family Care** (☎ **504/486-4001**); licensed, bonded, insured; 24 hours

➤ **Kinder Friend** (☎ **504/469-5059**); licensed, bonded, and insured; 24 hours

Travel Advice for the Senior Set

People over the age of 60 are traveling more than ever before. And why not? Being a senior citizen entitles you to some terrific travel bargains. If you're not a member of **AARP** (American Association of Retired Persons), 601 E St. NW, Washington, DC 20049 (☎ **202/434-AARP**), do yourself a favor and join. You'll get discounts on car rentals and hotels.

Sears' Mature Outlook, P.O. Box 9390, Des Moines, IA 50306-9519 (☎ **800/336-6330;** fax 847/286-5024), is a similar organization, offering discounts on car rentals and hotel stays at many Holiday Inns, Howard

Johnson's, and Best Westerns. The $20 annual membership fee also gets you $100 in Sears coupons and a bimonthly magazine. Membership is open to all Sears customers 18 and over, but the organization's primary focus is on the 50-and-over market.

In addition, most of the major domestic airlines, including American, United, Continental, US Airways, and TWA, all offer discount programs for senior travelers—be sure to ask whenever you book a flight. In most cities, people over the age of 60 get reduced admission at theaters, museums, and other attractions, and they can often get discount fares on public transportation. Carrying identification with proof of age can pay off.

The Mature Traveler, a monthly 12-page newsletter on senior-citizen travel is a valuable resource. It is available by subscription ($30 a year) from GEM Publishing Group, Box 50400, Reno, NV 89513-0400. GEM also publishes *The Book of Deals,* a collection of more than 1,000 senior discounts on airlines, lodging, tours, and attractions around the country; it's available for $9.95 by calling ☎ **800/460-6676.** You get this book for free when you order the newsletter. Another helpful publication is *101 Tips for the Mature Traveler,* available from Grand Circle Travel, 347 Congress St., Suite 3A, Boston, MA 02210 (☎ **800/221-2610** or 617/350-7500; fax 617/350-6206).

Grand Circle Travel is one of hundreds of travel agencies specializing in vacations for seniors. But beware: Many of these trips are of the tour bus variety, with free travel thrown in for those who organize groups of 20 or more. Seniors seeking more independent travel should consult a regular travel agent. **SAGA International Holidays,** 222 Berkeley St., Boston, MA 02116 (☎ **800/343-0273**), offers inclusive tours and cruises for travelers 50 and older.

Advice for Travelers with Disabilities

There are more options and resources out there than ever before, so there's no reason to let a disability stop you from traveling. *A World of Options,* a 658-page book of resources for travelers with disabilities, covers everything from biking trips to scuba outfitters. It costs $45 and is available from **Mobility International USA,** P.O. Box 10767, Eugene, OR 97440 (☎ **541/343-1284,** voice and TDD; **www.miusa.org**). For more personal assistance, call the **Travel Information Service** at ☎ **215/456-9603** or 215/456-9602 (for TTY).

Many of the major car rental companies now offer hand-controlled cars for drivers with disabilities. **Avis** can provide such a vehicle at any of its locations in the United States with 48-hour advance notice; **Hertz** requires 24 to 72 hours advance notice at most of its locations. **Wheelchair Getaways** (☎ **800/642-2042** or 800/536-5518; www.blvd.com/wg.htm) rents specialized vans with wheelchair lifts and other features for travelers with disabilities in more than 100 cities across the United States.

Travelers with disabilities may also want to consider joining a tour that caters specifically to their needs. One respected company is **FEDCAP Rehabilitation Services,** 211 W. 14th St., New York, NY 10011. Call ☎ 212/727-4200 or fax 212/721-4374 for information about membership and summer tours.

Vision-impaired travelers should contact the **American Foundation for the Blind,** 11 Penn Plaza, Suite 300, New York, NY 10001 (☎ 800/232-5463), for information on traveling with seeing-eye dogs.

Building Accessibility

Most of the historic sites and a few of the older hotels and restaurants in New Orleans are exempt from the provisions of the Americans with Disabilities Act (ADA) and may present problems for people with disabilities. I've noted in the relevant chapters which places will be problematic, but be sure to call ahead and check.

All of the major hotels are in compliance with the ADA, although some of the smaller hotels and most notably the bed and breakfasts are either not in compliance or only partially so. Among hotels, the **Westin** receives the biggest thumbs-up, and the **Dauphine Orleans, Hotel de la Poste, Monteleone,** and **Royal Orleans** are also rated highly.

The following helpful sources will make your visit easier:

➤ **Terry's Taxis** is owned by, and caters especially to, people with disabilities. They have two vans equipped to handle wheelchairs. Call ☎ 504/283-4100 for reservations.

➤ The **Regional Transit Authority** also has lift-equipped buses available for individuals as well as for groups. Call ☎ 504/242-2600.

➤ If you're hearing-impaired and have a Telecommunication Device for the Deaf (TDD), the **Louisiana Relay Service** (☎ 800/947-5277) offers a connection service that connects you with non-TDD users.

➤ Travelers with disabilities can also call **Resources for Independent Living** at ☎ 504/522-1955.

Advice for Gay & Lesbian Travelers

New Orleans is one of the most gay- and lesbian-friendly cities in the United States and perhaps in the world. Bars, restaurants, hotels, and other businesses owned by or catering to gays and lesbians abound (the majority of them in or near the French Quarter), and there's always a big gay turnout for Mardi Gras, Halloween, and especially the Southern Decadence Festival.

I've listed and reviewed good gay-friendly choices for hotels, restaurants, and nightlife in the relevant chapters of this book, but here's some hints:

➤ **Best hotel choices** for gay and lesbian travelers are the **Lafitte Guest House,** the **New Orleans Guest House,** and the **Ursuline Guest House,** all in the French Quarter.

➤ **Best restaurant picks** are **Lucky Cheng's** and the **Quarter Scene** in the French Quarter and **Feelings** and **La Peniche** in the Faubourg Marigny.

➤ **Best lesbian nightlife choices** are **Charlene's** and **Rubyfruit Jungle,** both in the Faubourg Marigny. (Rubyfruit also welcomes gay men.)

➤ **Best gay nightlife choices** are **The Bourbon Pub/Parade Disco,** the **Golden Lantern, Good Friends, Café Lafitte in Exile, MRB, Oz,** and **Rawhide 2010** (all in the French Quarter) and **Phoenix** in the Faubourg Marigny.

New Orleans Publications for Gays & Lesbians

When you get to town, pick up one of these publications to find out what's what and where it's at. (And when you're planning your trip, their Web sites are invaluable.)

➤ *Pink Pages* (☎ **504/947-3969;** www.neworleanspinkpages.com)

➤ *Ambush 2000* (☎ **800/876-1484** or 504/522-4087; www.ambushmag.com)

➤ *Impact* (☎ **504/944-6722;** www.impactnews.com)

Miscellaneous Resources for Gay & Lesbian Travelers

➤ The **Gay and Lesbian Community Center,** 816 N. Rampart St. (☎ **504/522-1103**)

➤ **Alternative Tours and Travel** (☎ **504/949-5815**)

➤ **Avalon Travel Advisors** (☎ **504/525-1303**)

➤ **Big Easy Lodging** (☎ **800/368-4876** or 504/433-2563; fax 504/391-1903; Web site **www.crescentcity.com/fql/**)

➤ **French Quarter Reservation Service** (☎ **504/523-1246;** e-mail fqrs@accesscom.net)

➤ **Tande Reservations/Community Travel** (☎ **504/552-2910;** e-mail hyxg55a@prodigy.com)

➤ **French Quarter Accommodations** (☎ **800/209-9408** or 504/552-2910; fax 504/552-2918; Web site **www.crescentcity.com/fqaccom/**)

➤ **Gay New Orleans Online** (**www.gayneworleans.com**)

➤ **Alternative Tours and Travel** (☎ **504/949-5815** or 504/943-5805)

➤ **Community Travel Advisors** (☎ **504/552-2913**)

Chapter 2

Money Matters

In This Chapter

➤ The lowdown on traveler's checks, cash, and credit cards

➤ Tips for traveling on the cheap

➤ Budgeting your trip

Money matters quite a bit to me—as I'm sure it does to you, too. They say it can't buy happiness, but since happiness in New Orleans often means a big pot of gumbo and a ticket to a jazz show, I'd say they're *wrong*.

Of course, to the vacationer happiness also means a comfortable seat on the plane, a decent hotel room, and the freedom to enjoy the town in style, so you'll want to stretch your money as far as you can and get the most bang for your vacation buck. In this chapter, I'll show you how to do just that and go into other bits of financial planning.

One way to save money is to read all the "Dollars and Sense" sidebars located throughout this book. These sidebars contain lists of things that are free or inexpensive. You'll be surprised how cheaply you can have fun.

Should I Carry Traveler's Checks or the Green Stuff?

Traveler's checks are something of an anachronism from pre-ATM days, when people used to write personal checks all the time instead of carrying bundles of cash. In those days, travelers could not be sure of finding a place that would cash their checks, and so traveler's checks—which could be recognized worldwide and replaced if they were lost or stolen—were a sound alternative to traveling with your fortune in your wallet. These days, traveler's checks are less necessary because most cities have 24-hour ATMs linked to a national network that most likely includes your bank at home.

ATMs to the Left of Me, ATMs to the Right of Me...

No matter how much you have in traveler's checks, you should always have some cash handy. After all, you can't ask a vending machine or parking meter if it takes traveler's checks, and most taxi drivers insist on cash as well. The amount you carry depends on your individual needs, but as a general rule you should only keep as much on your person as you'll need for a day or two. After all, you can always go to an ATM for more.

Dollars & Sense

Although you'll be able to get in touch with your money through ATMs, you may have to pay a price for the privilege, particularly at non-bank locations. There are cash machines in such out-of-the-way places as supermarkets and indoor arcades, which is convenient if you've been forgetful, but you may be charged $1 or more for the transaction.

The merchants of New Orleans most certainly do *not* want you to run out of money, and for that reason you'll find 24-hour ATMs almost everywhere. In the French Quarter and the Central Business District, you'll find them in almost every major hotel as well as on the streets and in many bars, daiquiri shops, smaller hotels, shopping centers, and restaurants. During larger events, mobile ATMs are even brought in, and there's often one next to the Hard Rock Cafe on Decatur Street. The following is a list of some of the most conveniently located streetside ATMs in the French Quarter:

➤ Corner of Chartres and St. Ann

➤ 400 block of Chartres near K-Paul's restaurant

➤ Corner of Chartres and Toulouse

➤ Corner of Royal and Iberville

➤ 240 Royal St.

Cirrus (☎ **800/424-7787** or 800/4CIRRUS) and **Plus** (☎ **800/843-7587**) are the two most popular networks; check the back of your ATM card to see which network your bank belongs to. The 800 numbers will give you specific locations of ATMs where you can withdraw money while on vacation. There are often limits on the amount of cash you can withdraw. Note, however, that many banks have begun to impose a fee ranging from 50¢ to $3 every time you use the ATM in a different city. Your own bank may also charge you a fee for using ATMs from other banks.

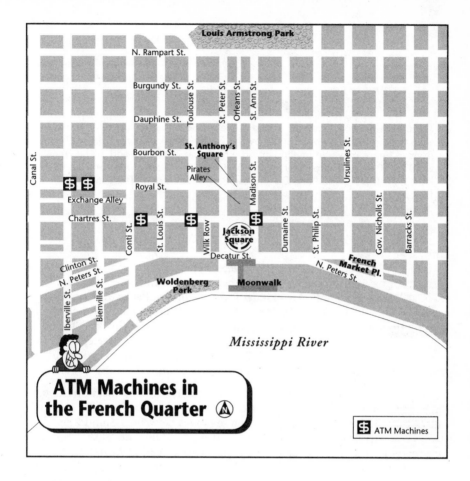

ATM Machines in the French Quarter

Local banks belonging to the Plus, Cirrus, and Pulse networks include:

➤ **Deposit Guaranty.** 321 St. Charles St. ☎ **504/837-3333.**

➤ **First NBC.** 210 Baronne St. ☎ **800/826-3390** or 504/561-8500.

➤ **Regions Bank.** 301 St. Charles St. ☎ **800/888-9293** or 504/587-1888.

➤ **Schwegmann Bank.** 6600 Franklin Ave. ☎ **504/361-5555.**

➤ **Whitney Bank.** 430 Chartres St. ☎ **504/838-6565.**

Bet You Didn't Know

The use of the word *Dixie* originated in New Orleans before the Civil War as a term for the $10 bank note issued by the Citizens Bank of New Orleans. The front of the note was in English, and the back was in French, and as the French word for 10 was *dix* (pronounced dee or dees), these bank notes came to be known as "Dixies," and New Orleans came to be known as "The Land of Dixies."

Check It Out

If you feel you need the security of traveler's checks and don't mind the hassle of showing identification every time you want to cash one, you can get them at almost any bank. **American Express** offers checks in denominations of $10, $20, $50, $100, $500, and $1,000. You'll pay a service charge ranging from 1 to 4%, although AAA members can obtain checks without a fee at most AAA offices. You can also get American Express traveler's checks over the phone by calling ☎ 800/221-7282; American Express gold and platinum cardholders who call this number are exempt from the 1% fee.

Citibank offers **Citibank Visa** traveler's checks at Citibank locations across the country and at several other banks. To find the Citibank closest to you, call ☎ 800/541-8882. The service charge ranges between 1.5 and 2%; checks come in denominations of $20, $50, $100, $500, and $1,000. For information on non-Citibank **Visa** travelers checks, call ☎ 800/732-1322. **MasterCard** also offers traveler's checks. Call ☎ 800/223-9920 for a location near you.

Plastic Money

Credit cards are invaluable when traveling. They're a safe way to carry money, and they provide a convenient record of all your travel expenses when you arrive home. Plus, if you run short of the green stuff, you can get cash advances from your cards at any bank (although you'll start paying interest on the advance the moment you receive the cash, and you won't receive frequent-flyer miles on an airline credit card). At most banks, you don't even need to go to a teller; you can get a cash advance at the ATM if you know your PIN number. If you've forgotten your PIN number or didn't even know you had one, call the phone number on the back of your credit card and ask the bank to send it to you. It usually takes 5 to 7 business days to get your PIN number, although some banks will give it to you over the phone if you give them your mother's maiden name or offer some other form of ID.

Dollars & Sense

To save time and money, get your information from the Internet. Both **American (www.americanair.com)** and **Continental Airlines (www.flycontinental.com)** have weekly electronic newsletters offering special fares. The **Marriott (www.marriott.com)** and **Hilton (www.hilton.com)** hotel chains have similar offers on their room rates. Also check out **www.traveler.net, www.expedia.com, www.travelweb.com, www.amtrak.com,** and **www.thetrip.com** for discount travel information, and see appendix B at the back of this book for even more helpful Web sites.

Stop, Thief! (What to Do If Your Money Gets Stolen)

Almost every credit card company has an emergency 800 number you can call if your wallet or purse is stolen. The company may be able to wire you a cash advance off your credit card immediately, and in many places you can get an emergency credit card in a day or two. The issuing bank's 800 number is usually on the back of the credit card, but that doesn't help you much if the card was stolen, does it? **Citicorp Visa**'s U.S. emergency number is ☎ **800/645-6556. American Express** cardholders and traveler's check holders should call ☎ **800/221-7282** for all money emergencies. **Master-Card** holders should call ☎ **800/307-7309.** Or you can call **800 information** at ☎ **800/555-1212** to find out your card's or traveler's check issuer's 800 number. If you opt to carry traveler's checks, be sure to keep a record of their serial numbers in a safe place so you can handle just such an emergency.

Odds are that if your wallet is gone, you've seen the last of it, and the police aren't likely to recover it for you. However, after you realize that it's gone and you cancel your credit cards, it's still worth a call to inform the police. You may need the police report number for credit card or insurance purposes later.

So What's This Trip Gonna Cost?

Budget, budget, who's got a budget? You will, if you want to avoid any nasty pocketbook surprises. The cost of some things, like hotels, is relatively inflexible and along with airfare or other transportation costs will be the largest part of your expenditure. Other things, such as transportation in the city, will be relatively cheap. The incredible number of restaurants and nightlife choices in New Orleans are as different in cost as they are in the kind of experience they offer, and it's entirely up to you whether you opt for the dress-up or dress-down variety. Check out the budget worksheet at the end of this chapter for help in figuring out where your money's going to go.

Lodging

Lodging is the least elastic part of your budget. Although you can find inexpensive rooms, they're often far from the center of town or they don't offer much in the way of amenities. You'll more than likely spend a minimum of $90 to $100 a night.

Transportation

Transportation around the city is a relative bargain. Most of the hotels and attractions are in the French Quarter or Central Business District and are within a mile of one another. If the sight you want to see is farther away than you want to walk—or if it's a really uncomfortably hot day—a taxi ride won't break the bank. Unless traffic is heavy, the average trip in or around the Quarter should be no more than $5.

If you want to take **public transportation,** you can hop one of the city's buses or the streetcar. Fares range from $1 to $1.25 each time you get on, but a three-day **VisiTour** pass costs only $8 and entitles you to unlimited bus and streetcar rides. Check with your hotel's concierge or call ☎ **504/ 248-3900** for regional transit information. Many hotels also offer free shuttles to and from the French Quarter or Central Business District. For more information on getting around the city, see chapter 9.

Tourist Traps

Here's a common scam: Someone will come up to you and bet that (a) they can tell you where you got your shoes, or (b) they can spell your last name. Here's what you tell them:
  (a) "I got my shoes right here on my feet."
  (b) "'Your last name' is spelled Y-O-U-R L-A-S-T N-A-M-E."
Better yet, don't even talk to them.

Dining

Dining options in New Orleans range from the very inexpensive to the astronomical. Since finding great food for high prices is never a problem, think about your bottom line. If you're really trying to eat cheap, you can get coffee and beignets for breakfast at Café du Monde for $2.40, a $5 po boy for lunch at any one of a hundred places, and dinner for under $15 at a place like the Café Maspero in the Quarter or Louisiana Pizza Kitchen in the Mid City area.

Dollars & Sense

Question: How many times a day can you stop to buy a soda or bottled water ($1 or more a pop) when it's 99 degrees and 95% humidity? Answer: a lot. Carry your own bottle and refill it at your various stops. A dumb way to save? It could be your lunch money.

Attractions
Your budget for entrance fees and admissions will depend, of course, on what you want to see, but unless you're traveling with your whole family it shouldn't make too much of a dent in your budget (at least not as much as food and lodging will). Refer to the attraction listings in chapter 14 and make a list of your "must sees," and then figure out your costs from the ticket prices given there.

Shopping
Again, money for shopping is a flexible part of your budget, and you don't have to buy anything at all if that's your style, but self-restraint can be a tough thing when you're faced with all the fine shops in town. As an international port city, New Orleans has access to more imported items than many other American cities. Therefore, you can find just about whatever you need from just about whatever place you can name. And if your interest is in antiques, New Orleans can oblige. It's been around for a while, after all, and many of the antiques you'll find in town came from Europe in the early days.

If you're just looking for some souvenirs to take home as proof of the trip, there are whole colonies of shops selling postcards, posters, sunglasses, and T-shirts in the French Quarter. You could go hog wild and blow your whole budget on Bourbon Street T-shirts, or you could shop for that one perfect $3 snow globe. It's up to you.

Entertainment
Unlike a city like New York, where you practically have to mortgage your house to afford tickets to the theater, most of the nightlife in New Orleans is relatively inexpensive—but again, it's your personal preferences that count; you'll obviously spend more if you go to the opera than if you head to the Dragon's Den for some jazz.

Turn to chapters 19 and 20 for the nightlife listings. I've put in detailed information on ticket prices and cover charges, so adding a few of these up (and padding your estimate to allow for a few drinks and sundries) should give you a good idea of how much you'll spend over the course of your trip. (*Hint:* You'll probably spend more than you think you will. Keep that in mind and think realistically.)

What Things Cost in New Orleans

Taxi from the airport to the Central Business District or French Quarter	$21
Bus from airport to downtown	$1.50
St. Charles streetcar ride for one (one-way)	$1
Riverfront streetcar ride for one (one-way)	$1.25
Bus ride for one (one-way)	$1
Average taxi ride for one (add 75¢ each for extra people)	$5
Inexpensive ($) hotel room for two	under $75
Low-moderate ($$) hotel room for two	$75–$125
High-moderate ($$$) hotel room for two	$125–$175
Expensive ($$$$) hotel room for two	$175–$250
Very expensive ($$$$$) hotel room for two	over $250
Inexpensive ($) breakfast for one	$3–$4
Moderate ($$) breakfast for one	$6–$8
Expensive ($$$) breakfast for one	$25–$50
Inexpensive ($) lunch for one	$5–$8
Moderate ($$) lunch for one	$10–$15
Expensive ($$$) lunch for one	$15–$20
Inexpensive ($) dinner for one	$15–$20
Moderate ($$) dinner for one	$25–$30
Expensive ($$$) dinner for one	$35–$50
Non-alcoholic drink	$1–$1.50
Bottle of beer	$1.50–$4
Cocktail	$3.50–$8
Cup of coffee	50¢–$1.50
Roll of ASA 100 Kodacolor film, 36 exposures	$7.50
Admission to New Orleans Museum of Art	$6
Theater ticket at Le Petit Theatre	$18–$25

Dollars & Sense

For an **inexpensive breakfast or snack,** try Café du Monde, located at the beginning of the French Market right by Jackson Square. It's open 24 hours a day and is famous for its **beignets**—a square, deep-fried doughnut that comes hot, crisp, and covered with confectioner's sugar. It's the official doughnut of Louisiana, and you can get a sack of three with a cup of coffee for $2.40 (tax included).

Tipping
The golden tipping rule for most services (including restaurants and taxis) is to add 15% to your bill, although you should make sure the tip hasn't already been added if you're with a large group, as restaurants will sometimes add a 15% to 20% gratuity to the bill for parties of 6 or more. If you're just drinking at a bar, 10% to 15% is typical. Bellhops get $1 or $2 per bag, maids $1 per day, coat check people $1 per garment, and automobile valets $1.

What Are All Those Dollar Signs?
In certain places in the book—for example, in the hotel and restaurant listings—you'll see one or more dollar symbols ($) attached to each item. These symbols are neither decorative nor arbitrary; they're keyed to a scale at the beginning of the chapter and help you tell at a glance what particular bracket that item falls into. For example, a hotel prefaced by "$$" will cost $75 to $125, and one marked "$$$" will cost $125 to $175.

What If I'm Worried That I Can't Afford It?
If you've been keeping a mental tally of what you think you'll spend on your trip and are worried that you can't afford it, relax. Go over the worksheet at the end of this chapter carefully. If the number comes out too high, think about where you can, or are willing to, economize.

There are plenty of ways, some little and some big, to cut down on costs. Note the "Dollars and Sense" boxes scattered throughout this book, which offer hints on places to trim your budget. Up front, here are a few ways to save a little money:

➤ **Go in the off-season.** If you can handle the heat, you can get some great deals from June through August—but be warned that when I say it's hot, I mean it's *hot*. The first three weeks of December are also downtime in the tourist industry and so are another good bet for getting a deal.

➤ **Travel on off days of the week.** Airfares vary depending on the day of the week. If you can travel on a Tuesday, Wednesday, or Thursday, you may find cheaper flights to your destination. When you inquire about airfares, ask whether you can obtain a cheaper rate by flying on a different day. Also remember that staying over a Saturday night can cut your airfare by more than half.

➤ **Reserve your flight well in advance** (taking advantage of APEX— Advance Purchase Excursion—fares), or watch the last-minute "e" fares online for bargains. (See "Surfing the Web to Fly the Skies" in chapter 3 for a discussion of online strategies.)

➤ **Try a package tour.** For many destinations, one call to a travel agent or packager can net you airfare, hotel reservations, ground transportation, and even some sightseeing, all for a lot less than if you tried to put the trip together yourself. (See the section on package tours in chapter 3 for specific suggestions of companies to call.)

➤ **Pack light.** That way, you can carry your own bags (don't forget to tip yourself) and take a bus rather than a cab from the airport.

➤ **Always ask for discount rates.** Always ask for corporate, weekend, or other discount rates. Membership in AAA, frequent-flyer plans, trade unions, AARP, or other groups may qualify you for discounted rates on plane tickets, hotel rooms, car rentals, and even meals. Ask about everything—you could be pleasantly surprised.

➤ **Ask whether your kids can stay in your room with you.** A room with two double beds usually doesn't cost any more than one with a queen-size bed, and many hotels won't charge the additional-person rate if the additional person is pint-sized and related to you. Even if you have to pay $10 or $15 for a rollaway bed, you'll save hundreds by not taking two rooms.

➤ **Try expensive restaurants at lunch instead of dinner.** Lunch tabs are usually a fraction of what dinner would cost at most top restaurants, and the menu often boasts many of the same specialties.

➤ **Get out of the Quarter.** Hotels outside the French Quarter tend to be less expensive than those within it, so if you don't mind the slightly longer trip to most of the attractions, book yourself into a hotel in the Faubourg Marigny, Uptown, or along the Esplanade Ridge. See chapters 6 and 7 on hotels for more information.

➤ **Study up on the public transit system.** What could be more romantic than traveling around New Orleans on the streetcar? Not much, and it only costs $1 or $1.25. The bus is somewhat less romantic, but it will still cost less than relying solely on taxis. See chapter 9 for more info.

➤ **Walk a lot.** You'll save money, get your exercise, and see the city the way it was meant to be seen: from the ground and at a slower pace. Be sure to pack a good pair of walking shoes—the last thing you need on vacation is sore feet. (*Note:* Don't overdo the walking if you're in town during a really hot spell.)

➤ **Skip the souvenirs.** Your photographs and your memories are the best mementos of your trip, so if you're worried about money, skip the tourist shops. After all, you don't really *need* those riverboat salt-and-pepper shakers, do you?

Budget Worksheet: You Can Afford This Trip

Expense	Amount
Airfare (multiplied by number of people traveling)	
Car rental (if applicable)	
Lodging (multiplied by number of nights)	
Parking (multiplied by number of nights)	
Breakfast (multiplied by number of nights) *Note: May be included in your room rate*	
Lunch (multiplied by number of nights)	
Dinner (multiplied by number of nights)	
Baby-sitting	
Attractions (admission charges to museums, monuments, tours, theaters, nightclubs, and so on)	
Transportation (cabs, streetcars, buses, and so on)	
Souvenirs (T-shirts, postcards, that thing you just gotta have)	
Tips (think 15% of your meal total plus $1 a bag every time a bellhop moves your luggage)	
The cost of getting to and from the airport in your hometown, plus long-term parking (multiplied by number of nights)	
Grand Total	

How Will I Get There?

Getting there may not *really* be half the fun, but it certainly gives you a lot of choices to make. Are you going to wrangle through them yourself, or get a travel agent to help you? And when you arrive, will you feel comfortable working the town on your own or will you want the kind of guidance you get with a group tour? This chapter will help you sort out the answers to these questions.

Travel Agent: Friend or Foe

A good travel agent is like a good mechanic or a good plumber: hard to find, but invaluable once you've found the right person. The best way to find a good travel agent is the same way you find a good plumber or mechanic or doctor—word of mouth.

Any travel agent can help you find a bargain airfare, hotel, or rental car, but a good travel agent will stop you from ruining your vacation by trying to save a few dollars. The best agents can tell you how much time you should budget in a destination, find a cheap flight that doesn't require you to change planes in every other city, get you a better hotel room than you can find on your own at no additional cost, and arrange for a competitively priced rental car.

Travel agents work on commission. The good news is that *you* don't pay the commission—the airlines, hotels, and tour companies do. The bad news is that unscrupulous travel agents will try to persuade you to book the vacations that net them the most money in commissions.

To make sure you get the most out of your travel agent, do a little home-work. Read about your destination (you've already made a sound decision by buying this book) and pick out some accommodations and attractions you think you'd like. If you have access to the Internet, check prices on the Web yourself in advance so you can do a little prodding. (See "Fighting the Airfare Wars" later in this chapter for more information on how to do that.) Then take your guidebook and Web information to the travel agent and ask him or her to make the arrangements for you. Because travel agents have access to more resources than even the most complete Web travel site, they should be able to get you a better price than you could get by yourself. They also can issue your tickets and vouchers. If they can't get you into the hotel of your choice, they can recommend an alternative, and you can look for an objec-tive review in your guidebook right there and then.

In recent years, most airlines and resorts have begun limiting travel agent commissions or eliminating them altogether. The immediate result has been that some travel agents are beginning to add a service charge. Be sure to ask your agent about these extra costs so you're not taken by surprise when the bill comes.

Should I Join a Guided Tour or Travel on My Own?

Do you like to let a bus driver worry about traffic while you sit in comfort and listen to a tour guide explain everything you see? Or do you prefer going out and following your nose, even if you don't catch all the highlights? Do you like to have lots of events planned for each day, or would you rather improvise as you go along? The answers to these questions will determine whether you should choose the guided tour or travel a la carte.

Some people love guided tours. These tours free you from spending lots of time behind the wheel; they take care of all the details; and they tell you what to expect at each attraction. You know your costs up front, and there aren't many surprises. Guided tours can take you to the maximum number of sights in the minimum amount of time with the least amount of hassle.

Other people need more freedom and spontaneity—and they can't *stand* guided tours. They prefer to discover a destination by themselves and don't mind getting caught in a thunderstorm without an umbrella or finding that a recommended restaurant is no longer in business. That's just the adventure of travel.

If you do choose a guided tour, ask a few simple questions before you sign on:

1. **What's the cancellation policy?** Do you have to put a deposit down? Can the tour company cancel the trip if it doesn't get enough people? How late can you cancel if you are unable to go? When do you pay? Do you get a refund if you cancel? If *the company* cancels?

2. **How jam-packed is the schedule?** Does the tour company try to fit 25 hours' worth of activities into a 24-hour day or is there ample time for relaxing and shopping? If you don't enjoy getting up at 7am every day and not returning to your hotel until 6 or 7pm at night, certain guided tours may not be for you.

3. **How big is the group?** The smaller the group, the more flexible it'll be and the less time you'll spend waiting for people to get on and off the bus. Tour operators may be evasive about this, because they may not know the exact size of the group until everybody has made their reservations, but they should be able to give you a rough estimate. Some tour companies have a minimum group size and may cancel a tour if they don't book enough people.

4. **What's included?** Don't assume anything. You may have to pay to get yourself to and from the airport. Or a box lunch may be included in an excursion, but drinks might cost extra. Or beer might be included, but wine might not. How much choice do you have? Can you opt out of certain activities, or does the bus leave once a day, with no exceptions? Are all your meals planned in advance? Can you choose your entree at dinner, or does everybody get the same chicken cutlet?

Here's a few reputable travel companies in New Orleans that provide guided tours:

➤ **Destination Management** (☎ **888/670-4638** or 504/524-5030; Web site http://dmi.accesscom.net)

➤ **First Discount Travel** (☎ **504/455-8747**)

➤ **Custom Tour & Travel** (☎ **800/414-4896** or 504/523-7939)

If you choose an guided tour, seriously consider purchasing trip-cancellation insurance, especially if the tour operator asks you to pay up front. But don't buy insurance from the tour operator! If the tour operator doesn't fulfill its obligation to provide you with the vacation you've paid for, there's no reason to think it'll fulfill its insurance obligations either. Get travel insurance through an independent agency. See the section on travel insurance in chapter 5.

The Pros & Cons of Package Tours

Package tours are not the same thing as escorted tours. With a package, you travel on your own but pay group rates for airfare and accommodation. For a popular destination like New Orleans, this type of tour can save you a ton of money. In many cases, a package that includes airfare, hotel, and transportation to and from the airport will cost you less than just the hotel alone if you booked it yourself. That's because packages are sold in bulk to tour operators, who resell them to the public. It's kind of like buying your vacation at Sam's Club, except that it's the tour operator who buys the 1,000-count box of garbage bags and resells them 10 at a time at a cost that undercuts what you'd pay at your neighborhood supermarket.

Tour packages vary as much as garbage bags too. Some packages offer a better class of hotels than others. Some offer certain hotels for lower prices than other packages. Some offer flights on scheduled airlines, and others book chartered flights. In some packages, your choices of accommodations and travel days may be limited. Some packages let you choose between escorted vacations and independent vacations; others will allow you to add on just a few excursions or escorted day trips (also at prices lower than if you booked them yourself) without booking an entirely escorted tour.

Each destination usually has one or two packagers that are usually better than the rest because they buy in even bigger bulk. The time you spend shopping around for a package tour will be well rewarded.

Pick a Peck of Pickled Packages

The best place to start looking for a package tour is the travel section of your local Sunday newspaper. Also check the ads in the back of national travel magazines like *Travel & Leisure, National Geographic Traveler,* and *Condé Nast Traveler.* **Liberty Travel** (many locations; check your local directory because there's not a central 800 number) is one of the biggest packagers in the Northeast and usually boasts a full-page ad in Sunday papers. You won't get much in the way of service, but you will get a good deal.

Extra! Extra!

Extra, indeed. Although your tour package will include most of your trip costs, there may be extras—such as airport transfers and optional tours or events—that you'll have to pay for separately. Read the fine print.

Extra! Extra!

Through the Web site **www.vacationpackager. com**, you can link up with many different operators and design your own package.

Another good resource is the airlines themselves, which often package their flights together with accommodations. When you pick the airline, you can choose one that has frequent service to your hometown and/or one on which you accumulate frequent-flyer miles. Disreputable packagers are uncommon, but they do exist, so buying your package through the airline is a safer bet—you can be pretty sure the company will still be in business when your departure date arrives. Among the airline packages, your options include **American Airlines FlyAway Vacations** (☎ 800/321-2121), **Delta Dream Vacations** (☎ 800/872-7786), and **US Airways Vacations** (☎ 800/455-0123).

The biggest hotel chains, casinos, and resorts also offer packages. If you already know where you want to stay, call the resort itself and ask whether it offers land/air packages.

Some other packagers you might try include **TWA Getaway Vacations** (☎ 800/438-2929), **American Express Vacations** (☎ 800/241-1700), and **Destination Management** (☎ 888/670-4638 or 504/524-5030; Web site http://dmi.accesscom.net), which specializes in New Orleans packages.

So What's in the Package?

The following examples of the kind of package tours you can get to New Orleans were being offered by **Destination Management** (☎ 888/670-4638 or 504/524-5030; Web site http://dmi.accesscom.net) as this book went to press. Prices are averages per person based on double occupancy, are offered for comparison only (they'll almost certainly change), and are based on only a few of the hotels that are available. Travel to the city is extra and will obviously depend on where you're traveling from and whether you intend to fly or take ground transportation.

Halloween package: The "Gathering of the Coven Ball" package includes accommodations for three nights with all taxes, "A stroll with the Mayfair Witches" Garden District tour, and the "Gathering of the Coven Ball." Many optional tours and services are available as add-ons. (With accommodation at the Hotel Provincial, $349; at the Hotel St. Pierre, $225.)

Mardi Gras package: Arthur Hardy publishes the annual and much respected *Mardi Gras Guide,* and the "Arthur Hardy Mardi Gras" package gives you five days and four nights of hotel accommodations including all taxes, a complete city tour, a Mississippi River cruise aboard the paddle wheeler *Creole Queen,* an official *Arthur Hardy's Mardi Gras Guide,* and a Riverwalk Shopping Center coupon book ($250 in savings). The deluxe Mardi Gras package (add $125 per person) also includes a Lundi Gras (Monday before Mardi Gras) tableau ball including a gourmet dinner with wine, dance band, and krewe presentation (black tie or costume); breakfast at world-famous Brennan's restaurant; and café au lait at Café du Monde, along with all taxes and gratuities. (With accommodations at Bienville House Hotel, $639; at Bourbon Orleans, $679; at Chateau LeMoyne, $579.)

New Orleans Jazz and Heritage Festival package: The "Jazz Fest" package includes three nights of hotel accommodations including all taxes, a two-day ticket for the festival with round-trip shuttle transportation from Downtown/French Quarter, a Mississippi River day cruise on the paddle wheeler *Creole Queen* or riverboat *Cajun Queen,* a Riverwalk Shopping Center coupon book with over $250 in savings/discounts, and discounts to Audubon Zoo and Aquarium of the Americas. (With accommodation at the Monteleone Hotel, $399; at the Holiday Inn Superdome, $229.)

Discover New Orleans package: This package is not available during special events, but includes a two nights' hotel stay (including taxes), a Mississippi River day cruise on the paddle wheeler *Creole Queen* or riverboat *Cajun Queen,* and a Riverwalk Shopping Center discount coupon book. (With accommodations at the St. Pierre, $139; at the Dauphine Orleans, $175.)

French Quarter Festival package: This package includes three nights of hotel accommodations (including taxes), a French Quarter walking tour, a Riverwalk Shopping Center discount coupon book, and discount coupons to the Audubon Zoo and Aquarium of the Americas. (With accommodation at the Holiday Inn Superdome, $239; at the Hotel St. Pierre, $239.)

Fighting the Airfare Wars

Airfares are capitalism at its purest, to the point that passengers in the same cabin on the same airplane rarely pay the same fare as each other; rather, they each pay what the market will bear. Business travelers who need the flexibility to purchase their tickets at the last minute, change their itinerary at a moment's notice, or get home before the weekend pay the premium rate or full fare. Passengers who can book their ticket long in advance, who don't mind staying over Saturday night, or who are willing to travel on a Tuesday, Wednesday, or Thursday pay the least, usually a fraction of the full fare. On most flights, even the shortest hops, the full fare is close to $1,000 or more, but a 7-day or 14-day advance purchase ticket is closer to $200 or $300. Obviously, it pays to plan ahead.

The airlines also periodically hold sales in which they lower the prices on their most popular routes. These fares have advance purchase requirements and date-of-travel restrictions, but you can't beat the price: usually no more than $400 for a cross-country flight. Keep your eyes open for these sales as you're planning your vacation, and then pounce on them. The sales tend to take place in seasons of low travel volume such as the summer and the first two weeks of December. You'll almost never see a sale around peak times like Mardi Gras week or around Thanksgiving or Christmas, when people have to fly regardless of what the fare is.

Consolidators, also known as bucket shops, are a good place to check for the lowest fares. Their prices are much better than the fares you could get yourself and are often even lower than what your travel agent can get you. You see their ads in the small boxes at the bottom of the page in your Sunday travel section. Some of the most reliable consolidators include ☎ **800/FLY-4-LESS** or **800/FLY-CHEAP.** Another good choice, **Council Travel** (☎ **800/226-8624**), caters especially to young travelers, but its bargain-basement prices are available to people of all ages.

Surfing the Web to Fly the Skies

Another way to find the cheapest fare is by using the Internet to do your searching for you. After all, that's what computers do best: search through millions of pieces of data and return information in rank order. The number of virtual travel agents on the Internet has increased exponentially in recent years, and agencies now compete the way locksmiths do in the yellow pages for the first alphabetical listing. At this writing, 007Travel, 1st Choice Travel, and 1Travel.com all preceded A Plus Travel in an alphabetical listing of online travel agents.

Dollars & Sense

Hint for all you west coasters: Try flying through Atlanta. The sale price from Los Angeles, San Diego, or San Franciso can drop to around $225 round trip, and as low as $140 one way. **Western Pacific** usually starts the sale, then the others (**Delta, American, Continental, US Air, America West, TransWorld, Frontier**) match it. Then **AirTran** (☎ **800/AIR-TRAN**) out of Atlanta will get you to New Orleans any time for $124 round trip, and sale prices sometimes go down to $98. Other airlines match AirTran's fares, especially Delta, which also flies non-stop to New Orleans. To find the lowest fares possible, check out the Web site **www.travelocity.com**.

There are too many companies now to mention, but a few of the respected ones are **Travelocity (www.travelocity.com)**, **Microsoft Expedia (www.expedia.com)**, and **Yahoo!'s Flifo Global (http://travel.yahoo. com/travel/)**. Each has its own little quirks—Travelocity, for example, requires you to register with them—but they all provide variations of the same service. Just enter the dates you want to fly and the cities you want to visit, and the computer looks for the lowest fares. The Yahoo! site has a feature called "Fare Beater," which will check flights on other airlines or at different times or dates in hopes of finding an even cheaper fare. Expedia's site will e-mail you the best airfare deal once a week if you so choose. Travelocity uses the SABRE computer reservations system that most travel agents use, and has a "Last Minute Deals" database that advertises really cheap fares for those who can get away at a moment's notice.

Great last-minute deals are also available directly from the airlines themselves through a free e-mail service called **E-savers.** Each week, the airline sends you a list of discounted flights, usually leaving the upcoming Friday or Saturday, and returning the following Monday or Tuesday. You can sign up for all the major airlines at once by logging on to **Epicurious Travel (http://travel.epicurious.com/travel/c_planning/02_airfares/ email/signup.html)**, or go to each individual airline's Web site:

➤ **American Airlines: www.americanair.com**

➤ **Continental Airlines: www.flycontinental.com**

➤ **TWA: www.twa.com**

➤ **Northwest Airlines: www.nwa.com**

➤ **US Airways: www.usairways.com**

See appendix B of this book for a complete list of airline Web sites.

The Inside Scoop on the Comfort Zone

The seats in the front row of each airplane cabin, called the **bulkhead seats,** usually have the most leg room. They have some drawbacks, however. Because there's no seat in front of you, you have to put your carry-on luggage in the overhead bin. The front row also may not be the best place to see the in-flight movie. Airlines often put passengers with young children in the bulkhead row so the kids can sleep on the floor. This is terrific if you have kids, but a nightmare if you have a headache and the kids sitting next to you start screaming.

Emergency-exit row seats also have extra leg room. They're assigned at the airport, usually on a first-come, first-serve basis. Ask when you check in whether you can be seated in one of these rows. In the unlikely event of an emergency, you'll be expected to open the emergency exit door and help direct traffic.

Ask for a seat toward the front of the plane. The minute the captain turns off the "Fasten Seat Belts" sign after landing, people jump up out of their seats as though Ken Griffey, Jr. just hit a home run. They then stand in the aisles and wait for 5 to 10 minutes while the ground crew puts the gangway in place. The closer to the front of the plane you are, the less hurry-up-and-waiting you'll have to do. Why do you think they put first class in the front?

Extra! Extra!

If you have special dietary needs, be sure to order a special meal. Most airlines offer vegetarian meals, macrobiotic meals, kosher meals, low-salt meals, meals for the lactose intolerant, and others. Ask when you make your reservation if the airline can accommodate your dietary restrictions. Some people without any special dietary needs order special meals anyway because they are made to order, unlike the mass-produced dinners served to the other passengers.

Wear comfortable clothes. The days of getting dressed up to ride an airplane went out with Nehru jackets and poodle skirts. And dress in layers; the supposedly controlled climate in airplane cabins is anything but predictable. You'll be glad to have a sweater or jacket that you can put on or take off as the temperature on board dictates.

Bring some toiletries aboard on long flights. Airplane cabins are notoriously dry places. Take a travel-size bottle of moisturizer or lotion to refresh your face and hands at the end of the flight. If you're taking an overnight flight (also known as the red eye), don't forget to pack a toothbrush to combat that feeling upon waking that you've been sucking on your seat cushion for six hours. If you wear contact lenses, take them out before you get on board and wear glasses instead. Or at least bring eye drops.

Jet lag is not usually a problem for flights within the United States, but some people are affected by three-hour time zone changes. The best advice is to get acclimated to local time as quickly as possible. Stay up as long as you can the first day, and then try to wake up at a normal time the second day. Drink plenty of water both days, as well as on the plane to avoid dehydration.

And **if you're flying with kids,** don't forget chewing gum for ear pressure problems, a deck of cards or favorite (preferably *quiet*) toys to keep them entertained, extra bottles or pacifiers, diapers, and so on.

Getting There by Car

If you choose not to fly, you can easily get to New Orleans by car. Interstate 10 runs directly through the city from east to west, and just north of the city is Interstate 12, which also travels from east to west. From I-12, you can connect with the Lake Pontchartrain Causeway and drive south to I-10 directly in the metro area or connect with either I-55 to the west of the city or I-59 to the east of the city. Both of these interstate highways flow from north to south and connect with I-10. In addition, the city is accessible by U.S. highways 11, 51, 61, and 90. See the "Greater New Orleans" map on page xv in the Introduction for help on planning your route into the city.

As I emphasize all throughout the book, New Orleans is not an easy driving city in terms of sightseeing. It's hard to find parking on the street and even harder to find a spot near anything you want to see. Parking in commercial lots is readily available, but these lots aren't cheap, and sometimes their locations are less than convenient.

Cruises from the Big Easy

Can't decide between visiting New Orleans and going to the Caribbean? Do both! New Orleans is an up-and-coming home port for cruise ships, which come in from the Gulf of Mexico via the Mississippi River and dock near the New Orleans Convention Center, not far from the French Quarter. Three cruise lines currently run ships from here: the budget-priced **Commodore Cruise Line** (☎ 800/237-5361), the luxurious (and pricey) **Crystal Cruises** (☎ 800/446-6620), and the everlastingly festive **Carnival Cruise Lines** (☎ 800/438-6744). Cruises from New Orleans follow a western Caribbean itinerary that usually includes stops in Grand Cayman and Playa del Carmen, and your travel agent can arrange packages that include your cruise and hotel accommodations in New Orleans. You'll get the best of both worlds: the old-world grandeur of New Orleans and the fun and relaxation of a cruise.

Getting There by Train

If you're planning on chugging into New Orleans on a train, you'll arrive at the **Union Passenger Terminal** (☎ **504/528-1610**) on Loyola Avenue in the Central Business District, just a few blocks from the French Quarter. Once you arrive at the station, **taxis** will be available to take you into town. (If by some fluke they're not, you can call **United Cab** at ☎ **504/522-9771.**)

For information on train schedules and fares, you can call **Amtrak** at ☎ **800/USA-RAIL** or 504/528-1610. Using the All Aboard America fares, you'll pay approximately $190 to $210 from New York or Chicago and $250 to $290 from Los Angeles. Amtrak frequently offers senior-citizen discounts and packages that include a rental car, so be sure to ask when you reserve. Note that many of Amtrak's discounts are dependent on early reservations, so plan ahead.

Amtrak also offers some very appealing tour packages, which can be arranged through your local Amtrak Tour Desk. Options might range from a ticket with hotel accommodations to an air/rail package—take the train and then fly back home.

Getting There by Bus

Buses to New Orleans come into the same station as the trains—**Union Passenger Terminal**—and if you have patience, a cast-iron butt, and fantasies about hitting the road like an old bluesman, this might be the way to go. If not—if, for instance, you live more than four hours from town and are not a masochist—you'll probably fly. Just in case, though, the number for **Greyhound** is ☎ **800/231-2222** or 504/524-7571.

Fare Game: Choosing an Airline

Arranging and booking flights is a complicated business—that's why a whole industry has grown up to handle it for you. If you're searching around for a deal, though, it helps to leave a trail of bread crumbs through the maze so you can easily find your way to your destination and back. You can use this worksheet to do just that.

1   Schedule & Flight Information Worksheets

Travel Agency: _____ **Phone #:** _____

Agent's Name: _____ **Quoted Fare:** _____

Departure Schedule & Flight Information

Airline: _____ Airport: _____

Flight #: _____ Date: _____ Time: _____am/pm

Arrives in _____ Time: _____ am/pm

Connecting Flight (if any)

Amount of time between flights: _____ hours/mins.

Airline:_____ Flight #:_____ Time: _____am/pm

Arrives in _____ Time: _____ am/pm

Return Trip Schedule & Flight Information

Airline:_____ Airport: _____

Flight #: _____ Date: _____ Time: _____am/pm

Arrives in _____ Time: _____ am/pm

Connecting Flight (if any)

Amount of time between flights: _____ hours/mins.

Airline:_____ Flight #:_____ Time: _____am/pm

Arrives in _____ Time: _____ am/pm

2   Schedule & Flight Information Worksheets

Travel Agency: _____ **Phone #:** _____

Agent's Name: _____ **Quoted Fare:** _____

Departure Schedule & Flight Information

Airline: _____ Airport: _____

Flight #: _____ Date: _____ Time: _____am/pm

Arrives in _____ Time: _____ am/pm

Connecting Flight (if any)

Amount of time between flights: _____ hours/mins.

Airline:_____ Flight #:_____ Time: _____am/pm

Arrives in _____ Time: _____ am/pm

Return Trip Schedule & Flight Information

Airline:_____ Airport: _____

Flight #: _____ Date: _____ Time: _____am/pm

Arrives in _____ Time: _____ am/pm

Connecting Flight (if any)

Amount of time between flights: _____ hours/mins.

Airline:_____ Flight #:_____ Time: _____am/pm

Arrives in _____ Time: _____ am/pm

3   Schedule & Flight Information Worksheets

Travel Agency: _____ **Phone #:** _____

Agent's Name: _____ **Quoted Fare:** _____

Departure Schedule & Flight Information

Airline: _____ Airport: _____

Flight #: _____ Date: _____ Time: _____am/pm

Arrives in _____ Time: _____ am/pm

Connecting Flight (if any)

Amount of time between flights: _____ hours/mins.

Airline:_____ Flight #:_____ Time: _____am/pm

Arrives in _____ Time: _____ am/pm

Return Trip Schedule & Flight Information

Airline:_____ Airport: _____

Flight #: _____ Date: _____ Time: _____am/pm

Arrives in _____ Time: _____ am/pm

Connecting Flight (if any)

Amount of time between flights: _____ hours/mins.

Airline:_____ Flight #:_____ Time: _____am/pm

Arrives in _____ Time: _____ am/pm

4   Schedule & Flight Information Worksheets

Travel Agency: _____   **Phone #:** _____

Agent's Name: _____   **Quoted Fare:** _____

Departure Schedule & Flight Information

Airline: _____ Airport: _____

Flight #: _____ Date: _____ Time: _____am/pm

Arrives in _____ Time: _____ am/pm

Connecting Flight (if any)

Amount of time between flights: _____ hours/mins.

Airline:_____ Flight #:_____ Time: _____am/pm

Arrives in _____ Time: _____ am/pm

Return Trip Schedule & Flight Information

Airline:_____ Airport: _____

Flight #: _____ Date: _____ Time: _____am/pm

Arrives in _____ Time: _____ am/pm

Connecting Flight (if any)

Amount of time between flights: _____ hours/mins.

Airline:_____ Flight #:_____ Time: _____am/pm

Arrives in _____ Time: _____ am/pm

Chapter 4

Kickin' Up Your Heels: Mardi Gras, Jazz Fest & the Rest

In This Chapter

➤ The inside scoop on Mardi Gras

➤ The lowdown on Jazz Fest

➤ All the other (and lesser known) festivals in town

New Orleans means festival—if you don't believe it, try this simple little free-association test. What's the first thing that comes to mind when someone says New Orleans? Mardi Gras, right? That's the biggie, of course, but it's only one of this lively city's celebrations. There's something about the frame of mind here that just won't tolerate inhibitions—whether there's a declared celebration in progress or not.

As for officially designated festival days, a calendar of events issued by the New Orleans Metropolitan Convention and Visitors Bureau lists no fewer than 26, spread over the year, that are observed either in the city proper or in its neighboring parishes. There's a festival of jazz and food; a celebration of spring, when women don the costumes of long ago and shepherd the public through gorgeous old mansions; and numerous food festivals that celebrate the fine art of eating as it's practiced here. Get out of town a ways, and you can even find a festival dedicated to frogs. If there's any possible reason to celebrate, New Orleans throws a party.

Plan Today, Party Tomorrow

Trying to arrange a few days of festivals and fun in New Orleans requires some careful planning. First, you can't just drop in. If you do, you may find yourself sleeping in Jackson Square or on a sidewalk somewhere.

Accommodations are booked solid in the city itself and in the nearby suburbs, *so make your plans well ahead and book a room as soon as your plans are finalized.* Most hotels won't accept reservations a full year in advance except from their best long-term customers, so I'd recommend that you begin checking about 10 to 12 months prior to Mardi Gras or Jazz Fest. Of course, prices are usually higher during peak festivals, and most hotels and guest houses impose minimum-stay requirements.

If you want to join the maskers in costume, it's best to plan ahead and come prepared, but if advance planning's not your strong suit, you can always visit one of the shops in town that specialize in Mardi Gras costumes and masks. One of the most reasonable is the **Mardi Gras Center,** 831 Chartres St. (☎ **504/524-4384**). If you come early enough, they can custom-make a costume to your specifications; if not, they're well stocked with new and used costumes, wigs, masks, hats, and makeup.

When's the Party, Man?

Not only are festivals in New Orleans a little wild, but so are their schedules—few events fall on the same date each year. The exact date of Mardi Gras varies each year by as much as 35 days. Because of this and other considerations, the dates of most other festivals vary too. The good news is that most of the festivals are usually planned over weekends and holidays, when the largest number of people will be able to come.

What follows is a list of the major festivals and events and the approximate dates on which they fall. For more detailed information about each festival, see the sections on Mardi Gras and Jazz Fest and the "Let the Good Times Roll: Other New Orleans Festivals" section later in the chapter.

Event	Approximate Date
Sugar Bowl	January 1
Carnival	Begins January 6; ends on Mardi Gras
Lundi Gras	The day before Mardi Gras
Mardi Gras	The Tuesday 46 days before Easter
Black Heritage Festival	March
St. Patrick's Day	March 17th; parade dates vary
St. Joseph's Day	March 19th; parade dates vary
Tennessee Williams Festival	March
Spring Fiesta	Late March/early April
French Quarter Festival	Second weekend of April
New Orleans Jazz and Heritage Festival (Jazz Fest)	Late April/early May
Greek Festival	Last weekend in May
Reggae Riddums Festival	Second weekend in June
Essence Festival	July 4th weekend
Southern Decadence Festival	Labor Day weekend

Event	Approximate Date
Louisiana Jazz Awareness Month	October
Gumbo Festival	October
Halloween	October 31
Bayou Classic	Thanksgiving weekend
Celebration in the Oaks	End of November through beginning of January
Christmas celebration	Throughout December
New Year's Eve	December 31

Party Mardi

Mardi Gras, of course, is the mother of all festivals. Volumes could be written about its history, and almost any New Orleanian you encounter will have his or her own store of Mardi Gras tales. What follows here is a brief sketch of its background and a quick rundown on present-day krewes and parades.

To begin with, the name *Mardi Gras* means "Fat Tuesday" in French, and that's a very appropriate name because it's always celebrated on the Tuesday before the Christian Ash Wednesday—the idea being that you have an obligation to eat, drink, and be as merry as you possibly can before the 40-day Lenten season of fasting and repentance sets in. The name *Carnival* is Latin in origin (from *carnisvale,* meaning "farewell to flesh") and refers to the six- to eight-week stretch from Twelfth Night, or January 6, to Mardi Gras.

In New Orleans, the Carnival season is officially opened by the Krewe of Twelfth Night Revelers' Ball, the only ball that has a fixed date.

When you think of Mardi Gras, images of drunken orgies and large rambunctious crowds probably come to mind. I can't vouch for the orgies, but the crowds are everywhere—particularly on Bourbon Street. The worst of Mardi Gras (some would say the best) is here, particularly from the 500 block to the 1000 block. People are packed in like sardines, but thanks to the New Orleans Police Department, who are great when it comes to crowd control, things don't get too out of hand.

Mardi Gras from 1999 to 2001

You can always figure out the date of Mardi Gras because it falls exactly 46 days before Easter. If you can't find your calendar, or just can't be bothered with the math, here's the next three years for you:
February 16, 1999
March 7, 2000
February 27, 2001

The lower French Quarter (from St. Ann Street to Esplanade) is where **Gay Mardi Gras** is celebrated. Gays and lesbians come from everywhere to strut around in costumes of their own design, competing for prizes. The contest is held on Mardi Gras day around noon in front of the **Rawhide Bar and Lounge** at St. Ann and Burgundy. The winner receives the much sought-after Bourbon Street Award.

Despite the crowds, Mardi Gras can be one of the safest and most entertaining experiences you've ever had. Read on, and I'll tell you how to avoid making the same mistakes most newcomers do and give you tips (if you want 'em) on getting away from the drunken bacchanalia and enjoying a family-style Mardi Gras.

Bet You Didn't Know

Carnival season begins with a series of dances and balls. The most traditional of these are exclusive invitation-only parties sponsored by old-time krewes. But newer and more liberal krewes have sprung up that sponsor more public "supper dances," where tickets aren't hard to come by. For more information, check out *Arthur Hardy's Mardi Gras Guide,* which you can pick up most anywhere in this city (it usually comes out right after Christmas). You can also order it ahead of time by calling ☎ **504/838-6111.**

Hey, You Got Your Lingo in My Gumbo

If you're going to Mardi Gras, you have to talk the talk and walk the walk. I can't help you with your posture, but I can teach you a few things about Mardi Gras–speak. Understanding these terms will make it seem as though you've been coming to Mardi Gras for years.

➤ **Ball or Tableau Ball:** Masked balls given by Mardi Gras krewes. The theme is different each year.

➤ **Boeuf Gras** ("the fattened calf"): Long the symbol of Mardi Gras, the calf represents the ritual sacrifice and last meal eaten before Lent. It is the first float of the Rex parade.

➤ **Captain:** The leader of a krewe.

➤ **Carnival:** A celebration beginning January 6 ("the twelfth night" after Christmas) and ending Mardi Gras day.

➤ **Court:** A krewe's king, queen, and attendants.

➤ **Doubloon:** A metal coin with the krewe's logo on one side and the theme for a particular year on the other, thrown during parades.

➤ **Fat Tuesday:** Also known as Mardi Gras day, Fat Tuesday is the last day before Ash Wednesday, which is the first day of Lent.

➤ **Favor:** A souvenir with the krewe's logo and date, which is given by krewe members to people attending their ball.

➤ **Flambeaux:** Flaming torches carried by paraders.

➤ **Float:** Decorated platform on wheels carrying members of the krewe, usually pulled by a tractor.

➤ **King Cake:** An oval, sugared pastry decorated with Mardi Gras colors (purple, gold, and green), containing a small doll. The doll represents the baby Jesus. When the cake is eaten, the person whose piece of cake contains the baby has to buy the next round of King Cake.

➤ **Krewe:** The traditional word for a Carnival organization.

➤ **Lagniappe** (pronounced *lan-yap*): A word that loosely means "a little extra"; it refers to any small gift or token, even a scrap of food or a free drink.

➤ **Mardi Gras:** French for "Fat Tuesday."

➤ **Mardi Gras Indians:** African-American groups of men who dress in elaborate native American Indian costumes. I've heard that the tradition developed as a way of showing thanks to Indians who helped escaped slaves. The Indian parades never follow an organized route, but roam at will. Fights used to break out when two different tribes met on the street. Today there's an elaborate ceremony instead.

➤ **Rex:** Latin for "king." The King of Carnival is Rex, and his identity is kept secret until the day before Mardi Gras. Being King of Carnival is the ultimate honor for a New Orleanian. He is usually chosen for his prominent standing and his work for the community. The King is almost always an older man, and his Queen is always a young debutante.

➤ **Second Line:** Group of people following a parade, dancing to the music. Also a music term, which specifies a particular tempo.

➤ **Throws:** Inexpensive trinkets thrown from the floats to the parade watchers.

Dollars & Sense

Buy a VisiTour pass from the Regional Transit Authority. It allows for unlimited rides of streetcars and buses during your stay. A one-day pass is $4, and a three-day pass is $8. You can buy these passes at the Marriott Hotel, Soniat House Hotel, Westin Hotel, Le Richelieu Motor Hotel, or Lenny's News Stand at 700 Decatur St. (across from Jackson Square). Call ☎ **504/248-3900,** or ask your hotel's concierge for details.

I Love a Parade

Whatever else you do or don't do, you surely won't miss seeing a Mardi Gras parade—if, that is, you come during the final 11 days of Carnival. To start with, you should NEVER park along a parade route for at least two hours before or after a parade. Signs with dates and times are posted all over the place. If you don't heed this advice, your car will be towed. If you're smart, you'll walk to Mardi Gras parades or take public transportation, and go EARLY! Traffic is impossible, even for those of us who know how to get around.

You'll know a parade is coming when you hear the scream of motorcycle sirens and see a herd of motorized police come into view. They're followed by people on horseback (sometimes mounted police, sometimes krewe members) who clear the edges of the streets for the approaching floats. The king's float is first in line, with the king enthroned and waving with his scepter to the mass of cheering humanity. Then comes a float with a banner proclaiming the theme of the parade. After that, each float will illustrate some facet of the theme.

It's a grand sight! The papier-mâchè lions, elephants, and other fanciful creatures are sometimes enormous (people work all year designing and building them), and there's much use of silver and gold tinsel that sparkles often in the sunlight or in the flare of torches. These torches, or *flambeaux,* are carried by costumed dancers. Each float has masked krewe members who wave and throw doubloons and other souvenirs.

Bet You Didn't Know

In the early days of Mardi Gras, paraders often threw small bags of flour, per-haps to symbolize snow, which New Orleans seldom gets. Miscreants sometimes substituted lye or flour mixed with black pepper, so safer alternatives were sought. Over time, strings of cheap beads and metal doubloons imprinted with the krewe's logo became popular. It became a contest to see who could come back with the most loot. Today, cheap favors of all kinds are thrown, but the most common are plastic beads, doubloons, and plastic cups imprinted with the krewe's logo.

So Much to Do, So Little Time: Mardi Gras Highlights & Schedules

Running around trying to cram all of Mardi Gras into one visit would make anyone crazy, and you'd probably be too tired to have any fun. To make your planning easier, I've included a list of some of the bigger and better parades and maps of their routes (so you can position yourself early), as well as a schedule of *all* the Carnival parades, with their approximate dates and times. **My main advice:** Catch at least one or two of the big daytime parades (such as Rex and Zulu) and at least one or two of the big nighttime parades, where floats are lit up and flambeaux carriers fling their torches around—it's a sight to be seen!

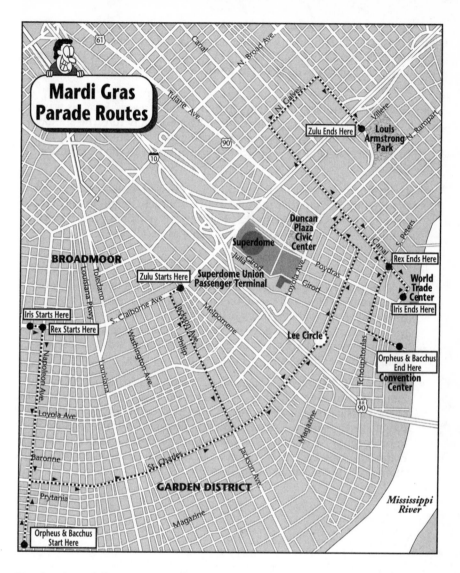

Here's a few of the major parades that take place over the last days of Carnival:

➤ **Iris** (founded 1917): Following the traditional Carnival rules of costume and behavior, this women's krewe parades in the afternoon on the Saturday before Mardi Gras along Napoleon Avenue to St. Charles Avenue, and then along Canal Street and along Convention Center Boulevard.

➤ **Endymion** (founded 1967): This krewe became one of the early "super krewes" in the 1970s by featuring a glut of floats (28 in 1997) and a

47

favorite celebrity guest (like Doc Severinsen, Alice Cooper, Charo, Tom Jones, Dolly Parton, John Goodman, and Chuck Norris). It runs Saturday evening down Canal Street to St. Charles Avenue, and then along Howard and Girod streets and into the Superdome for a big party.

➤ **Bacchus** (founded 1968): The original "super krewe," Bacchus was the first to host international celebrities. It traditionally runs the Sunday before Mardi Gras from Napoleon Avenue to St. Charles Avenue, and then along Canal Street and Tchoupitoulas Street to the Convention Center.

➤ **Orpheus** (founded 1994): One of the youngest krewes, Orpheus was founded by a group that includes Harry Connick, Jr. and usually features celebrities from the world of music. The parade is on the evening of Lundi Gras and follows the same route as Bacchus.

➤ **Zulu** (founded 1916): This Carnival krewe spoofs the King of Carnival by having its king wear a lard can as a crown and wield a banana stalk as a scepter. It's the liveliest parade, with float riders decked in wooly wigs and blackface, and krewe members carry the most prized of Mardi Gras souvenirs: gold and black painted coconuts. The parade begins the festivities on Mardi Gras day and runs from Claiborne Avenue to Jackson Avenue, along St. Charles Avenue to Canal Street, and then along Galvez and Orleans streets to Armstrong Park.

➤ **Rex** (founded 1872): Rex, the original Mardi Gras parade, follows the Zulu parade down St. Charles. It features the King of Carnival and some of the classic floats of New Orleans' Carnival. In my opinion, if you only have time for one parade, this should be it. Mardi Gras as we know it today—day parades, throwing of souvenirs, and the Mardi Gras colors—all hark back to this parade. Various independent walking clubs often precede the parade along its route.

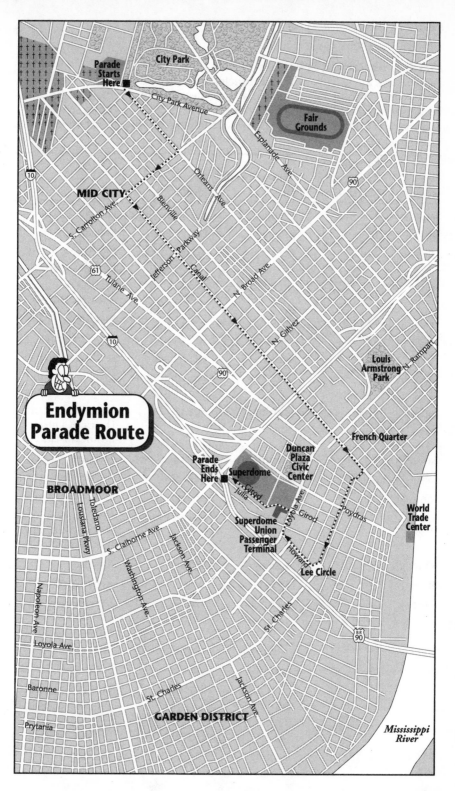

Mardi Gras Parade Schedule

Parade dates are usually not made official until the end of the year preceding Mardi Gras, so those below are tentative—check before you make plans. Also keep in mind that the parades seldom start or finish according to schedule, and that the number of krewes is always evolving as old krewes fold and new ones develop.

Day of week	Number of days before Mardi Gras	Approximate time	Krewe name	City
Saturday	17	evening	Krewe of Vieux	French Quarter
Sunday	16	midday	Little Rascals	Metairie
Friday	11	evening	Ashanti-Vesta	Mid City/Central Business District
Friday	11	evening	Oshun	Mid City/Central Business District
Friday	11	evening	Atlas	Metairie
Friday	11	evening	Cleopatra	Algiers/Gretna
Friday	11	evening	Gladiators	St. Bernard Parish
Saturday	10	midday	Pontchartrain	Mid City/Central Business District
Saturday	10	evening	Sparta	Uptown/Garden District/Central Business District
Saturday	10	evening	Caesar	Metairie
Saturday	10	evening	Choctaw	Algiers/Gretna
Saturday	10	evening	Shangri-La	St. Bernard Parish
Sunday	9	midday	Carrollton	Uptown/Garden District/Central Business District
Sunday	9	midday	Rhea	Metairie
Sunday	9	midday	Alla	Algiers/Gretna
Sunday	9	evening	Camelot	Uptown/Garden District/Central Business District
Sunday	9	evening	Centurions	Metairie
Sunday	9	evening	Juno	St. Bernard Parish
Monday	8	evening	Neptune	Metairie
Tuesday	7	evening	Pegasus	Uptown/Garden District/Central Business District
Tuesday	7	evening	Sinbad	Metairie

Day of week	Number of days before Mardi Gras	Approximate time	Krewe name	City
Wednesday	6	evening	Saturn	Uptown/Garden District/Central Business District
Wednesday	6	evening	Thor	Metairie
Thursday	5	evening	Babylon	Uptown/Garden District/Central Business District/ Basin Street
Thursday	5	evening	Aquila	Metairie
Friday	4	evening	Hermes	Uptown/Garden District/Central Business District
Friday	4	evening	d'Etat	Uptown/Garden District/Central Business District
Friday	4	evening	Diana	Metairie
Friday	4	evening	Aphrodite	St. Bernard Parish
Saturday	3	midday	Iris	Uptown/Garden District/Central Business District
Saturday	3	midday	Tucks	Uptown/Garden District/Central Business District
Saturday	3	midday	Nomtoc	Algiers
Saturday	3	midday	Ulysses	Gretna
Saturday	3	midday	King Arthur	Gretna
Saturday	3	evening	Endymion	Mid City/Central Business District
Saturday	3	evening	Isis	Metairie
Sunday	2	midday	Thoth	Uptown/Garden District/Central Business District
Sunday	2	midday	Okeanos	Uptown/Garden District/Central Business District
Sunday	2	midday	Mid City	Mid City/Central Business District
Sunday	2	midday	Mercury	Metairie
Sunday	2	midday	Poseidon	Gretna

Day of week	Number of days before Mardi Gras	Approximate time	Krewe name	City
Sunday	2	evening	Bacchus	Uptown/Garden District/Central Business District/Warehouse District
Sunday	2	evening	Napoleon	Metairie
Monday	1	evening	Bards of Bohemia	Uptown/Garden District/Central Business District
Monday	1	evening	Orpheus	Uptown/Garden District/Central Business District
Monday	1	evening	Zeus	Metairie
Tuesday	0	morning	Zulu	Uptown/Garden District/Central Business District/Armstrong Park
Tuesday	0	morning	Rex	Uptown/Garden District/Central Business District
Tuesday	0	follows Rex	Elks	Uptown/Garden District/Central Business District
Tuesday	0	follows Elks	Crescent City	Uptown/Garden District/Central Business District
Tuesday	0	midday	Argus	Metairie
Tuesday	0	midday	Jefferson	Metairie
Tuesday	0	midday	Elks/Jefferson	Metairie
Tuesday	0	midday	Grela	Gretna
Tuesday	0	evening	Krewe of America	Uptown/Garden District/Central Business District/Warehouse District

Mardi Gras, Family-Style

For a slightly more family-friendly Mardi Gras experience, check out the parades along **Veterans Highway** in Metairie on the East Bank of Jefferson Parish, the parades along the **Westbank Expressway** in Jefferson Parish, or those in **St. Bernard Parish.** It's a whole 'nother atmosphere. Sure, there's some drinking and partying going on, but for the most part, it's a family outing. Make sure your kids get plenty of sleep the night before, so they won't tire out early. Mardi Gras certainly won't bore them, but it can be a long day. And to avoid spending the kids' college fund on overpriced Mardi Gras food, bring snacks and drinks with you.

Extra! Extra!

Everyone has different strategies for catching beads and other throws, and each strategy has a different success rate. A few of the more popular ones are to wave your hands, jump up and down and shout, wear a unique costume, turn an umbrella inside out and use it to catch beads, stand on a ladder, have a cute kid on your shoulders, or show lots of skin.

The **Louisiana Children's Museum (☎ 504/523-1357;** see chapter 14) offers Mardi Gras activities for children, such as mask-making and a second line parade through the museum. These activities are free after you pay the $5 admission fee (children under one are free).

Be sure to decide in advance on a meeting place in case someone gets lost or separated. It's a good idea to choose a tall building or other recognizable landmark.

Letting the Good Times Roll Without Breaking the Bank

Whenever thousands of people cram together in a small area and go wild, prices for even the smallest things are bound to go up. Food and drink, for instance, are outrageously priced along the parade route, so if money matters, bring your own snacks and drinks.

To save money on beads or other Mardi Gras supplies, go to a Mardi Gras supply store. Supplies will cost you a fraction of what you'll pay buying from street vendors and souvenir shops. Here are a few of the best:

➤ **Accent Annex,** 633 Toulouse St., French Quarter. ☎ **504/592-9886.**

➤ **Accent Annex,** 1120 S. Jefferson Davis Pkwy., Mid City. ☎ **504/821-8885.**

➤ **Blaine Kern Artists,** 233 Newton St., Algiers. ☎ **504/362-8211.**

➤ **Laine's,** 810 Royal St., French Quarter. ☎ **504/523-2911.**

If you can't walk from your hotel to the festivities, try to take public transportation. If you have to take your car, though, you'll probably have to park in a **commercial parking lot.** Be sure that the person you pay is an employee in uniform, with appropriate identification. Here are a couple of good bets:

➤ **Blaise Parking**, 210 N. Rampart, French Quarter. ☎ **504/525-3295.**

➤ **Dixie Parking**, 528 Chartres, French Quarter; 716 Iberville, French Quarter; 722 Union St, Central Business District. ☎ **504/523-4521.**

How to Not Get Ripped Off

As in any crowded urban area, there's crime to be contended with at Mardi Gras. A few simple precautions should make you less of a mark:

Call of the Wild: Useful Telephone Numbers to Have During Mardi Gras

➤ All emergencies: ☎ 911
➤ New Orleans police (non-emergency): ☎ 504/821-2222
➤ General parking questions: ☎ 504/826-1900
➤ Parking enforcement: ☎ 504/826-1880

➤ Keep your money where a pickpocket can't get at it, and don't keep it all in one pocket.

➤ Take no more than one credit card to a parade.

➤ Keep your ID separate from your money and credit card.

➤ Don't leave anything of value in your car.

➤ Unless you know where you're going, stay with the crowd and don't venture onto side streets. You can easily wander into a dangerous neighborhood.

Staying Comfortable & Seeking Relief

Little niceties, such as physical comfort and hygiene, sometimes get forgotten in the mad Mardi Gras rush. As for comfort, be sure to wear comfortable shoes and clothing that can be removed or added if the temperature changes—and bring along a poncho in case it rains.

Finding a restroom along a parade route can be a traumatizing experience. Port-O-Lets are placed along the routes, but the lines are always long, and the facilities are not very clean. The owners of a house next to the po boy sandwich shop at **St. Charles and 6th Street** (2846 St. Charles Ave.) allow people to use their facilities—for a fee. More and more homeowners are beginning to do this. Several enterprising homeowners along St. Charles have begun renting their own Port-O-Lets and charging a fee for their use. The good news is that they hire someone to keep them clean. One such location last year was on **St. Charles near 7th Street.** The **McDonald's** restaurant at **Louisiana and St. Charles** always has several Port-O-Lets as well. As with toilets, you'll have a hard time finding any place to wash your hands, so if you're fastidious, you may want to carry a stash of disposable, pre-moistened towelettes.

Cajun Mardi Gras

For a unique Mardi Gras experience, drive out to Cajun country. Lafayette (130 miles west of New Orleans—just get on I-10 West and go straight for three hours until you hit Lafayette) is a booming but charming town in the very heart of French Acadiana, and it celebrates Carnival in a distinctive way that reflects the Cajun heritage and spirit. The three full days of activities leading up to Mardi Gras are designed to *laissez les bons temps rouler* ("let the good times roll"—an absolute creed around these parts during Carnival). This celebration is second in size only to New Orleans', but there's one *big* difference: The Cajuns open their final pageant and ball to the general public. You can don your formal wear and join right in.

Instead of Rex and his queen, the Lafayette festivities are ruled by King Gabriel and Queen Evangeline. They are the fictional hero and heroine of Longfellow's epic poem *Evangeline,* which was based on real-life lovers who were separated during the British expulsion of Acadians from Nova Scotia just after the French and Indian War. Their story is still very much alive here among the descendants of those who shared their wanderings.

Things get off to a joyous start with the **Children's Krewe** and **Krewe of Bonaparte parades and ball** the Saturday before Mardi Gras, following a full day of celebration at Acadian Village. On Monday night, Queen Evangeline is honored at the **Queen's Parade.** The **King's Parade,** held the following morning, honors King Gabriel and opens a full day of merriment. Lafayette's African-American community stages the **Parade of King Toussaint L'Ouverture and Queen Suzanne Simonne** about noon, just after the King's Parade. And following that, the Krewe of Lafayette invites everyone to get into the act as its parade winds through the streets. Krewe participants trot along on foot or ride in the vehicle of their choice—some very imaginative modes of transportation turn up every year. The Mardi Gras climax, a brilliantly beautiful, exciting formal ball presided over by the king and queen and their royal court, takes place that night. Everything stops promptly at midnight, as Cajuns and visitors alike depart to observe the solemnity of Lent with the fondly remembered glow of Mardi Gras to take them through to Easter.

Out in the Cajun/Creole countryside that surrounds Lafayette, there's yet another form of Mardi Gras celebration, and I'll guarantee you won't find another like it anywhere else in the world. It's very much tied to the rural lifestyle of these displaced people, who have created a rich culture out of personal disaster, and since Cajuns firmly believe that nothing is ever quite as much fun alone as it is when shared, you're entirely welcome to come along. The rural celebration goes like this: Bands of masked men dressed in patchwork costumes and peaked hats (*capichons*) set off on horseback on Mardi Gras morning, led by their *capitaine.* They ride from farm to farm, asking at each, *"Voulez-vous reçevoir le Mardi Gras?"* ("Will you receive the Mardi Gras?") and dismounting as the invariable "Yes" comes in reply. Then each farmyard becomes a miniature festival, as the revelers "make monkeyshines" (*faire le macaque*) with song and dance, much drinking of beer, and other antics loosely labeled as "entertainment." As payment for their show, they demand, and get, "a fat little chicken to make a big gumbo."

When each band has visited its allotted farmyards, all the bands head back to town, where everyone else has already begun the general festivities. There's dancing in the streets, rowdy card games, storytelling, and the like until the wee hours, and you may be sure that all those "fat little chickens" go into the "gumbo gros" pot to make a "big gumbo." It's a down-home sort of festival, and if you've never heard Cajun music or eaten gumbo cooked by real Cajuns, you're in for a treat.

You can write or call ahead for full particulars on both of these Mardi Gras celebrations. Contact **Lafayette Parish Convention and Visitors Commission,** P.O. Box 52066, Lafayette, LA 70505 (☎ **800/346-1958** or 318/232-3737 in the United States, 800/543-5340 in Canada).

Music to My Ears: New Orleans Jazz & Heritage Festival

By the time mid-April rolls around, Easter has passed, Mardi Gras is history, and New Orleanians turn to another celebration: the New Orleans Jazz and Heritage Festival (usually known as Jazz Fest). The Jazz and Heritage Festival combines two fetes, as its name implies. From one weekend to another (usually the last weekend in April and the first weekend in May), musicians, mimes, artists, craftspeople, and chefs head out to the Fair Grounds Race Course on the weekends and settle into hotel ballrooms, jazz joints, concert halls, and special evening concert sites to put on a never-ending show of what New Orleans is all about.

More than 4,000 performers turn up—and that's not counting the street bands. Big-name jazz, rock, pop, R&B, Cajun, zydeco, Latin, ragtime, Afro-Caribbean, folk, rap, country, bluegrass, and gospel musicians are drawn to this festival, and they very happily share 12 stages at Fair Grounds with lesser-known and local groups. Some of the artists who have attended in the past are Dr. John, James Taylor, Santana, Bela Fleck and the Fleckstones, Allen Toussaint, the Indigo Girls, Buckwheat Zydeco, the Neville Brothers, Joan Osborne, Phish, the Dave Matthews Band, The Radiators, Wynton Marsalis, Van Morrison, and Joan Baez.

You can find your favorites and stand in front of the stage all day long or make the rounds and come back to see which new group has taken the stage. Remember that this is a New Orleans festival—completely unstructured, with the emphasis on pure enjoyment. If you think this sounds like a lot of entertainment, keep in mind that it's only what's happening out at the Fair Grounds; on weeknights, street bands are everywhere, and if you can't find a performance of your kind of music going on somewhere, it must not exist. If traditional jazz happens to be your preference, you'll be in heaven.

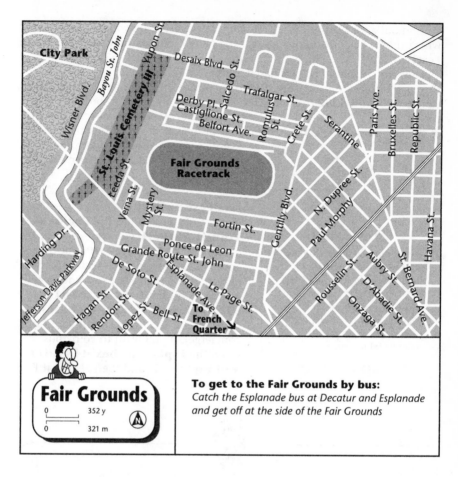

To get to the Fair Grounds by bus:
Catch the Esplanade bus at Decatur and Esplanade and get off at the side of the Fair Grounds

As for the "heritage" part of the festival, local craftspeople and out-of-town artisans arrive at Jazz Fest en masse with their wares, and demonstrations are offered throughout the festival. You might get to see Louisiana Native American basket making; Cajun accordion, fiddle, and triangle making; decoy carving; boat building; and Mardi Gras Indian beading and costume making. Contemporary arts and crafts, such as jewelry, furniture, hand-blown glass, and paintings, are also featured.

You could also probably call Jazz Fest a food fest. Over 50 food booths at the racetrack serve traditional fare such as jambalaya, gumbo, and red beans and rice, as well as soft shell crab po boys, *cochon de lait* (Cajun roast pig) sand-wiches, sausage and crawfish bread, alligator sausage, oyster sacks, crawfish sushi, and even vegetarian specialties, plus Caribbean and African delicacies. Your only problems will be having enough time to sample everything (and you'll want to) and deciding what was the most delicious.

To find out about current Jazz Fest dates, the artists who will be there, and where they'll be performing, contact the **New Orleans Jazz and Heritage Festival,** 2200 Royal St., New Orleans, LA 70177 (☎ **504/522-4786**). Tickets, which should be purchased as early as February, are available through Ticketmaster. To order tickets by phone, or to get ticket information, call ☎ **800/488-5252** or 504/522-5555 within Louisiana. To order by fax, dial 504/379-3291. Daily tickets for the festival cost $12 in advance and $16 at the gate for adults, and $2 in advance and $3 at the gate for children.

Evening events and concerts cost an additional $17.50 to $30, depending on the concert.

Extra! Extra!

The annual 20,000+ Computer Associates convention is usually held in July. In 1998, it will be held in conjunction with Jazz Fest (April 26 to May 1). Four cruise ships will be brought in to provide extra hotel rooms.

Jazz Fest or Bust

To get to Fair Grounds, the **Regional Transit Authority** operates special buses. Call ☎ **504/248-3900** for routes and pick-up points. Taxis charge $3 per person or the meter fare (whichever is greater). Call **United Cab ☎ 504/522-9771.** Several companies offer shuttle service as well (check with your hotel concierge). If you want to go by bus, catch the **Esplanade bus** at **Decatur and Esplanade** and then get off at Fair Grounds.

Dollars & Sense

If you're flying to New Orleans specifically for the Jazz and Heritage Festival, you should consider calling the **special convention number of Northwest Airlines** (☎ 800/328-1111). In 1998, Northwest is the official airline for the Jazz and Heritage Festival, and they offer special fares during the event. If you order your tickets 60 days in advance, you'll receive a 10% discount off the lowest fare available; it's a 5% discount for all you last-minute planners. You'll need to give a special promotional code—in 1998 is **NE4DT**. Please note that the official sponsor changes every year (last year it was Continental). You can call the Jazz and Heritage Festival information line (☎ 504/522-4786) for the scoop on special promotions related to the festival.

The Jazz Fest Beat: Insider Tips

➤ **Don't drive.** It's next to impossible to park your car at Fair Grounds. A few spots are available at $10 a day, but I don't know anyone who has ever been lucky enough to get one (and certainly not for the entire weekend). I strongly recommend that you take public transportation or one of the shuttles (see the preceding section).

➤ **See the big shows.** During Jazz Fest, special concerts, usually featuring the superstars, are held throughout the city after the festival's normal hours. Check the *Gambit, OffBeat,* or *Times-Picayune* newspapers for specific information.

➤ **See the little shows.** If you're not into crowds, check out the lesser-known performers. They're often just as good as the well-known ones.

➤ **Pack some jumbo garbage bags.** They're great to sit on if the ground is muddy or dusty. They also make great ponchos if it begins to rain.

➤ **Bring your own water to the festival.** The powers that be don't allow it, but many people sneak it anyway. (Use plastic bottles.)

➤ **Dine early.** The restaurants will be packed by 7pm. If you don't have reservations, beat the rush by eating around 5 or 6pm and be out having a good time while others are standing in line.

Let the Good Times Roll: Other New Orleans Festivals

After Mardi Gras and Jazz Fest wind down, the party is far from over. In New Orleans, there's always something to celebrate. Here are just a few of my favorite parties.

Winter

The **Sugar Bowl** is an annual college football classic that's been held since 1934. It takes place in the Superdome as early as December 30th and as late as January 3rd. Call ☎ **504/525-8573** for dates and information.

The **Black Heritage Festival** celebrates Louisiana's black history with food, music, and arts and crafts. Festivities take place throughout the city in late February or early March, including the Riverwalk, Audubon Zoo, the New Orleans Museum of Art, and the Old U.S. Mint. Call ☎ **504/581-4629** for more information.

St. Patrick's Day is March 17th and **St. Joseph's Day** is March 19th, but the parade dates vary and are often held in conjunction with one another. For St. Patrick's Day, the beer flows green, and celebrations are held throughout the city. For St. Joseph's Day, many Italian-Americans offer bountiful and beautifully prepared **St. Joseph's altars** of food, which are blessed by a priest and then given to strangers in thanks to St. Joseph for favors granted. Both groups have several parades. The Mardi Gras Indians also march through parts of the city, though their routes are not known in advance. For **St. Patrick's Day** information, call ☎ **504/525-5169** or 504/565-7080. For **St. Joseph's Day** information, call ☎ **504/566-5055**.

The **Tennessee Williams Literary Festival** occurs in March, when more than 7,000 people attend a four-day series of events including live performances, lectures, walking tours, and seminars about this famous writer. New Orleans was one of Williams's favorite cities, and he lived here while writing many plays, including *A Streetcar Named Desire*. Call ☎ **504/581-1144** for info, or visit the Web site at **www.gnofn.org/~twfest**.

Spring

The **Spring Fiesta,** when the wealthy open their homes and gardens to the public, takes place in late March or early April. Guides in period costume conduct tours of these otherwise private homes. Call ☎ **504/581-1367** for info.

The **French Quarter Festival,** the local version of the New Orleans Jazz and Heritage Festival, normally occurs on the second weekend in April. Free concerts are held in Jackson Square, Woldenberg Park, Royal Street, Bourbon Street, and elsewhere throughout the city. Food booths are set up where local delicacies can be sampled at reasonable prices. Though still a local event, the festival is getting bigger every year and may someday rival Jazz Fest. Call ☎ **504/522-5730** for info.

The **Greek Festival,** held over the last weekend in May, is a three-day event featuring Greek food, dancing, music, arts, and crafts. The food is great, and the music and dancing is lively. Profits go to the Greek church. Call ☎ **504/282-0259.**

Summer

Can't afford a Caribbean vacation? Take one in New Orleans. More than 25,000 people attend the two-day **Reggae Riddums Festival** in City Park. This event features calypso, reggae, ethnic arts and crafts, and great regional food. It occurs the second weekend in June and gets bigger each year. Take the Esplanade bus from the French Quarter to City Park. Call ☎ **504/367-1313** for information.

The **Essence Festival** takes place over the July 4th weekend. An estimated 40,000 to 50,000 African Americans and others flock to New Orleans to hear over 40 performers and personalities, including big names like **Gladys Knight, Patti LaBelle,** the **Isley Brothers, Kenny G, Maya Angelou, Clarence Carter,** and **Irma Thomas.** Call ☎ **504/523-5652** or visit the Web site at **www.gnobtn.com** for specific information.

The **Southern Decadence Festival** is an annual Labor Day weekend event when as many as 50,000 gays and lesbians from all over the country gather in New Orleans for a parade and accompanying celebration. Assembling in the 1200 block of Royal Street by the **Golden Lantern** bar, thousands of costumed marchers (many in drag) take to the streets of the French Quarter in a route only the Grand Marshal knows. When the Grand Marshal blows his or her whistle, they weave a drunken path through the streets of the Quarter. Call ☎ **800/876-1484** for more information, or check out the Web site at **www.southerndecadence.com**.

To prove my point that just about any-thing is cause for celebration in New Orleans and its environs, I'll tell you about the **Rayne Frog Festival.** It's held every September in Cajun country, just a few miles west of Lafayette. The Cajuns can hold their own when it comes to drumming up reasons for festivals: a har-vest, a new season, a special tradition, or just the job of being alive. In this case, they turn to the lowly frog as an excuse for a *fais-dodo* (dance) and a waltz contest. Not to forget the reason for it all, the fes-tivities get under way with frog races and frog-jumping contests—and if you arrive without your frog, there's a "Rent-a-Frog" service. To wind things up, there's a lively frog-eating contest. For dates and full details, contact **Lafayette Parish Convention and Visitors Commission,** P.O. Box 52066, Lafayette, LA 70505 (☎ **800/346-1958** or 318/232-3808 in the United States, 800/543-5340 in Canada).

Bet You Didn't Know

Fats Domino still lives in New Orleans. Want to see his house? Look for the big pink and yellow house at 5525 Marais St., on the cor-ner of Marais and Caffin avenues in the working class Ninth Ward, downriver of the French Quarter. Sorry, no tourists allowed inside.

Fall & the Holidays

October is **Louisiana Jazz Awareness Month.** Throughout the month, there are nightly concerts (some free), lectures, and television and radio spe-cials all sponsored by the Louisiana Jazz Foundation. For specifics, call ☎ **504/522-5267** or check *Gambit, OffBeat,* or the *Times-Picayune.*

The **Gumbo Festival** occurs in October and is held in Bridge City by the foot of the Huey P. Long Bridge, not far from my house in Avondale. You can find seafood gumbo, chicken and sausage gumbo, andouille gumbo, and gumbos of every description, along with music, dancing, and other food at this annual event. If you see a big, ugly guy eating a bowl of gumbo, it might be me. Call ☎ **504/436-4712** for information.

Halloween is wild in New Orleans, especially in the French Quarter. Costumes in the gay section of the Quarter (roughly between St. Ann, Rampart, Gov. Nicholls, and Royal streets) are quite elaborate. Contests, par-ties, and special events are held throughout the city. A few of them include the **Boo at the Zoo** (for kids), **Monster Bash** at the Convention Center, **Anne Rice's Gathering of the Coven Ball** and her other parties, and the **Moonlight Witches' Run.** Call ☎ **504/566-5055** for more information.

The Celebration in the Oaks begins in the end of November and runs through the beginning of January. The ancient oaks in City Park are decorat-ed with more than a million lights, neon, and fiber optics in fanciful designs. You can walk through, drive, or take a carriage tour. Call ☎ **504/483-9366** or 504/483-9415 for more information.

New Orleans celebrates Christmas throughout December. The first three weeks of December are a great time for tourists to visit New Orleans. The crowds are gone, hotels offer special **Papa Noel rates** to lure customers, and restaurants offer specially priced **Reveillion dinners.** Reveillion grew out of a custom whereby each guest to a party supplied a dish of food. Restaurants have a fixed-price menu that helps to keep costs and prices down. Call ☎ **504/522-5730.**

New Orleans' **New Year's Eve** celebration is beginning to resemble the one in New York's Times Square. New Orleanians have a big street party in front of the Jax Brewery and watch the ball drop from the pole at the top of the building. The city begins filling up right after Christmas for this celebration and the upcoming Sugar Bowl football classic as well, so make your reservations early. Call ☎ **504/566-5055** for information.

Chapter 5

Tying Up the Loose Ends

In This Chapter

➤ Tips on renting a car

➤ Tips on buying travel insurance and on what to do in case of illness

➤ Tips on making reservations

➤ What to bring to town

So you've figured out how you're going to get to New Orleans. Now all you need to do is decide where you're going to stay (I'll deal with that question separately in chapters 6 and 7), what you're going to do there, make the reservations, put the dog in the kennel, pack your bags, and do 50 other last-minute things. Organizing these details ahead of time will save you precious vacation time waiting in line, calling around town, being miserable, buying the swimsuit you forgot to bring, and dealing with all the other annoyances that plague the unprepared traveler. In this chapter, I'll help you make sure you've got everything covered, from getting travel insurance to packing comfortable walking shoes. The worksheet at the end of the chapter will help you keep track.

Do I Need to Rent a Car in New Orleans?

The short answer is "no," but that's assuming you plan to confine yourself to the French Quarter and other central areas of town (or plan to take an escorted tour to outlying destinations, such as the plantations). For sightseeing in the Quarter, a car is more of a hindrance than a help: All streets there are one-way, parking is almost impossible, and on weekdays during daylight hours, Royal and Bourbon streets are closed to automobiles between the 300 and 700 blocks. Driving is also trying in the Central Business District, where congested traffic and limited parking make life difficult for the motorist. To make matters worse, New Orleans meter maids hand out more tickets than krewes throw beads during Mardi Gras, and tow trucks will drag your car away in a heartbeat.

For all these reasons, I strongly suggest that if you do rent a car you use it only for longer jaunts out of congested areas and use public transportation for your more central sightseeing. Most hotels provide parking for their guests (although a daily fee is usually charged); smaller hotels or guest houses (particularly in the French Quarter) may not have parking facilities but will be able to direct you to a nearby public garage.

Dollars & Sense

Most car rentals are worth at least 500 miles on your frequent-flyer account. Inquire about this benefit when arranging your rental.

If you plan to get around the Greater New Orleans area, though, you will need to rent a car, and you can do so from any of these major national rental companies, all of which have desks at the airport: **Alamo (☎ 800/327-9633), Avis (☎ 800/331-1212), Budget (☎ 800/527-0700), Dollar (☎ 800/800-4000), Hertz (☎ 800/654-3131), National (☎ 800/227-7368). Swifty's Car Rental (☎ 504/524-7368)** has offices at 2300 Canal St.

As in making most other travel arrangements, it pays to plan ahead in renting a car. You can arrange car rental yourself or through your travel agent. If you're doing it yourself, shop around and ask questions. Weekend rates, for example, may be lower than weekday rates. Remember to ask whether the rate is the same if you pick up the car Friday morning as it is if you pick up the car Thursday night. If you're keeping the car five or more days, a weekly rate may be cheaper than the daily rate. Some companies may assess a drop-off charge if you do not return the car to the same renting location; others, notably National, do not. Ask if the rate is cheaper if you pick up the car at the airport or at a location in town.

If you see an advertised price in your local newspaper, be sure to request that specific rate; otherwise you may be charged the standard (higher) rate. Don't forget to mention if you're a member of AAA, AARP, a trade union, or any frequent-flyer programs, as these memberships may entitle you to discounts ranging from 5% to 30%. Use the worksheet in this section to keep track of the rates as you call the various rental companies.

Car Rental over the Web

Internet resources can make comparison shopping for rental cars easier. For example, Yahoo!'s partnership with Flifo Global travel agency enables you to look up rental prices for any size car at more than a dozen rental companies in hundreds of cities. Just enter the size car you want, the rental and return dates, and the city where you want to rent, and the server returns a price. It will even make your reservation for you. Point your browser to **http://travel.yahoo.com/travel/** and then choose "Reserve car" from the options listed.

On top of the standard rental prices, other optional charges apply to most car rentals. The **Collision Damage Waiver** (CDW), which requires you to pay for damage to the car, is illegal in some states but is covered by many credit card companies. Check with your credit card company before you go; you may be able to avoid paying this hefty fee (as much as $10 a day).

Car rental companies also offer additional **liability insurance** (if you harm others in an accident), **personal accident insurance** (if you harm yourself or your passengers), and **personal effects insurance** (if your luggage is stolen from your car). If you have insurance on your car at home, you are probably covered for most of these unlikely situations. If your own insurance doesn't cover rental cars, or if you don't have auto insurance, consider buying the additional coverage, though it may cost as much as $20 a day.

Some companies also offer refueling packages, which require you to pay for an entire tank of gas up front. The price is usually competitive with local gas prices, but you don't get credit for any gas remaining in the tank. If you reject this option, you pay only for the gas you use, but you have to return the car with a full tank or face charges of $3 to $4 a gallon for any shortfall. If you're always arriving at the airport a few minutes before your flight leaves, you may want to take advantage of the fuel purchase option. Otherwise, skip it.

Car Rental Comparison Worksheet

Company	Type of Car	No. of Days	Rate
Avis (800/331-1212)			
Budget (800/527-0700)			
Dollar (800/800-4000)			
Hertz (800/654-3131)			
National (800/227-7368)			
Thrifty (800/367-2277)			
Other			
Other			
Other			

What About Travel Insurance?

There are three kinds of travel insurance: trip cancellation insurance, medical insurance, and lost luggage insurance. Trip cancellation insurance is a good idea if you've paid a large portion of your vacation expenses up front and would lose out if your trip were canceled or if you or someone in your family became sick and you couldn't go. But the other two types of insurance don't make sense for most travelers.

Your existing health insurance should cover you if you get sick while on vacation (if you belong to an HMO, you should check to see whether you're fully covered when away from home), though you may want to insure yourself against emergency medical evacuation in case you have to fly home in a hurry and forfeit the second half of your round-trip ticket. Your homeowner's insurance should cover stolen luggage. Check your existing policies before you buy any additional coverage. The airlines are responsible for $1,250 on domestic flights if they lose your luggage; if you plan to carry anything more valuable than that, keep it in your carry-on bag.

Some credit cards (American Express and certain gold and platinum Visas and MasterCards, for example) offer automatic flight insurance against death or dismemberment in case of an airplane crash. If you still feel you need more insurance, try one of the companies listed below. But don't pay for more insurance than you need. For example, if you only need trip cancellation insurance, don't purchase coverage for lost or stolen property. Trip cancellation insurance costs approximately 6% to 8% of the total value of your vacation. The following are some of the reputable issuers of travel insurance:

➤ **Access America,** 6600 W. Broad St., Richmond, VA 23230 (☎ 800/284-8300)

➤ **Mutual of Omaha,** Mutual of Omaha Plaza, Omaha, NE 68175 (☎ 800/228-9792)

➤ **Travel Guard International,** 1145 Clark St., Stevens Point, WI 54481 (☎ 800/826-1300)

➤ **Travel Insured International, Inc.,** P.O. Box 280568, East Hartford, CT 06128 (☎ 800/243-3174)

What If I Get Sick Away from Home?

It can be hard to find a doctor you trust when you're away from home or to get in touch with your doctor back home if you need a prescription phoned in. Bring all your medications with you, as well as a prescription for more if you worry that you'll run out. If you have health insurance, be sure to carry your identification card in your wallet. Bring an extra pair of contact lenses in case you lose one. And don't forget over-the-counter medications for common travelers' ailments such as upset stomach or diarrhea.

If you suffer from a chronic illness, talk to your doctor before taking the trip. For such conditions as epilepsy, diabetes, or a heart condition, wear a **Medic Alert Identification Tag,** which will immediately alert doctors to your condition and give them access to your medical records through Medic Alert's 24-hour hot line. Membership is $35, plus a $15 annual fee. Contact the Medic Alert Foundation, P.O. Box 1009, Turlock, CA 95381-1009 (☎ 800/825-3785).

If you do get sick, ask the concierge at your hotel to recommend a local doctor—even his or her own doctor. This recommendation is probably better than one from any national consortium of doctors available through an 800 number. If you can't get a doctor to help you right away, try the emergency room at the local hospital (see appendix A of this book for a listing of hospital addresses and phone numbers). Many hospital emergency rooms have walk-in clinics for emergency cases that are not life-threatening. You may not get immediate attention, but you won't pay the high price of an emergency room visit (usually a minimum of $300 just for signing your name, on top of whatever treatment you receive).

Making Reservations & Getting Tickets Ahead of Time

For most events in New Orleans (other than football games and special concerts), you won't need to buy tickets or make reservations in advance, but if there's something you *really* want to see—a Saints game, for instance, or a production of the New Orleans Ballet—by all means get your tickets ahead of time. After all, why put yourself through the worry of missing the event, and why waste valuable vacation time in line to buy tickets? Tickets for most events are available through **Ticketmaster** (☎ **504/522-5555** or www. ticketmaster.com).

Once you get to New Orleans, the *OffBeat, Times-Picayune,* and *Gambit* newspapers will be your best bet for finding out what's going on while you're in town. The *Times-Picayune,* available at most newsstands throughout the city, features a daily entertainment section, as well as a special extra section called "Lagniappe" on Fridays. *Gambit* is available free most anywhere. If you can't find it or would like a copy before you come, call ☎ **504/486-5900** or check out the online version at **www.bestofneworleans.com**. *OffBeat* is also available free almost everywhere or by calling ☎ **504/522-5533**. They too, have their information available online at **www.offbeat.com**. If Jazz music is what you've come to New Orleans to hear, **WWOZ** always has the latest on the jazz scene. You can find them on your radio at **90.7 FM** or call them at ☎ **504/568-1234** or 504/ 568-1238. You can also listen to them online and get other information at **www.wwoz.org**.

Bet You Didn't Know

At one time, New Orleans was a walled city with an earthen embankment, a wooden palisade fence, and five forts around it. Rampart Street was named for the ramparts that ran along the walls.

For all you gourmands out there, keep in mind that many restaurants don't take reservations at all and that the ones that do sometimes book up months in advance, so make your reservations as soon as you have your flight confirmed. You can find restaurant information (including notes on reservations) in chapters 10 and 11. Some restaurants that fill up early include Bayona, Brigtsen's, Emeril's, Grill Room, and Pascal's Manale.

Pack It Up

Start your packing by laying everything you think you'll need on the bed. Then get rid of half of it. I don't say this because the airlines won't let you take it all—they will, with some limits—but because you don't want to get a hernia from lugging half your house around with you. A suitcase on wheels is a good investment whether you take this advice or not—they're handy and a real pleasure to use. A foldover garment bag will help keep dressy clothes wrinkle-free, but can be a nuisance if you'll be packing and unpacking a lot. Hard-sided luggage protects breakable items better, but weighs more than soft-sided bags.

When packing, start with the biggest, hardest items (usually shoes), and then fit smaller items in and around them. Pack breakable items in between several layers of clothes, or keep them in your carry-on bag. Put things that could leak, such as shampoos and suntan lotions, in plastic reclosable bags. Lock your suitcase with a small padlock (available at most luggage stores, if your bag doesn't already have one), and put an identification tag on the outside.

Airlines allow either one or two pieces of carry-on luggage on planes (call for their latest policy), and it must fit in the overhead compartment or under the seat in front of you. Carry on any breakable items, a book or something else for you to do on the plane, a snack in case you don't like the airline food, any vital documents you don't want to lose in your luggage (such as your return tickets, passport, and wallet), and perhaps a sweater or jacket in case the air-conditioning in the plane is on overdrive.

Dressing for Success

When packing, remember that New Orleans is best explored on foot, so be sure to bring a pair of comfortable walking shoes. Also, if you're visiting in the summer, remember that that stylish black linen number you have in the closet will soak up sun like Bounty soaks up spills—light (and light-colored) cotton is a better idea.

Men should pack a jacket and women should pack a nice dress or suit if **Antoine's, Galatoire's,** the **Grill Room,** or **Christian's** are on your list for dinner. If you're going to one of these places for lunch, however, the dress code is much more relaxed. If you plan to attend the opera or the phil-harmonic orchestra, the standard dress is business attire, although you'll probably spot a few gowns and tuxes in the crowd.

Here are some other essentials: a versatile sweater and/or jacket, a belt, toi-letries and medications (pack these in your carry-on bag so you'll have them if the airline loses your luggage), a traveler's alarm clock, a camera and film, and something to sleep in. Use the following checklist to help you make sure that you have everything you need.

The Big Roundup

Okay, by now all your reservations should be in order and you should be all packed up and ready to go. So fasten your seatbelts and let's go!

Packing Checklist: Don't Forget Your Toothbrush!

- ☐ Socks
- ☐ Underwear
- ☐ Shoes (try not to pack more than two or three pairs; don't forget a good pair of walking shoes)
- ☐ Pants and/or skirts
- ☐ Shirts or blouses
- ☐ Sweaters and/or jackets
- ☐ Umbrella (the folding kind, so you can carry it with you)
- ☐ A belt
- ☐ A jacket and tie or a dress (only if you plan to go someplace fancy in the evening)
- ☐ Shorts (in warm weather)
- ☐ Bathing suit (if your hotel has a swimming pool or if you're trekking to a beach)
- ☐ Workout clothes (if you plan to use the hotel gym)
- ☐ Toiletries (razor, toothbrush, comb, deodorant, makeup, contact lens solution, hair dryer, extra pair of glasses, sewing kit, and so on)
- ☐ Camera and film
- ☐ Medications (pack these in a carry-on bag so you'll have them even if you lose your luggage)

Part 2

Finding the Hotel That's Right for You

Finding the hotel that's right for you is one of the most important things you can do to enhance your stay in New Orleans. In this part of the book, I do more than just list the hotels—I tell you about the city's different neighborhoods and give you the pluses and minuses about staying in each one.

As a native, I know a few secrets about finding hotel bargains. I'll share these with you and tell you about "rack rates" and how to avoid paying them. I'll explain the taxes and service charges, tell you how to comparison shop, explain how to bargain with some hotels, compare all the different kinds of lodgings, and give you the lowdown on the whole hotel scene, from making your reservations to finding the ice machine.

Chapter 6

Pillow Talk: The Lowdown on the New Orleans Hotel Scene

In This Chapter

➤ How to choose a neighborhood

➤ How to choose a hotel

➤ How to choose a room

Despite the annual influx of hundreds of thousands of visitors needing a place to stay, New Orleans has managed to keep historic districts such as the French Quarter free of the kind of skyscraper hotels that have defaced many a formerly gracious and historic city. The dedication to preserving the Quarter's architectural style has been so faithful that it's almost impossible to tell if some of the new French Quarter hotels have been built from scratch or lovingly placed inside the shell of an older building. Even motor hotels (which have alleviated the ever-present problem of on-street parking) have a look that is distinctly New Orleans. You'll find those high-rise hotels, of course, but they're more appropriately located uptown, in commercial sections, where they seem to fit just fine.

As for **guest houses,** they really do make you feel like a guest. Presided over by New Orleanians (or people who picked up and moved here after falling under the city's spell) and imbued with a special brand of hospitality, many are furnished with antiques, and all provide a very homelike atmosphere. You'll be treated as one of the family, and there's no better way to experience the history of New Orleans—most guest house owners know the story of their home and are more than willing to share it with you.

Time-Savers

The **Bed & Breakfast Reservation Service,** 1021 Moss St. (P.O. Box 52257), New Orleans, LA 70152 (☎ **800/729-4640** or 504/488-4640), provides a sort of passkey to homey New Orleans accommodations. Personable Hazell Boyce can put you up in luxury in 19th-century, turn-of-the-century, or modern residences. Or you can opt for a cottage in the French Quarter or Garden District areas. Prices range from $35 to $225 single or double occupancy, and she delights in arranging modest lodging for students. Hazell will send you free listings upon request that include rates and locations.

Location! Location! Location!

New Orleans wasn't built in a day. It started out as a series of small neighborhoods and cities that over time came together to form the city as we know it. Each of those neighborhoods has its own distinctive style and character, which I'll tell you about in the following sections. The majority of visitors to New Orleans usually opt to stay in one of the three main areas: the **French Quarter,** the **Central Business District,** and the **Garden District.** There are other options, however. The following list of neighborhoods should help you better understand the lay of the land. In chapter 7, I'll list the hotels by neighborhood as well as by other categories to help you make your choice a little easier; then I'll give you the detailed lowdown on each hotel.

The French Quarter

The historic French Quarter is definitely where a great deal of the action is. Just walking around it is a trip—it looks like no place else in the United States, except maybe for portions of Disneyland (and they ripped it off from here). The Quarter is only 6 blocks wide and 13 blocks long, so nothing is far away. You won't lack for restaurants, shops, or sights. Unfortunately, you also won't lack for other tourists. At least half of your fellow visitors will be staying there, and the rest will be milling around.

In terms of safety, the general rule is that once you start going above Bourbon Street, heading away from the river, you're entering increasingly dicey areas. Although these areas may be fine to walk through during the daytime, you should use taxis at night, particularly as you get farther away from the crowds and closer to the far border of the Quarter at Rampart Street. Taxis are readily available at taxi stands throughout the Quarter and throughout the area.

A Room over Bourbon Street

Bourbon Street is the center of the party universe in New Orleans. Here's a few things to keep in mind if you're considering getting a room right at ground zero:

- 👍 Rooms with balconies right on Bourbon Street are considered the tops: They let you watch the free human show on the street all night long.
- 👎 On the other hand, hotels with rooms on or near Bourbon Street are going to be noisy, and around Mardi Gras time, sleep will be impossible.
- 👍 The hotels closest to the intersection of Bourbon and Canal are the most sought-after and are usually the most expensive. The farther away from the center you get, the lower the price.
- 👎 On the other hand, the farther away from the center you get, the more careful you have to be at night. (Though most hotels on the outskirts of the Quarter usually have security guards.)

In a way, because much of your sightseeing will probably be centered in the Quarter, it might be better *not* to stay there. Why? Because a lot of visitors never get out of the Quarter, which is like going to New York and never leaving Greenwich Village. You haven't seen the whole city. Staying in another neighborhood (such as the Garden District) forces you to see more of what New Orleans has to offer. I've reviewed a number of options in these other neighborhoods, so the choice is yours.

In a nutshell:

- ☺ It's right at the center of things
- ☺ All the restaurants, shops, and sights are nearby
- ☺ It's an easy trip from here to the rest of town

But...

- ☹ It can be very loud, depending on how close you are to Bourbon Street
- ☹ It can be overrun with tourists
- ☹ You risk getting complacent and never seeing more of the city

The Faubourg Marigny

The Faubourg Marigny is just outside the Quarter on the other side of Esplanade Avenue. It's an easy walk to anything in the Quarter, though at night I'd take a taxi. (You can usually hail a taxi on the street, but if you aren't so lucky, you can always call one at ☎ **504/522-9771.**) There aren't any big hotels in the Marigny, but if you enjoy small bed-and-breakfasts or guest houses, this neighborhood is for you. The hotels closest to the river have the safest location. The Frenchmen area, a center of music and nightlife, is located here as well.

In a nutshell:

☺ It's close to the French Quarter

☺ It's great if you prefer a small guest house to a big hotel

☺ One of the best areas for music is right here in the Frenchmen area

But...

☹ You'll have a short walk to most of the sights

☹ You'll probably have to take a taxi home at night from the Quarter

☹ You'll have to learn how to pronounce "Faubourg Marigny" (Foe-berg Mar-a-nee)

The Central Business District

Home to about 30% of the tourist population, the Central Business District is within convenient walking distance to the Quarter and the Superdome, and public transportation to any other part of the city is readily available. If Mardi Gras parades are what you're going to New Orleans to see, this is the place to be—that is, if you don't mind the crowds.

Taxis are available at stands located by most major hotels and many pass through this area looking for fares or on their way back from one. As with the Quarter, most hotels are located in sections that are quite safe. At night, however, some hotels are best reached by taxi.

In a nutshell:

☺ It's an easy walk to the Quarter and the Garden District during the day

☺ Public transportation is right at hand

☺ It's ground zero for the Mardi Gras parades

But...

☹ You'll have to take a taxi to and from the Quarter at night

☹ It's ground zero for the Mardi Gras parades (hey, some people don't want that)

The Garden District

One of the most beautiful areas in New Orleans, the Garden District features one spectacular home after another. Anne Rice's vampires and witches walk and live here, and the St. Charles Streetcar means you are only a picturesque ride away from the Quarter (it lets you off on Canal Street at the entrance to Bourbon). Sure, you won't have several restaurants right at your fingertips, but on the other hand, you won't have drunken sailors howling at your window, either.

The area is extremely convenient for Mardi Gras parades and there's great shopping along St. Charles and Magazine streets. At night, I recommend taking a taxi. Some hotels have taxi stands, and many taxis regularly cruise through the area. If you don't see one, call ☎ **504/522-9771.**

In a nutshell:

☺ It's a quiet, beautiful part of town

☺ The St. Charles Streetcar runs right through it

☺ There's great shopping on St. Charles and Magazine streets

But...

☹ The area isn't as thickly clustered with restaurants and shops as the French Quarter

☹ You'll have to take a taxi back from the Quarter at night

The Lower Garden District

The *Utne Reader* magazine recently named the Lower Garden District the hippest neighborhood in the United States. Hip it is, but it's not quite as convenient as the Quarter, the Marigny, or the Central Business District, though accommodations are a bit cheaper. It's more funky than the stately, old-money Garden District, but it's just as lovely, and there are tons of shops and restaurants on Magazine Street. The St. Charles Streetcar and the Magazine bus are not far away.

In a nutshell:

☺ This is the hippest neighborhood in the country

☺ It's cheaper than some other parts of town

☺ There's great shopping on St. Charles and Magazine streets

But...

☹ It's a bit of a hike (or taxi ride) to the more central parts of town

☹ You can't just roll out of bed and see the big sights

Mid City

Mid City is an uncommon choice for lodging, as it's not really within walking distance of the Quarter and most of the sights visitors want to see. There's one exception to this, though: If you're coming specifically for Jazz Fest, Mid City is absolutely the most convenient location to Fair Grounds Race Course (where most of the events take place).

In a nutshell:

☺ It's close to the action at Jazz Fest

But...

☹ It's pretty far from everything else the other 51 weeks of the year

Uptown

The Uptown area, upriver and past the Garden District, is about as far as you can get from the Quarter and still be in New Orleans proper (its northwest border is the boundary between Orleans Parish and Jefferson Parish). Do I have to say that it's not the most convenient place to stay? On the other hand, it's where Tulane and Loyola Universities and Audubon Park and Zoo are located, so if you're visiting a student or have an overwhelming passion for botany or zoology, this neighborhood might be your best bet. It's a wealthy, mostly residential area with a goodly number of restaurants and shops, and during Mardi Gras, several parades wind through its streets. The St. Charles Streetcar and the Magazine bus run right through the center of the area, connecting it with the rest of the city.

In a nutshell:

☺ It's close to the universities and to Audubon Park and Zoo

☺ It's a good location for watching Mardi Gras parades

But...

☹ It's far from most of the sights and restaurants you'll probably want to visit

☹ It's far away from the nightlife of the Quarter

The Price Is Right

The **rack rate** is the maximum rate that a hotel charges for a room. It's the rate you'd get if you walked in off the street and asked for a room for the night. You sometimes see the rate printed on the fire/emergency exit diagrams posted on the back of your door. Hotels are happy to charge you the rack rate, but you don't have to pay it! Hardly anybody does. Perhaps the best way to avoid paying the rack rate is surprisingly simple: just ask for a cheaper or discounted rate. You may be pleasantly surprised.

In all but the smallest accommodations, the rate you pay for a room depends on many factors, not the least of which is how you make your reservation. A travel agent may be able to negotiate a better price with certain hotels than you could get by yourself. (That's because the hotel gives the agent a discount in exchange for steering his or her business toward that hotel.) Reserving a room through the hotel's 800 number may also result in a lower rate than if you called the hotel directly. On the other hand, the central reservations number may not know about discount rates at specific locations.

For example, local franchises may offer a special group rate for a wedding or family reunion, but they may neglect to tell the central booking line. Your best bet is to call both the local number and the 800 number and see which one gives you a better deal.

Here's a few other ways to save money on your room:

➤ **Weekend packages.** The most common package deal offered by hotels is for a weekend. Hotels with many business clients, for example, discount their weekend rates to keep their volume up. If you can't find one at your first-choice hotel, try another. Many package deals are advertised in the travel section of major newspapers.

➤ **Holiday rates.** If you're thinking of traveling on a holiday, ask if there's a special holiday rate.

➤ **Corporate rates.** Many hotels, particularly those in the mid to upper range, have corporate rates. Find out whether these rates apply to you.

➤ **Senior citizen rates.** If you're 65 or older, there's a good chance you may be able to get a senior discount.

➤ **All-in-one/inclusive packages.** Sometimes a package is offered that includes meals, tours, and tickets to the theater. If you were planning on doing these things anyway, the package may save you money.

➤ **Family rates.** Packages and discounts for families vary a great deal from hotel to hotel. Ask what's available, and be sure to find out exactly how many kids of what age can stay in the parents' room for free. Ask how much you'll pay for an extra bed in a room or for an extra child. For more about families, see the section "Family Ties: Hotel Strategies for Traveling with Kids" later in the chapter.

Room rates also change with the season and as occupancy rates rise and fall. A nearly full hotel is less likely to extend discount rates; a nearly empty one may be willing to negotiate. Resorts are most crowded on weekends and usually offer discounted rates for midweek stays. The reverse is true for business hotels in downtown locations. Room prices are subject to change without notice, so even the rates quoted in this book may be different from the rate you receive when you make your reservation. Be sure to mention membership in **AAA, AARP, frequent-flyer programs,** and any other corporate rewards program when you make your reservation. You never know when it might be worth a few dollars off your room rate.

What About the Off Season?

If you're looking for bargains, try New Orleans during June, July, and August. It's hot and humid—boy, is it hot and humid—but unless there's a big convention in town, tourism is slow, and hotels are practically giving rooms away. Remember, there are still a few big events, such as Essence Festival and Southern Decadence, even during this slow season.

If the thought of being in New Orleans in July leaves you feeling a little slug-gish, consider visiting in the weeks between Thanksgiving and Christmas, which are also slow times for tourism. It can be quite lovely and pleasant. Right after Christmas, however, the city begins filling up again.

Taxes & Service Charges

When figuring the price of your room, don't forget that there will be other fees on top of the basic rate you pay. Remember, for instance, that you'll have to pay hotel taxes, which add a whopping 11% to your bill. In addition, many hotels charge an additional $1 or $2 per room as an occupancy charge. When you reserve, make sure you know whether the price you're being quot-ed includes taxes. Ditto for packages.

Tourist Traps

Hotel telephones and minibars are a perennial source of nasty misunderstand-ing. Many hotels in the moderate to expensive range now have free local call-ing from rooms, but don't count on it. Ask when you reserve, or you may wind up with a big service charge for those 30 restaurants you called on Saturday night, trying to get a reservation for six people and a dog. Minibars in rooms are also a potential rude surprise: Just because it's stocked, doesn't mean it's free. It's generally cheaper to bring your own drinks.

What's in It for Me? What You Get for Your Money

In the next chapter, you'll see that each hotel listing is prefixed by a number of dollar signs, ranging from one ($) to five ($$$$$). The ranges are for two people and run like this:

➤ **$ (inexpensive)** hotels will cost you under **$75.** Such accommoda-tions are usually not in the best neighborhoods. At night, you should take a taxi to get to and from these places. (In same cases, this is true during the day as well.) The accommodations are usually clean and rel-atively comfortable, but some may be on the shabby side. After all, the hotels figure you spend most of your time sightseeing anyway, so why pay for all that extra glitz? In some cases, the linen may not be changed daily. Check to make sure.

➤ **$$ (low moderate)** hotels run from **$75 to $125.** Like the really inexpensive places, they're also usually located in marginal areas where at night you'll be safest getting around by taxi. Rather than luxury, the name of the game here is value, so don't be surprised if the wallpaper is cracked and faded. You'll probably get a towel, a wash cloth, and a small bar of soap, but don't expect a mint on your pillow.

➤ **$$$ (high moderate)** hotels run from **$125 to $175** and may have some of the amenities associated with more expensive hotels, but the rooms are smaller and service is geared more toward providing you with a nice, clean room in a safe and convenient location than on making you feel like the Duchess of York. They probably won't have a restaurant, or if they do, not a great one. Room service may take longer, and there may be fewer conveniences. For instance, you might have to get some personal items from vending machines rather than just wait for them to appear magically (and free) while you're out.

➤ **$$$$ (expensive)** hotels run from **$175 to $250.** They're conveniently located and have nice-sized rooms and very nice furnishings. They'll have all of the trappings of the most expensive hotels (uniformed doormen, nice furnishings, and so on) but to a lesser extent. Personal items in these places aren't usually free, either, but there will probably be a small boutique in the hotel lobby where you can pick up what you need.

➤ **$$$$$ (very expensive)** hotels usually run over **$250.** These hotels are in very safe and convenient locations and usually have huge rooms and elegant furnishings. Your bed will be turned down each night, and there will probably be a mint on your pillow. You'll probably have a minibar in your room and individual bottles of shampoo, mouthwash, and other niceties. You'll be pampered and your every whim catered to—but of course, it'll cost you.

What Kind of Place Is Right for You?

There are hotels, motels, bed-and-breakfasts, guest houses, inns, hostels, campgrounds, and private residences—it's enough to make your head spin. Don't fret, though: Deciding between them is a lot easier than it sounds.

What says "vacation" to you? A sleek, marbled modern high-rise hotel with all the conveniences? Or a cozy little guest house where you get fresh muffins in the morning? Frankly, staying in an expensive "classy" hotel that could be just about anywhere doesn't seem quite right for New Orleans. The city calls for a little character, which can means that some things are frayed around the edges, but can also mean a place with antiques, gas lamps, and banana tree-filled courtyards. It just seems like part of the whole package. But if you're from England, say, and get plenty of "olde" and atmosphere every day, you might just prefer a more glossy modern locale—just for the change.

I've made my recommendations concerning hotels and other lodgings on the basis of value and location (convenience and safety). I've recommended a few expensive hotels and a few inexpensive ones, but concentrated mostly on the moderate ones. Because the French Quarter and the Central Business District are the most popular neighborhoods and most convenient to restaurants and attractions, that's where I've focused my energy. However, you can find good value in other parts of the city, so I've also recommended some hotels in the Garden District and other outlying areas.

Don't waste time trying to figure out which of these hotels are dumps; the places listed in this book are all decent and reputable, and I've screened out those in dire need of renovation. Of course, the amenities in a $$$$$ room are a bit more substantial than those in a $ one.

Breakfast in Bed

Although most bed-and-breakfasts don't serve breakfast in bed, they do *provide* both beds and breakfast. Rather than calling around to all the B&Bs in the area, you can call a B&B agency, which will do all the work for you. Here's a list of agencies that handle reservations for local bed-and-breakfasts. Be aware that these places are quite popular and that regular visitors to Mardi Gras and Jazz Fest can reserve rooms up to a year in advance.

➤ **Bed and Breakfast & Beyond** (☎ 504/822-8525)

➤ **Bed & Breakfast and Accommodations** (☎ 504/838-0071)

➤ **Bed & Breakfast Travel** (☎ 800/926-4320)

➤ **Garden District Bed & Breakfast** (☎ 504/895-4302)

➤ **New Orleans Bed & Breakfast Reservation Service** (☎ 504/488-4640)

Getting the Best Room

Somebody has to get the best room in the house, and it might as well be you. Always ask for a corner room. They're usually larger, quieter, have more windows and light than standard rooms, and don't always cost any more.

When you make your reservation, ask whether the hotel is renovating; if it is, request a room away from the renovation work. Inquire, too, about the location of the restaurants, bars, and discos in the hotel—these could all be a source of irritating noise. Lastly, ask for an inside room if you're a light sleeper, otherwise you might be disturbed by the street noise (especially if your hotel is on or near Bourbon Street).

If you aren't happy with your room when you arrive, talk to the front desk. If they have another room, they should be happy to accommodate you, within reason.

Watching Your Ifs & Butts: A Word About Smoking

In 1983, after smoking up to five packs a day for over 20 years, I finally quit. The farther my smoking days drift into the past, the more adverse reaction I have to other people's smoke. Many hotels now offer non-smoking rooms; by all means ask for one if smoke bothers you. If you're like me, make sure you specify a room where smoking is *never* allowed (there may be lingering odors if smoking is allowed). Most of the larger hotels set aside several rooms or even an entire wing where smoking is strictly forbidden.

Family Ties: Hotel Strategies for Traveling with Kids

Kids generally appreciate the finer things in life, and that, of course, means swimming pools and video games—you can dangle these amenities as a reward for getting through a busy day of sightseeing. Remember, too, that some things you just shrug over will be like a burning bush on a hilltop to most kids—soda machines right down the hall, for instance. (I used to get excited over hotel ice machines.) For the most part, the sheer novelty of staying in an unfamiliar place will be enough to stun most kids into submission.

In terms of economy, look for a hotel that will let your child/children stay for free in your room. If you have teenage kids, though, hotels may not be so agreeable to this. If you have teenagers, try to get adjoining rooms; that way, your kids will have the illusion of privacy, but you'll still be able to hear if they're doing anything evil.

Hotel Strategies for Travelers with Disabilities

Not all hotels, especially the old ones (and most in New Orleans *are* old), have been brought up to date with access regulations. Small hotels, B&Bs, and budget hotels are unlikely to be very advanced in this respect. Some hotels, however, have special facilities for folks that need 'em, such as roll-in showers to accommodate wheelchairs, lower sinks, and extra space to move around. In any case, you'll have to ask for one of these accessible rooms when you reserve. Also, some chains (like Hilton) have specially accessible rooms in all their hotels. I've mentioned in the "Hotels A to Z" listing (chapter 7) which hotels are especially good for people with disabilities.

What If I Didn't Plan Ahead?

If you didn't make reservations before you left, don't despair; you can still probably find a room. Go to any of the major hotels in the French Quarter or on Canal Street; if they're full, they'll check around for you and see what's available. If they won't, or if they can't find anything, ask them to check your luggage for you in case they have a cancellation while you check around on your own. And now you've got a couple of options:

1. Use a hotel house phone (or get yourself some quarters and find a pay phone) and start ringing every hotel listed in the next chapter. If you run out and still haven't found a place, you'll have to throw caution to the wind and just dive into the Yellow Pages, where hotels are listed both alphabetically and by location.

2. If that doesn't work, or if you just don't have the energy, call **Room Finders U.S.A., Inc.** (☎ **800/473-STAY**) or the **French Quarter Reservation Service** (☎ **504/523-1246**).

Hotels A to Z

Now that you've read through the last chapter and gotten an idea of the best areas to stay in New Orleans, this chapter gets down to the nitty-gritty and deals with the individual hotel options. I've started this chapter with some handy-dandy lists that break down my favorite hotels by neighborhood and price; then, for the grand finale, I've reviewed them all, giving you all the information you'll need to make your decision. I may not be Nostradamus, but I think I see some hotel reservations in your future.

The reviews are arranged alphabetically so they're easier to refer back to, and the neighborhood each hotel is located in appears right beneath its name—check them against the maps to give yourself a better idea of where they are in relation to what you want to see and where you want to be.

As far as price goes, I've noted rack rates in the listings and also preceded each with dollar signs to make quick reference easier. The more $$$ signs under the name, the more you pay:

$	=	under $75
$$	=	$75–$125
$$$	=	$125–$175
$$$$	=	$175–$250
$$$$$	=	over $250

I've also added a "kid friendly" icon (🌟kids) to those hotels that are especially good for families and included special features throughout that will direct you to the best hotels for those of you with special considerations in mind— if you're in the mood for love, if you want to be close to a Mardi Gras parade route, and so on.

Hint: As you read through the reviews, keep track of the ones that appeal to you. I've included a chart at the end of this chapter where you can rank your preferences, but to make matters easier on yourself now, why don't you just put a little checkmark next to the ones you like? Remember how your teachers used to tell you not to write in your books? Now's the time to rebel. Scrawl away.

Quick Picks: New Orleans' Hotels at a Glance
Hotel Index by Location

French Quarter

Best Western Inn on Bourbon Street ($$$$)

Bienville House ($$$$$)

Bourbon Orleans Hotel ($$$$$)

Chateau Hotel ($$)

Chateau Sonesta Hotel ($$$$)

Dauphine Orleans Hotel ($$$$$)

Holiday Inn–Chateau LeMoyne ($$$)

Hotel de la Poste ($$$)

Hotel Maison de Ville ($$$)

Hotel Provincial ($$$)

Hotel Ste. Hèléne ($$$)

Hotel Ste. Pierre ($$)

Hotel Villa Convento ($$)

Lafitte Guest House ($$)

LaMothe House ($$$)

Le Richelieu Motor Hotel ($$)

Maison Dupuy ($$$$)

Monteleone Hotel ($$$)

New Orleans Guest House ($$)

Omni Royal Orleans ($$$$)

Place d'Armes Hotel ($$)

Prince Conti Hotel ($$$)

Royal Sonesta ($$$$)

Soniat House ($$$$$)

St. Louis ($$$$)

Westin Canal Place ($$$$$)

Faubourg Marigny

B&W Courtyards Bed & Breakfast ($$)

Frenchmen ($$)

Melrose Mansion ($$$$$)

Central Business District

Holiday Inn Downtown Superdome ($$$)

Hotel La Salle ($$)

Le Pavillion Hotel ($$$$)

Windsor Court Hotel ($$$$$)

Garden District

Avenue Plaza Suite Hotel & Spa ($$$)

McKendrick-Breaux House ($$)

Pontchartrain Hotel ($$$$)

Lower Garden District

Prytania Inn ($)

Prytania Park Hotel ($$)

Mid City

House on Bayou Road ($$$$)

Mechling's Guest House ($$$)

Quality Inn Midtown ($$)

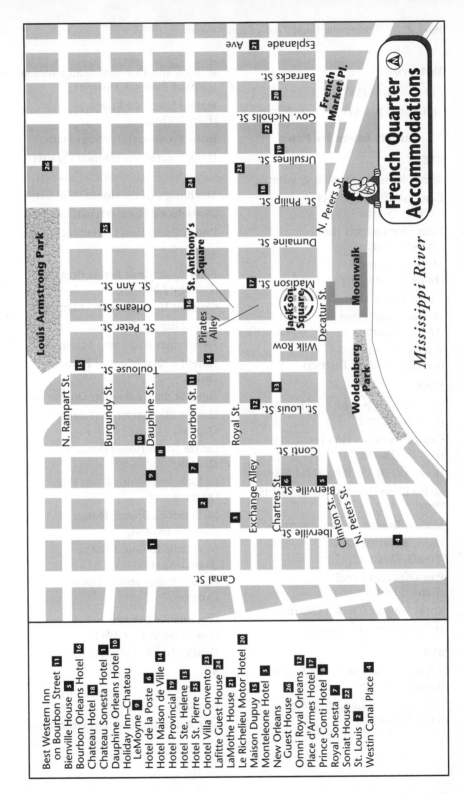

French Quarter Accommodations

Mississippi River

Louis Armstrong Park

St. Anthony's Square

Jackson Square

Pirates Alley

Moonwalk

Woldenberg Park

French Market Pl.

Esplanade Ave 21
Barracks St. 20
Gov. Nicholls St. 22
Ursulines St. 19
23
St. Philip St. 18
24
Dumaine St.
25
St. Ann St. 16
Orleans St.
St. Peter St. 14
Toulouse St. 15
St. Louis St. 13
Conti St. 12
Exchange Alley
Bienville St. 6 5
Iberville St.
Canal St.
Clinton St.
N. Peters St. 4
Decatur St.
Madison St. 17
Wilk Row
Royal St.
Bourbon St. 11
Dauphine St. 8 10
Burgundy St. 7 9
N. Rampart St.
Chartres St.
26
2
3
1

Best Western Inn on Bourbon Street 11
Bienville House 5
Bourbon Orleans Hotel 16
Chateau Hotel 18
Chateau Sonesta Hotel 1
Dauphine Orleans Hotel 10
Holiday Inn–Chateau LeMoyne 9
Hotel de la Poste 6
Hotel Maison de Ville 14
Hotel Provincial 19
Hotel Ste. Helene 13
Hotel St. Pierre 25
Hotel Villa Convento 23
Lafitte Guest House 24
LaMothe House 21
Le Richelieu Motor Hotel 20
Maison Dupuy 15
Monteleone Hotel 3
New Orleans Guest House 26
Omni Royal Orleans 12
Place d'Armes Hotel 17
Prince Conti Hotel 8
Royal Sonesta 7
Soniat House 22
St. Louis 2
Westin Canal Place 4

85

Uptown

The Columns ($$)

St. Charles Inn ($)

Hotel Index by Price

$$$$$

Bienville House (French Quarter)

Bourbon Orleans Hotel
(French Quarter)

Dauphine Orleans Hotel
(French Quarter)

Melrose Mansion
(Faubourg Marigny)

Soniat House (French Quarter)

Westin Canal Place
(French Quarter)

Windsor Court Hotel
(Central Business District)

$$$$

Best Western Inn on Bourbon Street
(French Quarter)

Chateau Sonesta Hotel
(French Quarter)

House on Bayou Road (Mid City)

Le Pavillion Hotel (Central Business
District)

Maison Dupuy (French Quarter)

Omni Royal Orleans
(French Quarter)

Pontchartrain Hotel
(Garden District)

Royal Sonesta (French Quarter)

St. Louis (French Quarter)

$$$

Avenue Plaza Suite Hotel & Spa
(Garden District)

Holiday Inn–Chateau LeMoyne
(French Quarter)

Holiday Inn Downtown Superdome
(Central Business District)

Hotel Maison de Ville
(French Quarter)

Hotel Provincial (French Quarter)

Hotel Ste. Hélène (French Quarter)

LaMothe House (French Quarter)

Mechling's Guest House (Mid City)

Monteleone Hotel (French Quarter)

Prince Conti Hotel (French Quarter)

$$

B&W Courtyards Bed & Breakfast
(Faubourg Marigny)

Chateau Hotel (French Quarter)

The Columns (Uptown)

Frenchmen (Faubourg Marigny)

Hotel La Salle (Central Business
District)

Hotel St. Pierre (French Quarter)

Hotel Villa Convento (French
Quarter)

Lafitte Guest House (French
Quarter)

Le Richelieu Motor Hotel (French
Quarter)

McKendrick-Breaux House
(Garden District)

New Orleans Guest House
(French Quarter)

Place d'Armes Hotel (French
Quarter)

Prytania Park Hotel
(Lower Garden District)

Quality Inn Midtown (Mid City)

$

Prytania Inn (Lower Garden
District)

St. Charles Inn (Garden District)

My Favorite Hotels

Avenue Plaza Suite Hotel & Spa
$$$. Garden District.

Just a quick streetcar ride from the Quarter, this recently renovated, all-suite hotel was once an 18th-century home. Each suite features a kitchenette and is furnished in a sophisticated Garden District style. Sun worshipers will appreciate the rooftop sun deck. There's also a courtyard swimming pool, a cafe, and a lounge.

2111 St. Charles (11 blocks from Lee Circle), New Orleans, LA 70130. ☎ *800/535-9575 or 504/566-1212. Fax 504/525-6899.* **Parking:** *$8.* **Rack rates:** *$89–$199 double. AE, CB, DC, DISC, MC, V.*

Don't Leave Home without This: Credit Card Abbreviations

AE	American Express
CB	Carte Blanche
DC	Diners Club
DISC	Discover Card
JCB	Japan Credit Bank
MC	MasterCard
V	Visa

B&W Courtyards Bed & Breakfast
$$. Faubourg Marigny.

The deceptively simple facade hides a sweet and very hospitable little B&B, complete with two small courtyards and a fountain. Owners Rob and Kevin went to ingenious lengths to turn five oddly shaped spaces into comfortable guest rooms. No two rooms are alike in layout—for example, you have to enter one room through its bathroom. Rob and Kevin are adept at giving advice not just about the city but about their own local favorites. Breakfast is light, but beautifully presented. The location means about a 10-minute walk (or $5 cab ride) from the Quarter. Prepare to be pampered—they take good care of you here.

2425 Chartres St., New Orleans, LA 70117. ☎ *800/585-5731 or 504/949-5313.* **Parking:** *Available on the street.* **Rack rates:** *$99–$115 double. AE, DISC, MC, V.*

Best Western Inn on Bourbon Street
$$$$. French Quarter.

Located on the site of the 1859 French Opera House (the first opera house built in the United States, it burned down in 1919), this place is in the middle of the most lively portion of Bourbon Street. Some of the rooms have balconies overlooking the street, and all have double or king-size beds and Deep South decor. The service can be slow, and the rooms along Bourbon Street can be noisy. There's a cafeteria (breakfast only), a small service bar, a fitness room, and an outdoor pool on the premises.

541 Bourbon St. (at the corner of Toulouse), New Orleans, LA 70130. ☎ *800/535-7891 or 504/524-7611. Fax 504/568-9427.* **Valet parking:** *$10.* **Rack rates:** *$185–$265 double. AE, CB, DC, DISC, MC, V.*

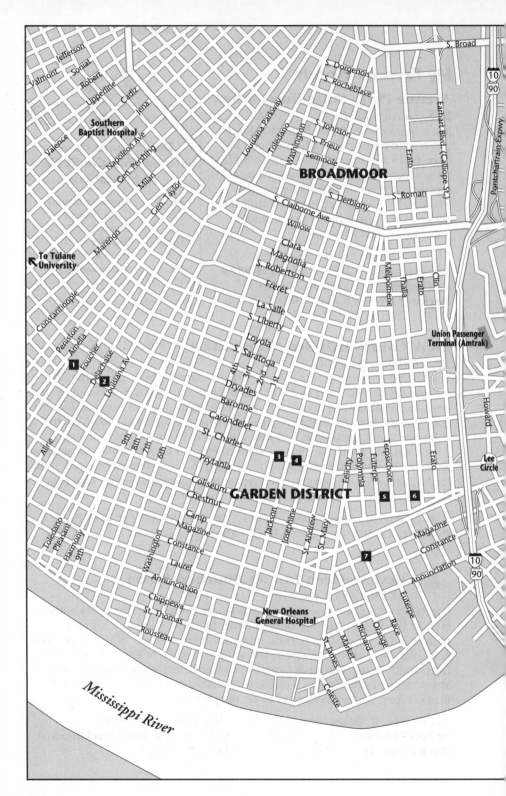

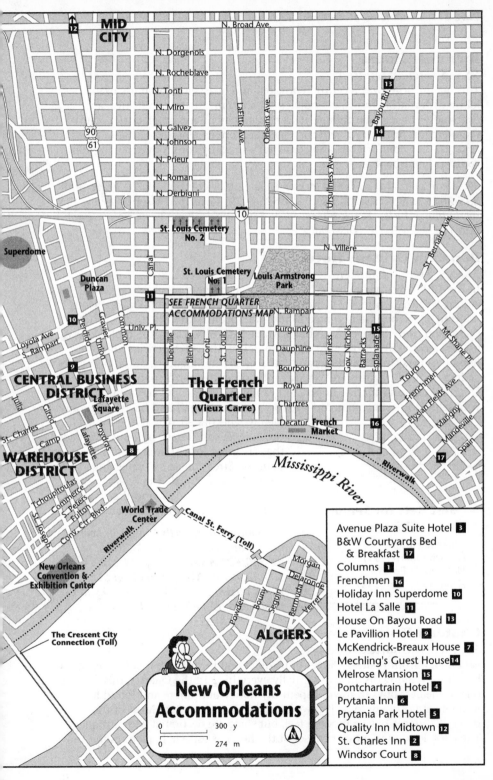

MID CITY

N. Broad Ave.

N. Dorgenois
N. Rocheblave
N. Tonti
N. Miro
N. Galvez
N. Johnson
N. Prieur
N. Roman
N. Derbigni

LaFitte Ave.
Orleans Ave.
Bayou Rd.
Ursulines Ave.
St. Bernard Ave.

90
61

10

St. Louis Cemetery No. 2

N. Villere

Superdome

Duncan Plaza

St. Louis Cemetery No. 1

Louis Armstrong Park

SEE FRENCH QUARTER ACCOMMODATIONS MAP

N. Rampart
Burgundy
Dauphine
Bourbon
Royal
Chartres
Decatur

Ursulines
Gov. Nichols
Barracks
Esplanade

McShane Pl.

Touro
Frenchmen
Elysian Fields Ave.
Marigny
Mandeville
Spain

The French Quarter (Vieux Carre)

Canal
Univ. Pl.
Iberville
Bienville
Conti
St. Louis
Toulouse

Loyola Ave.
S. Rampart
Perdido
Gravier
Union
Common

CENTRAL BUSINESS DISTRICT

Lafayette Square

Julia
Girod
Camp

St. Charles

Poydras
Lafayette

WAREHOUSE DISTRICT

French Market

Mississippi River

Riverwalk

Tchoupitoulas
Commerce
S. Peters
Fulton
Conv. Ctr. Blvd.
St. Joseph

World Trade Center

Canal St. Ferry (Toll)

Riverwalk

New Orleans Convention & Exhibition Center

The Crescent City Connection (Toll)

Morgan
Delaronde
Bermuda
Verret
Powder
Bouny
Seguin

ALGIERS

New Orleans Accommodations

0 ——— 300 y
0 ——— 274 m

Avenue Plaza Suite Hotel **3**
B&W Courtyards Bed & Breakfast **17**
Columns **1**
Frenchmen **16**
Holiday Inn Superdome **10**
Hotel La Salle **11**
House On Bayou Road **13**
Le Pavillion Hotel **9**
McKendrick-Breaux House **7**
Mechling's Guest House **14**
Melrose Mansion **15**
Pontchartrain Hotel **4**
Prytania Inn **6**
Prytania Park Hotel **5**
Quality Inn Midtown **12**
St. Charles Inn **2**
Windsor Court **8**

Bienville House
$$$$$. French Quarter.

This quaint hotel was recently renovated and boasts a small but elegant lobby with marble floors, chandelier, Mediterranean-style paintings, and overstuffed sofas. Even though it's a moderately priced hotel, antique and reproduction furniture give it the feel of a more expensive one. The rooms are small but comfortable, and some have small balconies overlooking the courtyard and pool area.

320 Decatur St. (3 blocks from Jackson Square), New Orleans, LA 70130. ☎ *800/535-7836 or 504/529-2345. Fax 504/525-6079. **Valet parking:** $11 cars; $15 sport utility vehicles. **Rack rates:** $179–$395 double. Rates include continental breakfast. AE, CB, DC, DISC, MC, V.*

Bourbon Orleans Hotel
$$$$$. French Quarter.

In the 19th century, having a creole mistress was very much in fashion among wealthy white New Orleanian men, and the Bourbon Orleans Hotel (built in 1815) originally served as the site of lavish quadroon balls, where these men came to meet free young women of color. Later, the building was used as a convent for the South's first order of African-American nuns. The hotel occupies three buildings and has recently undergone a $6-million renovation. Its public spaces are extravagantly decorated with chandeliers, Oriental rugs, and marble floors. You can even order room service through your television. Their standard-size rooms are not small and have been completely redecorated. The living rooms in the bi-level suites have pull-out sofa beds that are good for children. Avoid Bourbon Street noise by requesting a room closer to Royal. The on-site restaurant offers good meals, and the elegant lobby features a nightly cocktail hour.

Best Bets for Senior Citizens

Chateau Hotel
(French Quarter, $$)
Hotel de la Poste
(French Quarter, $$$)

717 Orleans St. (directly behind St. Louis Cathedral), New Orleans, LA 70116. ☎ *800/521-5338 or 504/523-2222. Fax 504/525-8166. **Valet parking:** $12. **Rack rates:** $240–$375 double. Extra person $20. AE, CB, DC, DISC, MC, V.*

Chateau Hotel
$$. French Quarter.

Far enough from Bourbon Street to be quiet and intimate, but close enough to be within walking distance of virtually everything in the Quarter, this hotel is one of the best buys in town. I spent my honeymoon here and found its intimate atmosphere to be just what my wife and I wanted. Most of the hotel's 27 rooms have a modern feel, but some are decorated with antiques. The pool, located in a quiet corner of the hotel, is especially picturesque and surrounded by a flagstone courtyard with chaise lounges. A continental break-fast and newspaper are included in the room fee, and seniors receive a 10% discount. Another plus: One of my favorite restaurants, **Irene's Cuisine,** is now located across the street from the hotel's Chartres Street side.

1001 Chartres St. (4 blocks from Jackson Square), New Orleans, LA 70116. ☎ **504/524-9636.** *Fax 504/525-2989.* **Rack rates:** *$79–$119 double. AE, CB, DC, MC, V. Free parking.*

Chateau Sonesta Hotel
$$$$. French Quarter.
Located on the site of the former D. H. Holmes Department Store building, the Chateau Sonesta opened in 1995, making it one of the newest hotels in the Quarter. Although the hotel has preserved its 1913 exterior, inside it has opted for a modern, luxurious ambiance. The rooms are large, and some have balconies overlooking Bourbon Street. The phones have a data port for guests who travel with their computers.

800 Iberville St. (at the corner of Dauphine St.), New Orleans, LA 70130. ☎ **800/SONESTA** *or 504/586-0800. Fax 504/586-1987.* **Valet parking:** *$14.* **Rack rates:** *$225–$285. Extra person $35. AE, CB, DC, DISC, MC, V.*

Bet You Didn't Know

For many years, it's been a New Orleans tradition to meet on Canal Street under the clock at the former D. H. Holmes Department Store (now the Chateau Sonesta Hotel). Now you can meet a New Orleans legend there: A statue of **Ignatius J. Reilly,** the protagonist from John Kennedy Toole's Pulitzer Prize-winning novel *A Confederacy of Dunces,* was recently unveiled and stands at the hotel's Canal Street entrance, where readers first meet him in the book.

The Columns
$$. Uptown.
The wide mahogany staircase of The Columns will seem familiar to anyone who has seen Louis Malle's film *Pretty Baby,* in which this hotel stood in for a Storyville brothel—and that should give you an idea of how it looks. The hotel was built in 1883 and is an elegant example of a late–19th century home. The grand columned veranda is a popular place to sip cocktails. The interior, however, is far from luxurious. There are 19 rooms, half of which lack private baths and none of which have televisions. All of the rooms, however, are clean and comfortable. The rooms that do have baths have claw-foot tubs, and those without bathrooms do have wash basins.

Best Bets for Travelers with Disabilities

Dauphine Orleans Hotel
(French Quarter, $$$$$)
Hotel de la Poste
(French Quarter, $$$)
Omni Royal Orleans
(French Quarter, $$$$)
Westin Canal Place
(French Quarter, $$$$$)

Bet You Didn't Know

The Union General Benjamin Butler, who controlled the city for seven months after taking it in 1862, was one of the most hated men in the South. He earned the nickname "Spoons" because he used to confiscate silverware, claiming it could otherwise be used to finance the Confederacy. When his daughter married, many New Orleanians gave her a single silver spoon as a wedding gift.

3811 St. Charles Ave. (halfway between Louisiana and Napoleon avenues), New Orleans, LA 70115. ☎ *504/899-9308. Fax 504/899-8170. Parking: available on the street. Rack rates: $95–$160. Rates include continental breakfast. AE, MC, V.*

Dauphine Orleans Hotel
$$$$$. French Quarter.

This small, charming hotel is located on a relatively quiet and peaceful block of the Quarter. In fact, as you sit in any of its three secluded courtyards, it's hard to believe that you're only a block away from the hullabaloo of Bourbon Street. Inside, all the rooms have been upgraded recently with marble bathrooms and new furnishings that are either modern or period pieces. Continental breakfast is included in the cost of your room and is served in the Coffee Lounge from 6:30am to 11am. Complimentary tea is also served daily from 3pm to 5pm. The hotel offers a guest library, a small fitness room, a Jacuzzi, and complimentary transportation to other areas of the French Quarter and downtown. The back buildings were once used as a studio by naturalist and renowned bird artist John James Audubon, and the hotel's bar was once a brothel; guests are given a copy of the 1857 license, the original of which hangs on the wall.

415 Dauphine St. (at the end of Arnaud's restaurant on Iberville), New Orleans, LA 70112. ☎ *800/521-7111 or 504/586-1800. Fax 504/586-1409. Valet parking: $12. Rack rates: $179–$399. Extra person $15. Children under 17 free in parents' room. AE, DC, DISC, MC, V. Wheelchair accessible.*

Frenchmen
$$. Faubourg Marigny.

Located at the intersection of Esplanade Avenue and Frenchmen Street, across from the Quarter, this hotel occupies two 19th-century buildings that were once grand New Orleans homes. It boasts a plush lobby, and rooms are individually decorated with antiques. The size of the rooms vary wildly, and some are downright tiny. The tropical courtyard features a Jacuzzi and a tiny pool (though the pool is overdue for its upcoming renovation). The hotel is a short block from the lively Frenchman area, which at night booms with a number of clubs and cafes and is quickly becoming one of the best spots for music in the city. Its bargain rates (which include breakfast and free parking) and convenience to both the Quarter and the Frenchman area make this place a favorite of savvy travelers.

417 Frenchmen St. (just across the street from the Old U.S. Mint on Esplanade), New Orleans, LA 70116. ☎ *800/831-1781 or 504/948-2166. Fax 504/948-2258.* **Rack rates:** *$84–$180. Rates include breakfast. AE, DISC, MC, V.*

Holiday Inn Downtown Superdome
$$$. Central Business District.
This 18-story hotel is a favorite of Saints fans because of its proximity to the Superdome, but that's not all it's close to—non-Saints fans will appreciate the easy access to New Orleans' business and financial centers as well as to the French Quarter (though it's probably a bit more of a walk than might be comfortable to the latter, particularly at night). It's also not as high-priced as the nearby Hyatt Regency. Jazz began in the clubs that used to dominate this area, and the hotel maintains a jazz theme, including a collection of jazz scene murals and a giant clarinet that hangs from the side of the building. Each room has a balcony and a city view and is decorated in typical Holiday Inn style. There's a heated pool on the roof.

Best Bets If You've Got the Kids in Tow

Best Western Inn on Bourbon Street
(French Quarter, $$$$)
Hotel Ste. Hélène
(French Quarter, $$$)
Omni Royal Orleans
(French Quarter, $$$$)
Prytania Park Hotel
(Lower Garden District, $$)

330 Loyola Ave. (across from the Louisiana Supreme Court building), New Orleans, LA 70112. ☎ *800/535-7830 or 504/581-1600. Fax 504/586-0833.* **Self-parking:** *$10.* **Rack rates:** *$94–$209 double. ($119 in summer; extra person $15.) Children 19 and under free in parents' room. AE, CB, DC, DISC, MC, V.*

Holiday Inn–Chateau LeMoyne
$$$. French Quarter.
Housed in buildings more than a century old and featuring winding staircases, this hotel is not a typical run-of-the-mill Holiday Inn. All the rooms are furnished in a comfortable, traditional style, and like the Dauphine Orleans, this hotel is located in a quiet section of the Quarter. Adding to the old New Orleans flavor, some of the bedrooms are converted slave quarters and overlook the courtyard. The restaurant serves breakfast only, but there's room service until 10pm.

301 Dauphine St. (just around the corner from the Deja Vu Bar & Grill), New Orleans, LA 70112. ☎ *800/HOLIDAY or 504/581-1303. Fax 504/523-5709.* **Valet parking:** *$12.* **Rack rates:** *$150–$185. Extra person $25. AE, CB, DC, DISC, MC, V.*

Hotel de la Poste
$$$. French Quarter.
Recently remodeled, the Hotel de la Poste has large comfortable rooms, most of which overlook either the Quarter or the courtyard and fountain. All in-room phones have data ports for those bringing computers. The courtyard features a beautiful staircase, which leads to a second-level outdoor pool. Within the hotel is the **Ristorante Bacco** (see chapter 11), run by brother and sister Cindy and Ralph Brennan of the famed Brennan restaurateur family.

316 Chartres St. (3 blocks from Jackson Square), New Orleans, LA 70130. ☎ *800/ 448-4927 or 504/581-1200. Fax 504/523-2910.* **Valet parking:** *$12.* **Rack rates:** *$75–$200. AE, CB, DC, DISC, MC, V. Children under 16 free in parents' room. AAA and senior's discounts available. Wheelchair accessible.*

Best Bets for Romantic Travelers

House on Bayou Road (Mid City, $$$$)
Hotel Maison de Ville (French Quarter, $$$)
Melrose Mansion (Faubourg Marigny, $$$$$)
Soniat House (French Quarter, $$$$$)

Hotel La Salle
$$. Central Business District
Low rates and clean, comfortable rooms make this one of the best values near the Quarter, but bear in mind that the rooms are plainly furnished and that many don't have private bathrooms. The high ceilings and vintage wooden reception desk give the lobby the feel of another era, and the location means a quick walk to Quarter action, though those first couple of blocks aren't the best after dark.

1113 Canal St. (4 blocks from Bourbon St.), New Orleans, LA 70112. ☎ *800/521-9450 or 504/523-5831. Fax 504/525-2531. Free parking.* **Rack rates:** *$58–$180. Children under 12 free in parent's room. AE, DISC, MC, V.*

Hotel Maison de Ville
$$$. French Quarter.
Ranked as one of the best small hotels in the world, the Maison de Ville is a terrific choice for a special-occasion splurge. It's like a fancy B&B, but with outstanding service and utter comfort. Tennessee Williams knew this—he lived here on and off (in room 6) for some years. Rooms (some of which can be quite small) are rich and elegant, mostly arranged around a small courtyard. A block or so away are the Audubon Cottages (one of which provided a temporary home for the famous naturalist, John James Audubon), which also

have a small pool. A continental breakfast is brought to your room on a silver tray along with the morning paper. Expect surprises on your pillow at night. The hotel also has a world-class (but tiny) bistro.

727 Toulouse St. (½ block from Bourbon St.), New Orleans, LA 70130. ☎ *800/634-1600 or 504/561-5858. Fax 504/528-9939.* **Valet parking: $15. Rack rates:** *$165–$185 (includes breakfast). AE, DC, MC, V.*

Hotel Provincial
$$$. French Quarter.
Located in a quiet stretch of the Quarter a mere two blocks from Bourbon Street, the Hotel Provincial is a series of 19th-century buildings with five different patios illuminated by gaslight. Rooms have the high ceilings of an earlier age, and each is decorated with French and Creole antiques. The moderately priced **Honfleur** restaurant is a good bet for breakfast, lunch, or dinner. The hotel was used as a hospital during the Civil War, and local ghost hunters swear it's haunted.

1024 Chartres St. (4 blocks from Jackson Square), New Orleans, LA 70116. ☎ *800/535-7922 or 504/581-4995. Fax 504/581-1018.* **Valet parking: $7. Rack rates:** *$150–$175. Summer package rates available. AE, CB, DC, DISC, MC, V.*

Hotel Ste. Hélène
$$$. French Quarter.
Two blocks from Jackson Square as well as Bourbon Street, the Ste. Hélène offers easy access to all of the action and yet is a retreat from the noise when you're ready to sleep. The outer courtyard, with its flagstone patio and cast-iron tables and chairs, is an ideal place to enjoy the free continental breakfast. Other amenities include a small pool.

508 Chartres St. (just 2½ very short blocks from Jackson Square), New Orleans, LA 70130. ☎ *800/348-3888 or 504/522-5014. Fax 504/523-7140.* **Parking: $14** *in a nearby lot.* **Rack rates:** *$145–$185 double. Rates include continental breakfast. AE, CB, DC, DISC, MC, V.*

Hotel St. Pierre
$$. French Quarter.
Located in a residential area of the Quarter only two blocks from Bourbon Street, this hotel was once a private home. The rooms vary in size; some are in the old slave quarters, several have fireplaces, and all are furnished in a modern style. Swimmers will enjoy the two outdoor pools. The hotel's proximity to Bourbon Street makes it an excellent value for the money, and though the neighborhood is relatively safe, it's best to keep your eyes open when on this side of Bourbon Street at night.

911 Burgundy St. (2 blocks from Bourbon St.), New Orleans, LA 70116. ☎ *800/535-7785, 800/225-4040, or 504/524-4401. Fax 504/524-6800.* **Parking:** *Free, but limited.* **Rack rates:** *$79–$175; extra person $20 (includes breakfast). Children under 12 are free in parents' room. AE, CB, DC, DISC, MC, V.*

95

Hotel Villa Convento
$$. French Quarter.
Local tour guides swear this small inn was the original House of the Rising Sun (the notorious bordello of story and song), so posing in robe or underwear on one of the balconies overlooking Ursulines Street as the tours pass by could be a cheap thrill. Guests are devoted to the personal attention they receive from the staff. Group rooms with twin beds in lofts overhead make this hotel a perfect choice for families. A continental breakfast served in the tropical courtyard is included in the room rates.

616 Ursulines St. (around the corner from the Old Ursuline Convent), New Orleans, LA 70116. ☎ *800/887-2817 or 504/522-1793. Fax 504/524-1902.* **Parking:** *available in public parking area at the riverfront ($15 per day).* **Rack rates:** *$89–$155 (breakfast included); additional person $10. AE, CB, DC, DISC, MC, V.*

Best Hotels with a History
Best Western Inn on Bourbon Street (French Quarter, $$$$)
Bourbon Orleans Hotel (French Quarter, $$$$$)
Hotel Provincial (French Quarter, $$$)
Hotel Villa Convento (French Quarter, $$)
House on Bayou Road (Mid City, $$$$)
Monteleone Hotel (French Quarter, $$$)

House on Bayou Road
$$$$. Mid City.
This Creole plantation home, built in the late 1700s, is located just off Esplanade Avenue. The 10-minute taxi ride from the French Quarter means it's a little isolated, but it's still one of the city's best B&Bs and is quite convenient for Jazz Fest, which is held not far from here. The House is an oasis of luxurious peace and quiet; its four rooms and two cottages are individually decorated with antiques. The small cottage with a skylight over the bed and a Jacuzzi is perfect for those looking for a romantic escape. A complimentary full plantation breakfast is served in the morning, and during the day and the evening guests can help themselves to a mini-refrigerator filled with beverages. The House also offers cooking classes as a special package.

2275 Bayou Rd. (drive 1 mile from the Quarter along Esplanade and turn right at Bayou Rd.), New Orleans, LA 70119. ☎ *800/882-2968 or 504/949-7711.* **Parking:** *Free.* **Rack rates:** *$150–$230 (plantation breakfast included). AE, MC, V.*

Lafitte Guest House
$$. French Quarter.
The location of this guest house gives you the best of both worlds; at the quiet end of Bourbon Street (yes, there is such a thing!), it's just a quick trot from the action. The Lafitte's three-story building was originally constructed in 1849 and has been completely restored. All of the rooms are decorated individually and feature period furniture, marble fireplaces, 14-foot ceilings, and exposed brick walls. The size of the rooms varies—for example, Room 4 covers the entire top floor and accommodates up to six people.

1003 Bourbon St. (at the corner of St. Philip), New Orleans, LA 70116. ☎ *800/ 331-7971 or 504/581-2678. Fax 504/581-2677.* **Parking:** *$7.50.* **Rack rates:** *$85–$165 double (breakfast included). AE, DC, DISC, JCB, MC, V.*

LaMothe House
$$$. French Quarter.
Somehow, a shiny new hotel doesn't seem quite right for New Orleans. A slightly faded, somewhat threadbare elegance is much more appropriate, and the LaMothe House fits the bill. The Creole-style plain facade hides the sort of atmosphere you're looking for: a mossy, brick-lined courtyard with a fish-filled fountain and banana trees, and antique-filled rooms that are worn in the right places, but not shabby. It's located on Esplanade, a short walk from Quarter action and just a couple blocks from the bustling Frenchman scene. On a steamy night, sitting in that courtyard breathing the fragrant air, you can feel yourself slip out of time.

621 Esplanade Ave., New Orleans, LA 70116. ☎ *800/367-5858 or 504/947-1161. Fax 504/943-6536.* **Parking:** *Free off-street.* **Rack rates:** *$99–$175. AE, DISC, MC, V.*

Le Pavillion Hotel
$$$$. Central Business District.
Established in 1907, Le Pavillion's prices and its location (about seven blocks from the Superdome and Bourbon Street) make it a great value. Le Pavillion is a member of Historical Hotels of America. It opened in 1907 and was the first hotel in New Orleans to have elevators—mercifully, they aren't still using the same ones. Its breathtaking lobby (11 crystal chandeliers!) and impressive columned motor entrance on Poydras Street make it a truly elegant hotel. Services available include baby-sitting, newspaper delivery, and complimentary shoe shine. Complimentary hors d'oeuvres are served Monday through Friday from 4pm to 7pm

Best Hotels If You Want an Antique Ambiance

Hotel Maison de Ville
(French Quarter, $$$)
Hotel Provincial
(French Quarter, $$$)
House on Bayou Road
(Mid City, $$$$)
Lafitte Guest House
(French Quarter, $$)
LaMothe House
(French Quarter, $$$)
Mechling's Guest House
(Mid City, $$$)
Ponchartrain Hotel
(Garden District, $$$$)
Prince Conti Hotel
(French Quarter, $$$)
Soniat House
(French Quarter, $$$$$)

in the Gallery Lounge, and complimentary peanut butter and jelly sandwiches are available in the evening in the lobby. There's a heated pool on the roof, a fitness center, and a whirlpool spa.

833 Poydras St. (8 blocks from the river or 7 blocks from the Superdome), New Orleans, LA 70140. ☎ 800/535-9095 or 504/581-3111. Fax 504/522-5543. **Valet parking:** *$14.* **Rack rates:** *$149–$230. AE, CB, DC, DISC, MC, V.*

Le Richelieu Motor Hotel
$$. French Quarter.
For the price, this is one of the nicest hotels in the Quarter. Located on the Esplanade edge of the Quarter, the Richelieu offers convenience as well as a tranquil Old World charm. Many of the rooms have balconies overlooking the courtyard and pool. A small in-house restaurant provides lunch in the courtyard, and the Terrace Lounge is adjacent to the pool as well. For those who wish to go first class, there's the VIP suite with three bedrooms, a kitchen, living area, dining area, and steam room. This is the only hotel in the Quarter that offers free self-parking. You keep your keys, so there's no wait for a parking attendant to bring your car.

1234 Chartres St. (6 blocks from Jackson Square or 1 block from Esplanade), New Orleans, LA 70116. ☎ 800/535-9653 or 504/529-2492. Fax 504/524-8179. **Parking:** *free.* **Rack rates:** *$85–$150 double (suites start at $190). Extra person or child $15. AE, CB, DC, DISC, MC, V.*

Maison Dupuy
$$$$. French Quarter.
Despite being made up of seven townhouses, the picturesque Maison Dupuy manages to combine large hotel efficiency and small hotel care. The large rooms have desks and comfortable armchairs, and many have balconies that overlook the courtyard. Jazz aficionados will enjoy the champagne and jazz brunch buffet served Sundays in the hotel restaurant. The Cabaret Lautrec Lounge, which has live entertainment, is a nice place to wind down at the end of the day. The hotel's amenities include a heated outdoor pool and a health club, twice-daily maid service, and newspaper delivery.

1001 Toulouse (2 blocks from Bourbon St.), New Orleans, LA 70112. ☎ 800/535-9177 or 504/586-8000. Fax 504/525-5334. E-mail maisonno@aol.com. **Valet parking:** *$12 when available.* **Rack rates:** *$159–$259 double. AE, CB, DC, DISC, MC, V.*

McKendrick-Breaux House
$$. Garden District.
Owners Lisa and Eddie Breaux saved this 1865 building just before it was about to fall down and turned it into one of the city's best B&Bs. It's not just that the antique-filled rooms are spacious and lovely (and some of the bathrooms are downright huge) or that the public areas are gorgeous and comfortable, it's the Breauxs themselves. Not only are they utterly hospitable (fresh flowers may be waiting in your room), but they totally love their city and are quite knowledgeable about it. They will help with all sorts of plans

and are particularly helpful and opinionated with restaurant choices. (What good New Orleanian isn't, though?) The Magazine Street location puts you right in the middle of the Lower Garden District, just named the Hippest Neighborhood in America by *Utne Reader* magazine.

1471 Magazine St., New Orleans, LA 70130. ☎ *888/570-1700 or 504/586-1700. Fax 504/522-7138.* ***Parking:*** *Free off-street parking is available.* ***Rack rates:*** *$90–$135 double (breakfast included). AE, MC, V.*

Mechling's Guest House
$$$. Mid City.

The Mechling, a lovingly restored 1860s mansion with large rooms, is located in a lovely setting along Esplanade Avenue, which is convenient for Jazz Fest but not so much for Quarter action the rest of the year—the two miles are not worth walking, so come with a car or cab fare. During restoration, care was taken to save and use as many of the original fixtures and woodwork as possible, including a leaded-glass front door window and black onyx marble fireplace mantels.

Best Seriously Fancy Hotels

Melrose Mansion
(Faubourg Marigny, $$$$$)
Omni Royal Orleans
(French Quarter, $$$$)
Westin Canal Place
(French Quarter, $$$$$)
Windsor Court (Central
Business District, $$$$$)

2023 Esplanade Ave. (10 blocks along Esplanade from the edge of the Quarter), New Orleans, LA 70116. ☎ *800/725-4131 or 504/943-4131. Fax 504/944-0956.* ***Parking:*** *free.* ***Rack rates:*** *$125–$155 double. Rates include full breakfast. AE, MC, V.*

Melrose Mansion
$$$$$. Faubourg Marigny.

With only eight rooms, this restored three-story 1884 Victorian mansion offers luxury and the warm hospitality of a private home. It's not cheap, but it's one of the most intimate, romantic, and elegant guest houses in the area. The pampering begins as soon as you step off the plane, right into a chauffeured limousine. Perhaps the most luxurious of their accommodations is the Donecio Suite with a wide balcony on which breakfast can be served, a four-poster bed, and a marble bathroom complete with Jacuzzi and separate dressing room (Lady Bird Johnson, its first tenant, raved about its elegance). The Sol Owens Suite houses a fitness and health area with weight machines, a Life Cycle, a Stair Master, and a treadmill. A breakfast of freshly baked muffins and fresh fruit is served on beautiful china along with fine crystal and a silver coffee service. This is a popular place, so it's wise to book as far in advance as possible.

937 Esplanade Ave. (at the corner of Burgundy across the street from Buffa's Lounge), New Orleans, LA 70116. ☎ *504/944-2255. Fax 504/945-1794.* ***Parking:*** *free on the street.* ***Rack rates:*** *$225–$425. Rates include the airport limousine service, full breakfast, and cocktail hour. AE, DISC, MC, V.*

Monteleone Hotel
$$$. French Quarter.

The Monteleone is the largest and oldest hotel in the Quarter, and, along with the Omni Royal Orleans, it's one of the best big hotels in all New Orleans. Despite its size, service is remarkably personal—Marvin, the night doorman, is the most personable guy I know. The Monteleone underwent huge renovations in 1995, and its 600 rooms provide a variety of styles, ranging from smallish spaces to plush, antique-filled suites to more modern, comfortable family rooms. The hotel is justifiably famous for its revolving **Carousel Bar,** which looks out onto Royal Street; plus, Truman Capote's parents were living in the hotel when he was born. Concierge service, babysitting, room service, and laundry are available for an extra charge. There's a heated rooftop swimming pool, and the rooftop bar is popular with locals as well as visitors.

214 Royal St. (at the corner of Iberville across the street from Mr. B's restaurant), New Orleans, LA 70140. ☎ ***800/535-9595** or 504/523-3341. Fax 504/528-1019.* ***Valet parking:** $12 when available.* ***Rack rates:** $140–$210 double. Extra person $25. Children under 18 are free in their parents' room. AE, CB, DC, DISC, MC, V.*

Best Bets for Gay & Lesbian Travelers

Frenchmen (Faubourg Marigny, $$)
Hotel Maison de Ville (French Quarter, $$$)
Hotel St. Pierre (French Quarter, $$)
Lafitte Guest House (French Quarter, $$)
New Orleans Guest House (French Quarter, $$)

New Orleans Guest House
$$. French Quarter.

Just outside the Quarter and painted hot pink, the New Orleans Guest House is hard to miss. Inside there are two types of tastefully decorated rooms: large ones in the old Creole main house and smaller ones in the former slave quarters. All of the rooms open onto a lush courtyard with a tropical garden complete with a banana tree and some intricately carved old fountains. This guest house is known for being gay-friendly (although the same could be said for virtually every other hotel and motel in the city—New Orleans is a laid-back, tolerant city).

1118 Ursulines St. (1 block outside the Quarter just across Rampart St.), New Orleans, LA 70116. ☎ ***504/566-1177.** **Parking:** Free.* ***Rack rates:** $79–$99 double (includes breakfast). AE, MC, V.*

Omni Royal Orleans
$$$$. French Quarter.

The Omni, with its gleaming marble, brass, and crystal chandeliers, is an elegant hotel smack dab in the middle of all of the Quarter's attractions. All the rooms are richly decorated (but some are small—try a suite if your budget allows) and come equipped with ironing boards, irons, umbrellas, terry-cloth bathrobes, and makeup mirrors. Kids will love the rooftop swimming pool/ observation deck, and parents will appreciate the relatively cheap baby-sitting service. The downside for families is that they only have a few rooms with two double beds; they'll supply a roll-away bed, but that can make the room *really* cramped. The hotel's **Rib Room** is a great place for a meal.

621 St. Louis St. (1 block from Bourbon, 2 from Jackson Square, and 5 from Canal St.), New Orleans, LA 70140. ☎ *800/THE OMNI or 504/529-5333. Fax 504/529-7089.* **Valet parking:** *$14.* **Rack rates:** *$141–$279 double. Children 17 and under free with parent. Wheelchair accessible. AE, CB, DC, DISC, MC, V.*

Place d'Armes Hotel
$$. French Quarter.
Boasting one of the most attractive courtyards and pools in the Quarter, this smallish hotel is furnished in a cozy, traditional style. Make sure you ask for a room with a window when you make your reservations, though; some interior rooms don't have any. A complimentary breakfast is included in the price of the room and is served in the breakfast room. Located just off Jackson Square, it's close to Bourbon, Royal, and Decatur streets, making sightseeing especially convenient.

625 St. Ann St. (just behind the Presbytere), New Orleans, LA 70118. ☎ *800/ 366-2743 or 504/524-4531.* **Parking:** *24-hour parking available next door for $12 a day.* **Rack rates:** *$100–$160 (breakfast included). AE, CB, DC, DISC, MC, V.*

Pontchartrain Hotel
$$$$. Garden District.
Anne Rice fans will recognize this grand hotel from *The Witching Hour;* it's where the characters Rowan and Michael stayed when they first came to town. The hotel was built in 1927 in an elegant Moorish architectural style and most of its rooms still contain their original antiques. The outstanding service makes the Pontchartrain a favorite among celebrities. The St. Charles Streetcar line passes right by and provides easy access to the French Quarter. The hotel's restaurant, the **Caribbean Room,** also serves up some truly amazing food.

2031 St. Charles Ave. (10 blocks from Lee Circle, just before Jackson Ave.), New Orleans, LA 70140. ☎ *800/777-6193 or 504/524-0581. Fax 504/529-1165.* **Parking:** *$13 per night.* **Rack rates:** *$145–$275. Extra person $25. Seasonal and promotional packages available. AE, CB, DC, DISC, MC, V.*

Prince Conti Hotel
$$$. French Quarter.
Named for the Prince Armand de Conti, the French aristocrat who helped back Bienville's expeditions to found New Orleans, this hotel and its friendly, helpful staff would no doubt please the prince himself. It's located in a busy but not noisy part of the Quarter, and its rooms—many of them furnished with antiques and period reproductions—are especially comfortable. The on-premises **Bombay Club** serves some of the biggest martinis anywhere and is a favorite among locals.

830 Conti St. (at the corner of Dauphine St.), New Orleans, LA 70112. ☎ *800/ 366-2743 or 504/529-4172. Fax 504/581-3802.* ***Valet parking:*** *$12.* ***Rack rates:*** *$120–$155 double (breakfast included). AE, DC, DISC, MC, V.*

Prytania Inn
$. Lower Garden District.

The Prytania, a cross between a hotel, a hostel, a guest house, and a B&B, offers comfortable digs at inexpensive rates. There's no standard type of room here, but the accommodations are quaint, and the service is friendly. For instance, you can get lower rates if you skip the $5 breakfast or share a bathroom (out of 100 rooms, only 8 do not have a bath). It's only a block from the streetcar that goes into the Quarter.

1415 Prytania (3 blocks from the elevated expressway and 1 block from St. Charles Ave.), New Orleans, LA 70130. ☎ ***504/566-1515.*** *Fax 504/566-1518.* ***Parking:*** *A limited amount of free off-street parking is available.* ***Rack rates:*** *$39–$69 double (breakfast included). Extra person $10–$15. AE, DC, DISC, MC, V.*

Best Hotels for Catching a Mardi Gras Parade

Avenue Plaza Suite Hotel & Spa (Garden District, $$$)
Chateau Sonesta Hotel (French Quarter, $$$$)
The Columns (Uptown, $$)
Hotel La Salle (Central Business District, $$)
Le Pavillion Hotel (Central Business District, $$$$)
Monteleone Hotel (French Quarter, $$$)
Pontchartrain Hotel (Garden District, $$$$)
Prytania Inn (Lower Garden District, $)
Prytania Park Hotel (Lower Garden District, $$)
St. Charles Inn (Garden District, $)
Westin Canal Place (French Quarter, $$$$$)
Windsor Court Hotel (Central Business District, $$$$$)

🌟 Kids **Prytania Park Hotel**
$$. Lower Garden District.

This hotel consists of a Victorian house decorated in period hand-carved English pine and dating back to 1834, plus a 49-room addition that has more modern furnishings. The house has been beautifully restored and the newer rooms, although more modern, still have a genuine New Orleans flavor. Each has its own microwave and refrigerator (perfect for Mardi Gras) and opens onto landscaped courtyards. The loft beds that are found in most double rooms are reached by spiral staircases that always seem to entertain the kids. The St. Charles Streetcar is half a block away.

*1519 Terpsichore (5 blocks from the elevated expressway and 1 block from St. Charles Ave.), New Orleans, LA 70130. ☎ 800/862-1984 or 504/524-0427. Fax 504/522-2977. **Parking:** free. **Rack rates:** $99–$119 (continental breakfast included). Extra person $10. Children under 12 free. AE, CB, DC, DISC, MC, V.*

Quality Inn Midtown
$$. Mid City.
A five-minute drive from the Central Business District, the location of the Quality Inn is not as convenient as that of other accommodations I've recommended (please note that the neighborhood is a little rough); however, this hotel does offer free shuttle service to the French Quarter and Convention Center. All rooms have balconies, are spacious, and have double beds, and there's a French Quarter–style courtyard with a swimming pool and Jacuzzi. There's a coin-operated laundry on the premises as well.

*3900 Tulane Ave. (2½ miles from Rampart, ½ mile from Canal, and ¼ mile from Carrollton Ave.), New Orleans, LA 70119. ☎ 800/486-5541 or 504/486-5541. Fax 504/488-7440. **Parking:** free. **Rack rates:** $59–$199 (continental breakfast included). AE, CB, DC, DISC, MC, V.*

Royal Sonesta
$$$$. French Quarter.
The only four-star hotel in New Orleans, the Sonesta offers the best of both worlds: a Bourbon Street location and a gracious, classy hotel. It's so large (reaching nearly a whole block back to Royal) that once you enter the elegant lobby, you promptly forget about the scene outside. (There is also a door heading out to Conti, so you can avoid having to deal with Bourbon Street.) Lying by the large pool, you can't imagine that such craziness is mere feet away. Rooms are decorated with antique reproductions, and many have French doors that open onto balconies, which either look out over Bourbon or a side street or the courtyard and pool—if you want a peaceful night's sleep, request one of the inner rooms. If you stay here and need anything, ask for Dennis, Alfred, Russel, or John, who are all adept at satisfying guests' requests (they've called me many times to provide specialized carriage services).

*300 Bourbon St. (3 blocks from Canal between Bienville and Conti), New Orleans, LA 70140. ☎ 800/766-3782 or 504/586-0300. **Parking:** $14. **Rack rates:** $185–$320. AE, CB, DC, DISC, MC, V.*

Soniat House
$$$$$. French Quarter.
This hotel, located between the Hotel Provincial and Le Richelieu Motor Hotel, occupies an 1839 home built by a wealthy plantation owner. An experience in total luxury, the rooms are furnished with fine French and English antiques, Oriental rugs cover the hardwood floors, and beautiful paintings (some borrowed from the New Orleans Museum of Art) adorn the walls. A continental breakfast is available for an additional $7 charge (it's worth it). The recently renovated townhouse across the street (formerly the French Quarter Maisonettes) has an additional seven suites with Jacuzzis.

103

Best Bets for Proximity to Shopping

Beinville House
(French Quarter, $$$$$)
McKendrick-Breaux House
(Garden District, $$)
Monteleone Hotel
(French Quarter, $$$)
Omni Royal Orleans
(French Quarter, $$$$)
Westin Canal Place
(French Quarter, $$$$$)

Best Hotels If You Want to be Pampered

B&W Courtyards (Faubourg
Marigny, $$)
Hotel Maison de Ville
(French Quarter, $$$)
McKendrick-Breaux House
(Garden District, $$)
Melrose Mansion (Faubourg
Marigny, $$$$$)
Windsor Court (French
Quarter, $$$$$)

1133 Chartres St. (4 blocks from Jackson Square across the street from the Old Ursuline Convent), New Orleans, LA 70116. ☎ *800/544-8808 or 504/522-0570. Fax 504/522-7208. **Valet parking:** $14. **Rack rates:** $160–$475. AE, MC, V.*

St. Charles Inn
$. Garden District.
Though certainly not as elegant as the nearby Avenue Plaza Suite Hotel & Spa (see earlier in this chapter), this small hotel offers clean, comfortable, and economical accommodations. It's on the St. Charles Streetcar line and is three miles uptown from the French Quarter. Its simple, contemporary-style rooms come equipped with either a king-size bed or two double beds.

3636 St. Charles Ave. (two miles from Lee Circle), New Orleans, LA 70115. ☎ *800/489-9908 or 504/899-8888. **Parking:** $3 outdoors. Fax 504/899-8892. **Rack rates:** $50–$100 (breakfast included). AE, DC, DISC, MC, V.*

St. Louis
$$$. French Quarter.
The St. Louis, a small hotel right in the middle of the Quarter, boasts an exquisite fountained courtyard. Throughout the hotel, Parisian-style decor is complimented by antique furniture, original oil paintings, and crystal chandeliers. Its main attraction, though, is the elegant **Louis XVI** restaurant, which serves fine French cuisine.

730 Bienville (½ block from Bourbon St.), New Orleans, LA 70130. ☎ *800/535-9111 or 504/581-7300. Fax 504/524-8925. **Valet parking:** $12. **Rack rates:** $159–$329. Children under 12 free in parents' room. AE, CB, DC, DISC, MC, V.*

Westin Canal Place
$$$$$. French Quarter.
If you're a shopper, this place is for you. It's situated above the elegant Canal Place Shopping Center, and an elevator takes you directly from the 11th

floor lobby down to the stores. All 30 floors of this large, luxurious hotel provide guests with marble foyers and baths, fine furnishings, and spectacular views of the Quarter and the Mississippi River. Equally appealing to business travelers are the free office supplies and in-room coffeemakers and copier/printer/fax machines.

100 Iberville St. (one block from the Aquarium), New Orleans, LA 70132. ☎ *800/228-3000 or 504/566-7006. Fax 504/553-5120.* **Parking:** *$12.* **Rack rates:** *$259–$279. Wheelchair accessible. AE, CB, DC, DISC, MC, V.*

Windsor Court
$$$$$. Central Business District.
Without a doubt, this is the most luxurious hotel in New Orleans. From its Italian marble and antique furnishings to its galleries of 17th- to 19th-century artworks, the Windsor is truly magnificent—and about as expensive as you'd expect. The public spaces are lavishly decorated with British antiques and artwork, and most guest rooms are suites featuring Italian marble bathrooms, balconies or bay windows, kitchenettes, living rooms, and dressing rooms. Suite service is 24 hours, including newspaper delivery and in-room massage. There's an Olympic-size pool, a health club, and a first-class restaurant, The Grill Room, but the real highlight is the full English tea served daily on the first floor.

300 Graver St. (1 block from Canal St.), New Orleans, LA 70130. ☎ *800/262-2662 or 504/523-6000. Fax 504/596-4513.* **Parking:** *$17.* **Rack rates:** *$275–$360 standard guest room. Children under 12 free in parents' room. AE, CB, DC, DISC, MC, V.*

Help! I'm So Confused!
For some of you, the decision about where to stay may be easy. Maybe ever since you saw Louis Malle's film *Pretty Baby*, you've known you wanted to stay at The Columns in Uptown. The rest of you will need to weigh priorities and decide exactly what works for you and your budget.

You probably read through the reviews in this chapter and said, at least a few times, "Hey, that one sounds good." If you put a little check next to those, you're ahead of the game (if not, I hope you have a good memory), but it would still be a royal pain to flip around among a few dozen pages comparing and contrasting hotels. To get organized (without paying a professional), jot down the names and vital statistics of the places you marked (or remembered) in the following chart, get everything lined up and orderly, and then scan the lines to see how they stack up against each other. As you rank them in your mind, rank them in the column on the right, too, so that you can have your preferences ready when making reservations. If there's no room at the inn for choice number 1, just move right on to number 2.

Hotel Preferences Worksheet

Hotel	Location	Price per night

Advantages	Disadvantages	Your Ranking (1–10)

Part 3

Learning Your Way around New Orleans

Roaming the streets of New Orleans is always an adventure. You never know what you might hear, who you might see, or what type of exotic food you might stumble upon. In this part of the book, I'll help you get a feel for the Big Easy by acting as your human compass: I'll tell you how to get into the city from the airport, how to get around once you're here, and how to decipher those confusing New Orleans directions. I'll also clue you in to the different neighborhoods that make up my hometown.

YOU ARE HERE

Chapter 8

Getting Your Bearings

In This Chapter

➤ Point A to Point B (from the airport to your bed)

➤ The key to the city: learning the lay of the land

➤ How to get unlost

You might want to bring your compass, but in a city where the sun rises in the east but first appears over the West Bank, going with the flow might make more sense—upriver is Uptown, downriver is downtown, and lakeside is toward Lake Pontchartrain. In this chapter, I'll show you the best ways to get into the city whether you arrive by land or by air, and then I'll take you down the river, telling you about the different neighborhoods and letting you know where they're located, what makes them unique, and how to get from one to the other.

You've Just Arrived: Now What?

Compared to the chaotic airports found in other big cities such as New York, Atlanta, and Chicago, the New Orleans International Airport is a relatively laid-back place. Signs clearly direct you to the baggage claim area, and all the concourses are attached to a single building, making it easy to find your way around. If you want information, information booths are scattered through the airport and also in the baggage claim area. The **Traveler's Aid Society** (☎ **504/464-3522**) also has a branch in the baggage claim area.

Where Can I Get a Cab?

If you want a taxi, there are always cabs waiting in line just outside the baggage claim area of the airport. You'll have no trouble finding one; just walk out the door. A taxi ride to the French Quarter or Central Business District is $21 for one or two people or $8 each if there are more than two in your group. A taxi can take a maximum of five passengers.

United Cabs (☎ 504/522-9771) is the biggest and most reliable taxi company in the city. However, their taxis don't wait in line with the others at the airport. As the city's premier taxi fleet, they're usually busy handling radio calls. If you want a **United Cab,** call and one will be dispatched to you. Usually a few are in the airport area, so you shouldn't have to wait too long.

> ## Bet You Didn't Know
>
> New Orleans is almost an island. If you look on a map, you'll notice that the metro area of New Orleans is only connected to the continental United States by a thin strip of land to the west. From any other direction, you must cross a body of water to enter the city.

The Magic Buses

The **Downtown/Airport Express bus** leaves from the upper level near the down ramp and departs about every 23 minutes from 6am to 5:30pm (every 12 to 15 minutes during rush hours). For $1.25, the bus will take you to the corner of Elk's Place and Canal Street, about five blocks from Bourbon Street. The last bus leaves the airport at 5:30pm going downtown, and the last one back to the airport leaves Canal Street at 6:10pm. After that time, you can use public transportation and a series of buses to get to the airport; however, it's a hassle to switch buses with luggage, so I wouldn't recommend this method. For more information, call the **Regional Transit Authority** (**☎ 504/248-3900**) or the **Jefferson Transit Authority** (**☎ 504/ 737-7433**).

The **Airport Shuttle** is $10 each way and leaves from right outside the baggage claim area and takes you directly to your hotel. If you're traveling with someone else, a taxi will cost about the same, or less, and will also be more convenient. The shuttle leaves every 10 to 15 minutes, but you may have to go to several hotels before getting to yours, and the ride can take up to an hour. A cab will take only about 25 to 30 minutes. If you intend to take the shuttle back to the airport when you leave, remember that it's by reservation only. You must either make arrangements through the hotel's concierge or call **☎ 504/522-3500.** The shuttle is wheelchair accessible.

May I Call You a Limousine, Ma'am?

If you want to go from the airport to your hotel in style, call a limousine. There are more than 50 limousine companies in New Orleans and prices vary. The average price into town is $50 for up to four passengers or $65 for six. The following limousine companies are among the best:

➤ **A Touch of Class** (**☎ 800/821-6352** or 504/522-7565)

➤ **Celebrity** (**☎ 800/253-1991** or 504/888-5466)

111

➤ **Chisholm** (☎ **800/799-5827** or 504/524-2171)

➤ **New Orleans Limousine Service** (☎ **800/214-0133** or 504/529-5226)

➤ **Orleans Limousine** (☎ **888/819-5466** or 504/288-1111)

Extra! Extra!

Starting in the beginning of 1998, the ride from the airport to downtown might become somewhat of a traffic nightmare. For the next three years (until 2001), construction work on Interstate 10 will be taking place to widen the I-10/I-610 split. Although all the work will be done at night and during off-peak hours, everyone will feel the effects. There's now a new 45 mph speed limit. I would guess that the delays would increase driving time to 30–45 minutes to and from the airport to downtown. Of the alternate routes available, the most direct and easiest route would be to take Airline Highway (Hwy. 61 South) into New Orleans. For up-to-date information on the highway construction, check out the Web site: **www.dotd.state.la.us**.

Life Is a Highway

If I've said it once, I've said it a million times: Don't try to get around New Orleans in a car. However, if you insist on renting one, the car rental counters are conveniently located near the baggage claim area of the airport. If you're a traveler with disabilities and want to rent a vehicle, call **Wheelchair Getaways, Inc.** (☎ **504/454-1178**). They have accessible vans with fully automatic wheelchair lifts, raised roofs, and hand controls.

The New Orleans International Airport is not actually in the city of New Orleans—it's in the city of Kenner in Jefferson Parish (parish is the term used for counties), a 25-minute drive to the Central Business District or French Quarter. For those of you who are driving into New Orleans, I've included a map with the best route into town, marked for your convenience. Start by finding one of the many signs at the airport indicating the way to I-10 East. Just get on this road and continue to the I-10/I-610 split. *Don't* take I-610. Continue on I-10 until you get to the Superdome (you can't miss that). If you're heading for the French Quarter, follow I-10 to the left of the Superdome and take the Vieux Carre (French Quarter) exit. If you're staying in the Central Business District, stay to the right of the Superdome and take the Loyola exit. If you'll be staying in the Garden District, stay to the right of the Superdome and take the St. Charles Street exit. Check with your hotel for exact directions.

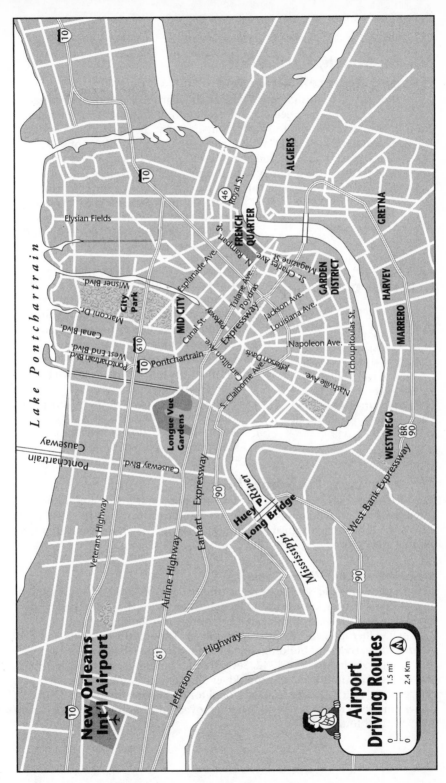

New Orleans Int'l Airport

Lake Pontchartrain

Elysian Fields

Pontchartrain Causeway

Veterans Highway

Airline Highway

Earhart Expressway

Jefferson Highway

Pontchartrain Blvd.
West End Blvd.
Canal Blvd.
Marconi Dr.
Wisner Blvd.

City Park

MID CITY

Pontchartrain

Longue Vue Gardens

Causeway Blvd.

Esplanade Ave.
N. Rampart St.
Royal St.
Canal St.
Tulane Ave.
Poydras
S. Carrollton Ave.
S. Claiborne Ave.
Jefferson Davis

FRENCH QUARTER

St. Charles Ave.
Magazine St.

GARDEN DISTRICT

Jackson Ave.
Louisiana Ave.
Napoleon Ave.
Nashville Ave.
Tchoupitoulas St.

Expressway

Huey P. Long Bridge

Mississippi River

West Bank Expressway

ALGIERS

GRETNA

HARVEY

MARRERO

WESTWEGO

BR 90

Airport Driving Routes

1.5 mi
2.4 Km

113

North, South, East, West: Getting Yourself Oriented

New Orleans is a confusing city. The French Quarter, where the city began, is a 13-block-long area between Canal Street and Esplanade Avenue running from the Mississippi River to North Rampart Street. Because of the bend in the river, much of the city is laid out at angles that make directions like north, south, east, and west pretty well useless. New Orleans solved this directional problem long ago by substituting *riverside, lakeside, uptown,* and *downtown.* It works, and you'll catch on quickly if you keep in mind that North Rampart Street is the "lakeside" boundary of the Quarter, Canal Street marks the beginning of "uptown," and the Quarter is "downtown."

As for building numbers, they begin at 100 on either side of Canal Street. In the Quarter they begin at 400 at the river (that's because four blocks of numbered buildings were lost to the river before the levee was built). Another reminder of Canal Street's old role as the border between the old, French New Orleans (the Quarter) and the new, American New Orleans is the fact that street names change when they cross it (for example, Bourbon Street "downtown" becomes Carondelet "uptown").

Bet You Didn't Know

Local legend has it that the only place in New Orleans you can tell you're facing north without a compass is Lee Circle. It's said that General Lee would never turn his back on a Yankee in life and surely wouldn't do so in death. His statue faces due north.

New Orleans Neighborhoods

The New Orleans metropolitan area consists of several towns and unincorporated areas that extend along both the east and west banks of the Mississippi River. The following is a great description of all the neighborhoods that make up this great city.

French Quarter (Vieux Carre)

The Vieux Carre (Old Square) was the original city of New Orleans, founded in 1718, and is now known as the French Quarter. It's the oldest neighborhood in New Orleans and is located between North Rampart Street, Esplanade, Iberville, and the Mississippi River. Though fires in 1788 and 1794 destroyed nearly every building, one of them, the old Ursuline Convent, is still around, dating back to 1742. Several other buildings were built prior to the 1800s. Fronting the Mississippi River and centered around Jackson Square, the French Quarter is most noted for its historic buildings, Bourbon Street, and the French Market. It's best enjoyed on foot, by buggy ride, or on an organized tour.

114

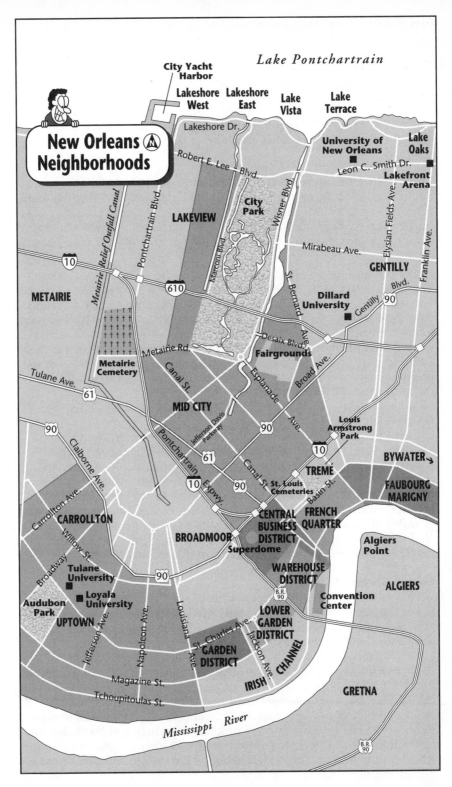

115

Canal Street/Central Business District/Warehouse District

There's no street more central to the life of New Orleans than Canal Street, which is used as the reference point to pinpoint the location of *everything*. The street took its name from a very shallow ditch that was dug along this border of the French Quarter in its early days. Although the ditch was given the rather grand name of canal, it was never large enough to be used for transport.

The Central Business District (CBD) is roughly bounded by Canal Street on the north and the elevated Pontchartrain Expressway (I-90) to the south, between Loyola Avenue and the Mississippi River. There are pleasant plazas, squares, and parks sprinkled among all the commercial high-rise buildings. Some of the most elegant of the city's hotels, restaurants, and stores are located here.

Part of this area, between Julia and St. Joseph's streets, is known as **The Warehouse District.** The neighborhood was once devoted almost entirely to warehouses, but revitalization has turned it into both an upscale residential neighborhood and a place for artists to display their work. It's also home to the Convention Center, Riverwalk Shopping Center, hotels and restaurants, museums, and art galleries. **The Contemporary Arts Center,** 900 Camp St. (just beyond St. Joseph toward Howard Avenue), has facilities for presenting not only art exhibitions but also performances. You'll also find the **Louisiana Children's Museum** in this area.

Garden District

Bounded by Jackson Avenue, St. Charles Avenue, Louisiana Avenue, and Magazine Street, the Garden District is best explored by the St. Charles Streetcar and on foot. This area was part of the original city of Lafayette and became a fashionable residential area when wealthy Americans took up residence around New Orleans after its purchase by the United States. The beautiful homes and gardens along St. Charles Avenue have been a favorite of visitors for many years. Unfortunately, most of the private gardens that used to flourish around the homes here (hence the name Garden District) no longer exist. Anne Rice's home is located in this neighborhood.

Lower Garden District

Developed in the early 1800s just downriver from the Garden District, the Lower Garden District is home to many modest cottages, attractive churches, and some elegant townhouses on Coliseum Square. Many of its streets were named for Greek Muses, though most have peculiar New Orleans pronunciations. This area is bounded by St. Charles Avenue, Jackson Avenue, the Pontchartrain Expressway, and the Mississippi River. The Magazine Street bus runs right through the heart of it. This area is okay to explore on foot during the daytime, but keep your eyes open and don't stray far from Magazine. You probably won't anyway, as Magazine is home to many great small antique shops, coffee shops, sidewalk cafes, neighborhood bars, and boutiques. The national magazine *Utne Reader* voted this "the hippest neighborhood in the U.S." It's only made a comeback in recent years, though, and some parts of it are still not super-safe.

Bet You Didn't Know

Heading away from the Quarter through the Lower Garden District, the streets between Lee Circle and Felicity are named for the Greek muses—the seven daughters of Mnemosyne and Zeus, each of whom presided over a different art or science. The spellings may be familiar, but we in New Orleans have our own pronunciations for them: There's Clio (usually pronounced *kli*-o but it's *cle*-o in New Orleans), the muse of history; Erato (er-*èh*-tó or è-*rat*-oh in New Orleans), the muse of lyric poetry and mime; Thalia (the-*li*-ah; *théyl*-yah), the muse of comedy and pastoral poetry and one of the three Graces; Melpomene (mèl-*pòm*-e-nêè; *mel*-puh-mean) the muse of tragedy; Terpsichore (tûrp-*sîck*-eh-rê; *tûrp*-sî-core), the muse of dancing and choral singing; Euterpe (yu-*tûrpê*; *ù*-turp), the muse of lyric poetry and music; and Polymnia (poly-*hymn*-ni-a; poh-*limb*-knee-ah), the muse of sacred song and oratory.

Mid City

Originally called "Back O' Town," the Mid City area was mostly swamp. Drained and developed in the early 20th century, it is most notable for its churches and the cemeteries at the end of Canal Street. The area stretches along Canal Street between Esplanade, Perdido, City Park, and Derbigny, though some say it begins at Rampart instead of Derbigny. It's best experienced on foot, but safety mandates a bus or organized tour. Plans call for the future expansion of the streetcar line into this area.

Uptown

Uptown, the largest neighborhood in the city, is bounded by Jackson Avenue, Claiborne, the Mississippi River, and Carrollton Avenue. The area is best explored on the St. Charles Streetcar or the Magazine bus, though you might want to get off the streetcar or bus and wander around some areas (such as the antique shops along Magazine) on foot.

The district is home to Tulane and Loyola universities, many fine mansions, the Audubon Park/Zoo, and some fine churches and synagogues. St. Charles Avenue runs through the heart of it for its entire length. The legendary music club **Tipitina's** is located here, as is **Pascal Manale's** and other restaurants. Magazine Street runs through this area, and features many antique galleries, boutiques, and art galleries.

Faubourg Marigny

The Faubourg Marigny area is located downriver from, and immediately adjacent to, the French Quarter. Its boundaries are Esplanade Avenue, St. Claude,

Bet You Didn't Know

Faubourg (pronounced faw-berg or foe-berg) was a French word meaning "false city." It was the equivalent to the modern-day suburb.

Press Street, and the Mississippi River. It's best explored on foot during daylight hours, though even then I recommend that you stick to Frenchmen Street, Chartres Street, Royal Street, Decatur Street, and the area by Washington Square.

This area is one of the earliest suburbs, developed in the late 1700s, and is home to many Creole cottages. Today, Frenchmen Street is developing its own reputation as a hip entertainment area, attracting young urban dwellers.

Irish Channel

Originally home to many of the city's Irish immigrants, the Irish Channel area is located between the Garden District's Magazine Street and the Mississippi River, with its sidewise boundaries at Jackson Avenue and Louisiana Avenue. It is best explored on foot with a large group of people, as it's not the safest neighborhood in town. The area was a working-class neighborhood during the 1800s and has many double-shotgun cottages built during the mid- to late 19th century. (Shotgun cottages got their name because a person could stand in his front doorway and fire a shotgun out the back without hitting anything.) To get a real feel for the area, walk around the **antique shop district** on Magazine Street and around Felicity Street and Jackson Avenue.

Bywater

Located just downriver from the French Quarter, past the neighborhood of Faubourg Marigny, Bywater is bounded by Press Street, St. Claude Avenue, Poland Avenue, and the Mississippi River. It is tempting to mis-speak and call this region "backwater," as at first glance it seems like a wasteland of light industry and run-down homes. In fact, Bywater has plenty of nice, modest residential sections and architecture that includes a mixture of Creole cottages and Victorian shotgun houses. Furthermore, it's home to the city's artists-in-hiding, and many local designers have set their shops here. This is in keeping with the history of the area, which was an early home to artisans, free persons of color, and communities of immigrants from Germany, Ireland, and Italy.

Algiers Point

Algiers Point is the only part of the city located on the west bank of the Mississippi, directly across from the Central Business District and the French Quarter and connected to them by the Algiers Free Ferry at the foot of Canal Street. One of the city's original Creole suburbs, it has changed the least over the decades. Today, you can't see many signs of the area's once-booming railroad and dry-docking industries, but you can see some of the best-preserved small gingerbread and Creole cottages in New Orleans. A large number of the area's Greek Revival and Italianate homes were destroyed by a fire in 1895, but many older buildings still survive. The neighborhood has begun to attract a lot of attention as a historic landmark in recent years, and it makes for a nice stroll.

Carrollton

This attractive residential and shopping area, shaded by oak trees, is a favorite among locals and visitors alike. It's located in a bend of the river just a few miles upriver from the French Quarter, between Broadway, South Claiborne Avenue, the Mississippi River, and the Jefferson Parish line. Carrollton is most easily explored on the St. Charles Streetcar, though you might want to get off the streetcar and explore the Riverbend area, where Carrollton Street meets St. Charles Avenue.

Relying on the Kindness of Strangers: Where to Get Information Once You're in New Orleans

A **Tourist Information Center** (☎ **504/568-5661** or 504/566-5031), operated by the State of Louisiana, is located in the French Quarter at 529 St. Ann St. in the historic Pontalba Buildings on the side of Jackson Square. Other information centers are located throughout the city, many of them owned and operated by tour companies or other businesses. Here's a list of where most of them are located:

➤ **Canal and Convention Center Boulevard** (☎ **504/587-0739**) at the beginning of the 300 block of Canal on the downtown side of the street

➤ Close to the **World Trade Center** (☎ **504/587-0737**) at 2 Canal St.

➤ Near the **Hard Rock Cafe** (☎ **504/587-0740**) on the 400 block of North Peters Street

➤ **Julia and Convention Center Boulevard** (walk-up booth)

➤ **Poydras and Convention Center Boulevard** (walk-up booth)

➤ **Vieux Carre Police Station** (☎ **504/565-7530**), located at 334 Royal St.

Extra! Extra!

Riding the waves in New Orleans isn't as impossible as you may think, if you're thinking about radio waves, that is. Listening to the local stations is a great way to find out what's going on when you're in town. Tune in to the following: **National Public Radio** (89.9 FM); **WWOZ** (90.7 FM), music with history; **WQUE** (93.3 FM), hip-hop, soul, R&B; **WEZB** (97.1 FM), top 40; **WNOE** (101.1 FM), country music; **KKND** (106.7 FM), alternative; **WODT** (1280 AM), blues.

Chapter 9

Getting Around

In This Chapter

➤ Using the streetcars, buses, and taxis

➤ Getting around on foot

Getting around New Orleans by car isn't easy, but it's a great town for walking, and there's an excellent public transportation system with buses and streetcars connecting all of the neighborhoods you might want to visit. This chapter includes all the information you'll need to navigate. For maps, passes, or other information about streetcars or buses, call the **Regional Transit Authority's Ride Line** at ☎ 504/248-3900 or drop into the Visitor Information Center at 529 St. Ann St. on the side of Jackson Square or any of the other information centers.

A Streetcar Named St. Charles

The Central Business District, Lower Garden District, Garden District, Uptown, and Carrollton neighborhoods are all served by the historic St. Charles Streetcar line, which began its life as the Carrollton Railroad in 1835 and used mule power and steam for propulsion before it was electrified in 1893. The present streetcars date from the 1920s and are listed on the National Register. The St. Charles Streetcar is the oldest railway system in continuous operation in the entire world.

The seven-mile streetcar ride from Canal Street through all of these historic neighborhoods costs only $1 (exact change or a VisiTour pass is required), and it'll cost you another buck to take it back. The round trip takes 90 minutes to two hours. You can purchase a one-day ($4) or three-day ($8) **VisiTour pass** that entitles you to unlimited bus and streetcar rides. Check with your hotel or call ☎ 504/248-3900 for information about where you can buy the pass. The St. Charles Streetcar operates 24 hours a day.

The $1 streetcar ride is not only a bargain—it's also a fun, relaxing way to experience the city. Riding through oak-lined avenues, looking at grand old residences, and taking in the sights, smells, and sounds of New Orleans is an unbeatable way to spend an afternoon.

If you pass by a historic building and wonder what its story is, or if you see an enchanting park and you want to learn more, pick up *St. Charles Avenue Streetcar Line—A Self-Guided Tour,* sold at the **Historic New Orleans Collection** at 533 Royal St. in the French Quarter and elsewhere. It only costs $4.95 and gives you a wealth of information about the streetcar line itself and about the buildings along the route.

Down by the Riverside: The Riverfront Streetcar

The Riverfront Streetcar line was established during the 1984 World's Fair. It runs along the riverfront from the Convention Center to the far end of the French Quarter at Esplanade with convenient stops along the way. It costs $1.25, and exact change or a VisiTour pass is required.

The Bus Stops Here

Buses in New Orleans are generally more convenient than streetcars, and they're air-conditioned; the streetcars are not. However, they don't cover the same route, and they're not anywhere *near* as picturesque. Most neighborhoods are connected by one or more bus lines, and the fare is $1 ($1.25 for express buses). Exact change or a **VisiTour pass** (see the previous section) is required.

Extra! Extra!

If you have even one romantic bone in your body, you'll find it hard to resist the authentic old mule-drawn carriages at Jackson Square. Each mule is decked out with ribbons, flowers, or even a hat, and each driver is in fierce competition with all other drivers to win the "most unique city story" award. No matter which one you choose, you'll get a nonstop monologue on historic buildings, fascinating events of the past, and a legend or two during the 2¼-mile drive through the French Quarter. Carriages congregate at the Decatur Street end of Jackson Square from 9am to midnight in good weather; the charge is $8 per adult and $5 for children under 12.

Note: The carriage ride described here is *not* the one that will take you on your own private tour. Private carriage tours offered by **Good Old Days Buggies** (☎ 504/523-0804), which include hotel or restaurant pick-up, will cost you significantly more. (See chapter 13 for info.)

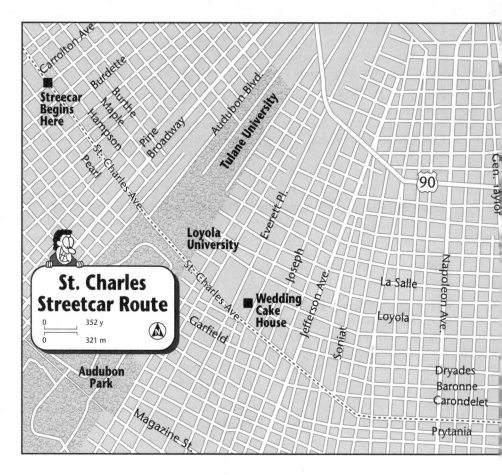

As a visitor, the only buses you're likely to need are the **Tulane bus** (if you happen to stay at a place on Tulane Avenue), the **Magazine bus** (which runs through the Central Business District, Lower Garden District, and Uptown between the Garden District and the Irish Channel), and the **Canal Street bus** (which runs the length of Canal Street).

You can catch a bus at bus stops every other block or so along its named route. You can also pick up the **Tulane bus** at the bus stop on the corner of **Elk's Place and Canal.** When Decatur Street crosses Canal Street, it becomes Magazine. You can also catch the **Magazine bus** at the bus stop on the corner of Canal and Magazine, near the Sheraton Hotel.

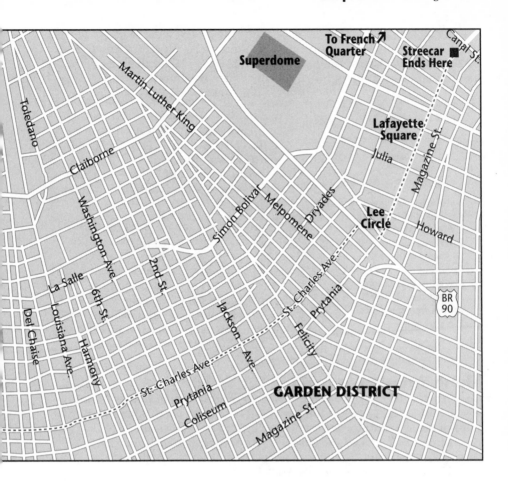

Taxi, Please

Public transportation is fine during the day, but I don't recommend it at night, though you probably won't have any problems if you get on and off at well-lit major intersections. If you're going somewhere that is not right on the line's route, however, I suggest a taxi. A neighborhood can go from good to bad in a very short distance.

A taxi ride for two people to most major tourist areas shouldn't run more than $10. There are more than 1,500 taxis in New Orleans, not to mention limousines and hotel shuttles. Except for busy times such as bad weather and rush hour, vacant taxis are everywhere.

Of course, the airport, the French Quarter, and the Central Business District are the easiest places to find a taxi. You'll find taxi stands near restaurants, at all of the major hotels, and at some smaller ones as well. Many cabs cruise the streets of the French Quarter, Central Business District, and other parts of

123

the city looking for fares. If you can't find a cab on the street, you can call a taxi company to have one dispatched to you by radio. **United Cab (☎ 504/ 522-9771)** is the largest and one of the most reliable taxi companies in the New Orleans area. Waiting time is usually under five minutes.

Dollars & Sense

Some parts of New Orleans are included in the **Jean Lafitte National Park Preserve** system. If you stop by their Folklife and Visitor Center at 419 Decatur St. (**☎ 504/589-2636**), you can get details about the various free tours given by the park rangers.

The fare for all taxis is $2.10 for the first one-sixth of a mile and 20¢ for each additional one-sixth of a mile. If the rate of travel is less than one-sixth of a mile per 40 seconds, the additional 20¢ is charged anyway. Add 75¢ for each additional person. The maximum number of passengers is five.

During football games, Jazz Fest, and other special events you're expected to pay $3 per person or the meter rate, whichever is greatest. Special events consist of regularly scheduled sporting events and/or concerts at the Superdome, Saenger Theater, Fair Grounds, and most other stadiums. You can also hire taxis for $22 an hour.

These Streets Were Made for Walking

The French Quarter, where you'll be spending most of your time, is basically 6 blocks wide and 13 blocks long, with a few irregular areas along the river; most of the action in the Quarter is confined to an even smaller area. For this reason—and because the Quarter's narrow streets, traffic congestion, strict traffic laws, and lack of on-street parking makes it a nightmare for driving—my advice to you is this: Walk.

But who'd want to drive anyway? If you're in a car, you can't enjoy the sights and sounds the same way you can from your own two feet. If you get tired, hop a carriage and let the horse or mule do the walking.

When exploring the French Quarter, or any area for that matter, use common sense. Do most of your exploring during daylight hours. After dark, stick to well-lit areas with other people around. On Bourbon Street, you watch out for pickpockets and stay away from scam artists.

Behind the Wheel

If you absolutely *need* to drive, here are a few rules: All streets in the Quarter are one-way, and on weekdays during daylight hours, Royal and Bourbon streets are closed to cars between the 300 and 700 blocks. Also, Chartres Street is closed on the blocks in front of St. Louis Cathedral. You can turn right on red throughout the city unless otherwise specified, but many of the streets are one-way, and some of them (most notably Tulane) do not allow left turns.

Parking is also a problem throughout the city. If you manage to find a parking place on the street, be careful: The city gets a large chunk of its operating budget from parking fines. Signs noting parking restrictions are often confusing. If you park too close to a driveway, corner, crosswalk, or fire hydrant, or too far from the curb, you're liable to be ticketed. Parking in a bad area could also result in your car being vandalized.

If you park on a parade route, block access to someone's driveway, or break other laws, you're liable to find your car towed away and impounded, and getting it back may cost you $100 or more. Believe me when I say that many of those given the power to enforce our parking regulations have little sense of humor. If you insist on driving, take my advice and park in a commercial lot. The small amount you pay is worth it for the peace of mind and safety.

Extra! Extra!

If you think your car has been towed, call the impounding lot (☎ 504/565-7235) or the Claiborne Auto Pound, 400 N. Claiborne (☎ 504/565-7450).

Time-Savers

Because many restaurants in New Orleans don't take reservations, you might be served a long line instead of some fine wine between 7pm and 9pm. To get around this problem, eat a light lunch and get to a popular restaurant early for dinner. Don't waste your time standing in line.

Part 4

New Orleans' Best Restaurants

In New Orleans, we live to eat, and some of the best restaurants in the country, if not the world, are right here. Throw your diet plans out the window during your stay—you just won't be happy otherwise. Not for nothing was New Orleans recently named "The Fattest City in America" by a panel of experts studying Americans' eating habits: If something isn't fried, it's probably covered in a sauce, and sometimes it's both. With luck, you'll be dancing and walking so much it'll all even out, and you won't notice much difference when you get home—except that all other food might suddenly seem bland and dull in comparison.

In chapter 10, I'll run through the basics of New Orleans eating for you, telling you what's what, where's where, and what to expect; then, in chapter 11, I'll tell you about all your best bets for lunch and dinner. Lastly, because those two meals are only the tip of the culinary iceberg, I'll share some thoughts on spots for serious snacking in chapter 12.

ALL-U-CAN EAT SPAGHETTI AND MEATBALLS

The Lowdown on the New Orleans Dining Scene

In This Chapter

➤ The news on New Orleans cuisine

➤ How to find the dining hot spots

➤ What you can expect to pay

➤ Some tips on tipping, taxes, and making reservations

It's hard to have a truly bad meal in New Orleans—the worst you can do is mediocre. But there's no excuse for even that. With some of the most innovative and exciting chefs around working right here, you should experience some of the most memorable meals of your life. Beyond Cajun cuisine, the hot chefs are employing ingredients and methods from Asian and California cuisines and are coming up with some marvelous new combinations. But even the humble po boy or muffuletta, not to mention that spicy boiled crawfish, will make your mouth sing.

What's Cooking in New Orleans

The national food spotlight hit New Orleans thanks to the **Cajun food** trend, which chef Paul Prudhomme brought to the American consciousness in the early 1980s. Cajun cooking came from the practical households of the Louisiana prairies and bayous, where economy dictated that everything available was chucked into a single pot to be cooked—a tradition that brought us jambalaya, ètouffèe, and the classic red beans and rice. The mistake outsiders make is assuming that Cajun food has to be smothered in spices. Not true: Although Cajun food is certainly hot stuff, the heat shouldn't overwhelm the flavor of the food it's covering.

Creole cooking, which originated in New Orleans proper, is a mix of French and Spanish cuisine, with an emphasis on sauces and sophisticated tastes and a kick provided by African and Caribbean spices. Thanks to this philosophy, what would otherwise be your basic plain-Jane seafood becomes Trout Almondine (trout prepared with white wine, almond sauce, and garlic) or Crabmeat Mornay (crab with white cheese and cream sauce).

Though Prudhomme got the early headlines, it's Emeril Lagasse who has come to define current New Orleans cooking, thanks to his show on the Food Network. His restaurants, **Emeril's** and **Nola,** continue to be where it's at. But don't overlook what's cooking at the **Upperline** or **Brigtsen's,** two other places working with innovative variations on Creole cuisine, or at **Uglesich's,** which delivers some of New Orleans' favorite seafood. And then there's the venerable **Commander's Palace,** which has been voted the best restaurant in the country by the James Beard Association. Taste for yourself.

Bet You Didn't Know

Legend has it that the famous New Orleans dish eggs Sardou was created especially for French playwright Victorien Sardou (author of *La Tosca*) by chef Antoine Alciatore.

Help, the Menu Is Confusing Me!

Although we speak English in New Orleans, when it comes to understanding what's on the menu, you may need a dictionary, so I'll give you one. These definitions should help you find your way through all of New Orleans' unique creations.

- ➤ **Andoille** (ahn-doo-*we*): A spicy, heavily smoked sausage made from pork.

- ➤ **Barbecued shrimp:** Shrimp served in a spicy butter sauce.

- ➤ **Cafè brûlot** (cah-*fay* brew-*low*): Coffee mixed with spices and liqueurs and served flaming.

- ➤ **Crawfish:** A tiny, lobsterlike creature plentiful in the waters around New Orleans and eaten in every conceivable way.

- ➤ **Dirty rice:** Rice cooked with chicken livers and gizzards, onions, chopped celery, green bell pepper, cayenne, black-and-white peppers, and chicken stock.

- ➤ **Dressed:** "Served with the works"—as when ordering a sandwich.

- ➤ **Eggs Hussarde:** Poached eggs with hollandaise, marchand de vin, tomatoes, and ham. (Marchand de vin is a wine sauce flavored with onions, shallots, celery, carrots, garlic, red wine, beef broth, and herbs.)

- ➤ **Eggs Sardou:** A dish that includes poached eggs, artichoke bottoms, anchovy fillets, hollandaise, and truffles or ham as a garnish.

➤ **Ètouffèe** (ay-too-*fay*): A spicy shrimp and crawfish stew served over rice. It means "smothered" in French.

➤ **Filè** (*fee*-lay): A thickener made of ground sassafras leaves. Filè is frequently used to thicken gumbo.

➤ **Grillades** (gree-*yads*): Thin slices of beef or veal smothered in a tomato-and-beef-flavored gravy. Often served with grits.

➤ **Gumbo:** A thick, spicy soup, always served with rice.

➤ **Hush puppies:** Fried balls of cornmeal, often served as a side dish with seafood.

➤ **Jambalaya** (jum-ba-*lie*-ya): The traditional Cajun rice dish that typically includes tomatoes, shrimp, ham, and onions, but can also include just about anything.

➤ **Lagniappe** (lan-*yap*): A little something extra that comes free with your order—like the 13th doughnut when you order a dozen.

➤ **Muffuletta:** Round Italian bread filled with an assortment of Italian cold cuts, cheese, and olive salad. Very large—best shared among friends. (See chapter 12.)

➤ **Oysters en brochette:** Oysters and crispy bacon fried in a batter.

➤ **Oysters Rockefeller:** Baked oysters on the half shell with a sauce of greens and anise liqueur. **Antoine's** is the home of this succulent dish.

➤ **Pain perdu** (pan *pair*-du): Literally translated as "lost bread," this is New Orleans' version of French toast, made with French bread.

➤ **Po boys:** Sandwiches similar to submarine sandwiches that are served on French bread with a huge variety of fillings. (See chapter 12.)

➤ **Pralines** (*praw*-lines): A very sweet confection made of brown sugar and pecans; they come in "original" and creamy styles. (See chapter 12.)

➤ **Remoulade:** A thick spicy sauce made in a variety of ways (expect mustard and/or horseradish) and used over seafood or salad.

➤ **Shrimp Creole:** Shrimp in a tomato sauce that's seasoned with what's known around town as "the trinity": onions, garlic, and green bell pepper.

➤ **Tasso:** Smoked, spicy Cajun ham.

➤ **Trout Nancy:** Filet of trout sautèed and topped with lump crabmeat, capers, and lemon-butter sauce.

Location! Location! Location!

Although the French Quarter has an almost unnatural number of standout restaurants, you'll also find that some of the best food happens elsewhere. Emeril's and Uglesich's, for instance, are just on the outskirts of the Quarter, and Commander's Palace, Brigsten's, and Upperline are cab rides away. Remember that when it comes to a gourmet feast, convenience isn't everything. This section gives you the lowdown on your banqueting options by neighborhood.

The French Quarter
As with most everything else in New Orleans, the Quarter is the center of things. Most of the famous, long-established restaurants, such as **Antoine's, Arnaud's,** and **Brennan's,** are here, as are some wackier options, such as **Lucky Cheng's** or the **Clover Grill.** In between these extremes, you can choose to dine in a fine but not budget-breaking place such as **Irene's Cuisine,** or enjoy a romantic meal at **Bella Luna** or the **Chart House.** Your choices are almost endless.

The Central Business District & Warehouse District
Although the selection of restaurants in the Central Business and Warehouse districts isn't quite as diverse as in the Quarter, the quality is right up there (as are the prices). The restaurant with the name is here (**Emeril's**), as is just about the ultimate dining experience in town (**Grill Room**). If you're more in the mood for a massive po boy than white-glove service, you can visit **Mother's,** which has fattened up many a tourist to proper New Orleans proportions. And if your mouth waters for the finest seafood this side of paradise, there's **Uglesich's** on Barrone Street.

The Garden District & Uptown
If you need any enticement to leave the Quarter for your evening meal, how about this: A few years ago, the James Beard Association picked the Garden District's own **Commander's Palace** as the best restaurant in the whole country. *In the whole country.* How can you beat that? If you want something a little less publicized, visit **Brigtsen's,** where Frank Brigsten cooks up the daily special and local foodies come running. Farther out, but worth the trip, **Upperline** serves inventive variations on Creole cuisine.

Bet You Didn't Know
There's a whole family of sausages used in New Orleans. In addition to a variety of smoked sausages, there's boudin (boo-DAN), which contains onions, spices, pork, and rice and comes in white or red varieties; chaurice (cho-REECE), a hard sausage used chiefly for flavoring beans or soups; and andouille (ahn-doo-WE), another hard pork sausage that's a bit saltier than chaurice.

Mid City

Though not exactly a hotbed of culinary invention, the Mid City area does boast a few standouts. The aptly named **Christian's** serves fine French/Creole selections in a converted church. (Talk about atmosphere!) If your mood wants something airier, try **Gabrielle,** where the mood is French cafe, and the food is Creole/Cajun. For the serious carnivore, Mid City's branch of **Ruth's Chris Steak House** will oblige—you'll be licking your chops big time over the 1½-inch-thick USDA prime beef served on a sizzling platter.

The Price Is Right

Naturally, the price of a meal will depend on what you order—if you pig out or order the most expensive dishes on the menu, you'll spend more than if you order moderately. The listings in chapter 11 give you two price elements for each restaurant: a dollar symbol that gives you an idea of what a complete meal will cost and the price range of the entrees on the menu. The two pieces of information combined should help you choose the place that's right for you and your budget. One dollar sign means inexpensive, and five dollar signs (the maximum) means extravagant. Prices include appetizer, entree, dessert, one drink, taxes, and tip (per person).

Tourist Traps

Remember that jambalaya, ètouffèe, red beans and rice, muffulettas, and po boys were invented as economy measures in the first place, so any place that charges a lot for them is trying to rip you off. Go elsewhere.

One important thing to note is that all the listings are for good (often excellent) restaurants where you get a satisfying meal. I didn't list any crummy places just because they were cheap; neither did I list any outrageously expensive places where you pay an arm and a leg for a leaf of well-arranged lettuce and a star-shaped blob of meat. All the places I've listed offer good quality food for a fair price. The difference between one category and the next has more to do with extras such as reputation, location, type of cuisine, interiors, service, atmosphere, and views.

Here's the breakdown:

➤ **$ (dirt cheap):** These popular places offer good food in a simple setting. You'll pay under $15 per person for a full meal.

➤ **$$ (inexpensive):** These are great choices. Don't expect designer decor, but do expect to have some great New Orleans food. You'll pay between $15 and $25 per person.

➤ **$$$ (medium):** These are probably the best bets for a fine, relatively fancy dinner that doesn't cost you a fortune (say, $25 to $35 dollars per person). In most of these restaurants, the food is classy, the decor is nice, and the service is good.

➤ **$$$$ (expensive):** These restaurants are among the best in New Orleans: top food, top chefs, top service, top location, and top decor (and it'll cost you between $35 and $45 per person).

➤ **$$$$$ (the ultimate):** These are the glamorous top of the top restaurants. They have achieved world fame, either for the celebrated skills of the chef or for the atmosphere, view, and location (and frequently for both). In these restaurants, you'll get a unique experience that you'll remember for the rest of your life (and probably run up a good bill on your credit card, too). Expect to spend more than $45 per person.

Paying Your Taxes & Giving Your Tip
The sales tax in New Orleans is one of the highest in the country: 9%. Add to that at least a 15% tip. Don't reward poor service, but keep in mind that some waiters have to split their tips with the rest of the wait staff and with the kitchen staff as well. If the service was great, be generous.

Top Hat, White Tie, & Tails? Dressing to Dine
Rumor has it that Mick Jagger was once turned away from Antoine's because he wasn't wearing a jacket. If you're going there or to Commander's Palace or one of the other top restaurants for dinner, men should wear a jacket and tie, and women should wear something appropriately sharp. Otherwise, don't sweat it. New Orleans depends on tourism, and most restaurants have a very casual dress code. Even the best restaurants usually allow casual wear at lunch. I've noted any special dress requirements in the individual restaurant reviews in chapter 11.

Do You Have a Reservation, Sir?
When I say in the reviews that reservations are recommended, I generally mean for dinner. At lunch, for a party of two, you can usually find a table without having to wait too long. With a couple of exceptions, the same goes for breakfast. (I've noted any exceptions in the reviews.)

Except during the hot summer months, the restaurants in New Orleans' do a very brisk business, so if you want to dine at a certain restaurant at a particular time, make reservations before you leave home. Some of the most famous restaurants are booked up a month or more in advance (particularly at Mardi Gras and Jazz Fest), so plan way ahead if you want to eat at them.

If you haven't made reservations and need to rely on the kindness of strange maitre d's, one of the best bets for finding a table and avoiding long waits is to arrive early—meaning before 12:30pm for lunch and before 7pm for dinner. It's not guaranteed to work, but it's worth a shot.

Chapter 11

Restaurants A to Z

In This Chapter

➤ Restaurant indexes by location, price, and cuisine

➤ Full reviews of all the best restaurants in town

➤ The best places to get deep-fried food, Sunday brunch, 24-hour eats, and oddball New Orleans specialties

➤ The best places for romance, for kids, for live entertainment with your meal, and more

---

Loosen your belts and pick up your forks: It's time to eat. I've started this chapter off with indexes you can use to figure out which are the best bets for your particular tastes and needs. I've indexed by location, so you can find a good restaurant near the sights you're seeing; by price, so you can budget yourself; and by cuisine, so you can more easily satisfy your cravings. Throughout the chapter, I've also provided various specialized listings so romantic couples, families with kids, and fans of exotic eats can find their place in the sun.

After that, it's on to my picks of the best restaurants in the city, listed alphabetically so they're easier for you to refer back to and with each name followed by its price range, what part of town it's in, and the type of cuisine you'll find there. As described in chapter 10, the price ranges per person, including appetizer, entree, dessert, one drink, taxes, and tip, run something like this:

$	=	under $15
$$	=	$15–$25
$$$	=	$25–$35
$$$$	=	$35–$45
$$$$$	=	over $45

From September through May (except for the first three weeks of December), restaurants in New Orleans do a very brisk business, so if you want to dine at a certain restaurant at a particular time, make reservations at least a week in advance. Some restaurants are booked up a month or more in advance (particularly at Mardi Gras and Jazz Fest times), so the earlier you can make your reservations, the better. If you forget to make reservations before you get to town, call anyway—the restaurant may have cancellations, or it may not be booked up in the first place, no matter how popular it is. It only takes a phone call. A few restaurants don't take reservations at all, but they make up for the informality by having a long line instead.

As far as dress is concerned, you can assume that restaurants listed as requiring jackets don't require ties (unless otherwise noted); that restaurants allowing casual wear don't allow shorts or jeans; that restaurants allowing shorts and T-shirts don't allow tank tops or cutoffs; and that restaurants that allow tank tops and cutoffs don't allow you to show up naked. They just have to draw the line somewhere.

I've identified restaurants that are especially good for kids with a 🌟Kids🌟 icon. I've also noted in the reviews which restaurants are wheelchair accessible, but some may still provide problems—tables may be packed a little too closely together, for instance—so you should call ahead to inquire.

Quick Picks: New Orleans' Restaurants at a Glance
Restaurant Index by Location

Faubourg Marigny
Praline Connection No. 1

French Quarter
Antoine's ($$$)
Arnaud's ($$$)
Bacco ($$$)
Bayona ($$$)
Bella Luna ($$$)
Brennan's ($$$$)
Broussard's ($$$$)
Café Maspero ($)
Chart House ($$$$)

Clover Grill ($)
Court of Two Sisters ($$$$)
G & E Courtyard Grill ($$)
Galatoire's ($$$)
Gumbo Shop ($)
Irene's Cuisine ($$)
K-Paul's Louisiana Kitchen ($$$)
Louis XVI ($$$$)
Lucky Cheng's ($$)
Maximo's ($$)
Mike Anderson's ($$)
Mr. B's ($$$)

135

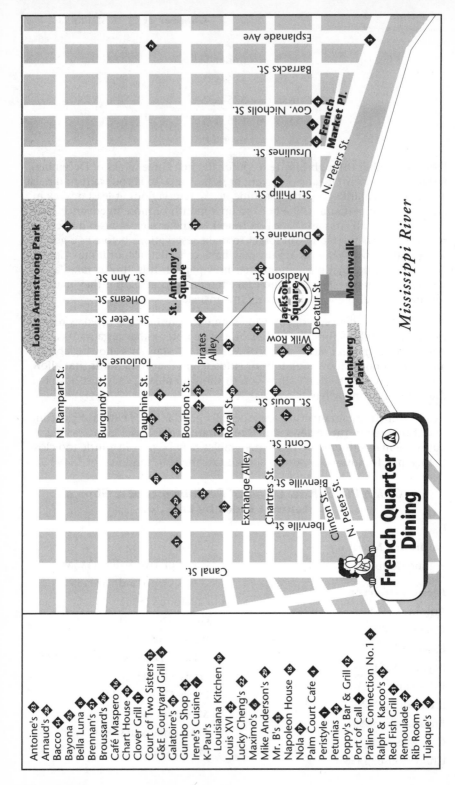

French Quarter Dining Ⓐ

Mississippi River

Louis Armstrong Park

Esplanade Ave

Barracks St.

Gov. Nicholls St.

French Market Pl.

Ursulines St.

N. Peters St.

St. Philip St.

Dumaine St.

Moonwalk

St. Ann St.

Orleans St.

St. Peter St.

Pirates Alley

St. Anthony's Square

Jackson Square

Madison St.

Decatur St.

Wilk Row

Woldenberg Park

Toulouse St.

Burgundy St.

Dauphine St.

Bourbon St.

Royal St.

St. Louis St.

N. Rampart St.

Conti St.

Exchange Alley

Chartres St.

Bienville St.

Iberville St.

Clinton St.

N. Peters St.

Canal St.

Antoine's 23
Arnaud's 28
Bacco 31
Bayona 25
Bella Luna 6
Brennan's 21
Broussard's 26
Café Maspero 16
Chart House 10
Clover Grill 11
Court of Two Sisters 13
G&E Courtyard Grill 5
Galatoire's 30
Gumbo Shop 14
Irene's Cuisine 7
K-Paul's
Louisiana Kitchen 19
Louis XVI 32
Lucky Cheng's 22
Maximo's 29
Mike Anderson's 18
Mr. B's 33
Napoleon House 4
Nola 17
Palm Court Cafe 4
Peristyle 1
Petunias 24
Poppy's Bar & Grill 12
Port of Call 2
Praline Connection No.1 3
Ralph & Kacoo's 15
Red Fish Grill 31
Remoulade 27
Rib Room 20
Tujaque's 9

136

Napoleon House ($)
Nola ($$$)
Palace Cafe ($$$)
Palm Court Café ($$)
Peristyle ($$$)
Petunias ($$)
Poppy's Bar and Grill ($)
Port of Call ($$)
Ralph & Kacoo's ($$)
Red Fish Grill ($$)
Remoulade ($)
Rib Room ($$$$$)
Tujaque's ($$$)

**Central Business District/
Warehouse District**
Bon Ton Cafe ($$$$)
Emeril's ($$$)

Grill Room ($$$$$)
Mike's on the Avenue ($$$)
Mother's ($)
Praline Connection No. 2 ($$)
Uglesich's ($)

Garden District/Uptown
Brigsten's ($$)
Commander's Palace ($$$$)
Gautreau's ($$)
Pascal's Manale ($$$)
Upperline ($$)

Mid City
Christian's ($$$)
Gabrielle ($$$)
Ruth's Chris Steak House ($$$$$)

Restaurant Index by Price

$$$$$
Grill Room (Central Business District)
Rib Room (French Quarter)
Ruth's Chris Steak House (Mid City)

$$$$
Bon Ton Cafe (Warehouse District)
Brennan's (French Quarter)
Broussard's (French Quarter)
Chart House (French Quarter)
Commander's Palace (Garden District)
Court of Two Sisters (French Quarter)
Louis XVI (French Quarter)

$$$
Antoine's (French Quarter)
Arnaud's (French Quarter)
Bacco (French Quarter)
Bayona (French Quarter)

Bella Luna (French Quarter)
Christian's (Mid City)
Emeril's (Warehouse District)
Gabrielle (Mid City)
Galatoire's (French Quarter)
K-Paul's Louisiana Kitchen (French Quarter)
Mike's on the Avenue (Warehouse District)
Mr. B's (French Quarter)
Nola (French Quarter)
Palace Cafe (French Quarter)
Pascal's Manale (Uptown)
Peristyle (French Quarter)
Tujaque's (French Quarter)

$$
Brigtsen's (Riverbend)
G & E Courtyard Grill (French Quarter)

137

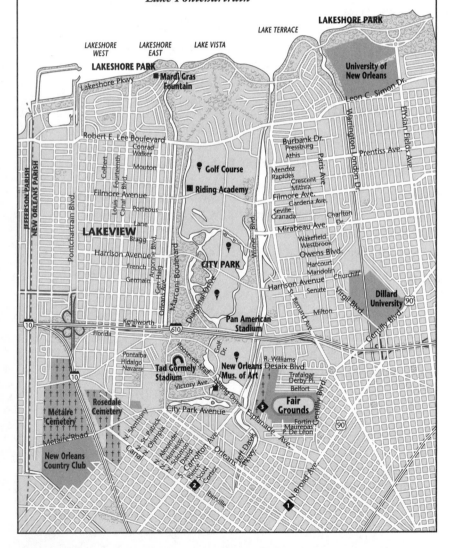

Gautreau's (Uptown)
Irene's Cuisine (French Quarter)
Lucky Cheng's (French Quarter)
Maximo's (French Quarter)
Mike Anderson's (French Quarter)
Palm Court Café (French Quarter)
Petunias (French Quarter)
Port of Call (French Quarter)
Praline Connection No. 1 (Faubourg Marigny)
Praline Connection No. 2 (Warehouse District)

Ralph & Kacoo's (French Quarter)
Red Fish Grill (French Quarter)
Upperline (Uptown)

$

Café Maspero (French Quarter)
Clover Grill (French Quarter)
Gumbo Shop (French Quarter)
Mother's (Central Business District)
Napoleon House (French Quarter)
Poppy's Bar and Grill (French Quarter)
Remoulade (French Quarter)
Uglesich's (Warehouse District)

Restaurant Index by Cuisine

American/New American
Emeril's (Warehouse District, $$$)
G & E Courtyard Grill (French Quarter, $$)
Mike's on the Avenue (Warehouse District, $$$)
Nola (French Quarter, $$$)
Peristyle (French Quarter, $$$)
Remoulade (French Quarter, $)

Asian
Lucky Cheng's (French Quarter, $$)

Breakfast
Bacco (French Quarter, $$$)
Brennan's (French Quarter, $$$$)
Clover Grill (French Quarter, $)
Court of Two Sisters (French Quarter, $$$$)
Grill Room (Central Business District, $$$$$)
Mother's (Central Business District, $)
Petunias (French Quarter, $$)
Poppy's Bar and Grill (French Quarter, $)
Rib Room (French Quarter, $$$$$)

Cajun
Bon Ton Cafe (Warehouse District, $$$$)
Brigtsen's (Riverbend, $$)
Gabrielle (Mid City, $$$)
K-Paul's Louisiana Kitchen (French Quarter, $$$)
Petunias (French Quarter, $$)

Contemporary Louisiana/ French Provincial
Gautreau's (Uptown, $$)
Irene's Cuisine (French Quarter, $$)

Creole
Antoine's (French Quarter, $$$)
Arnaud's (French Quarter, $$$)
Bacco (French Quarter, $$$)
Brennan's (French Quarter, $$$$)
Brigtsen's (Riverbend, $$)
Broussard's (French Quarter, $$$$)
Christian's (Mid City, $$$)
Commander's Palace (Garden District, $$$$)
Court of Two Sisters (French Quarter, $$$$)

139

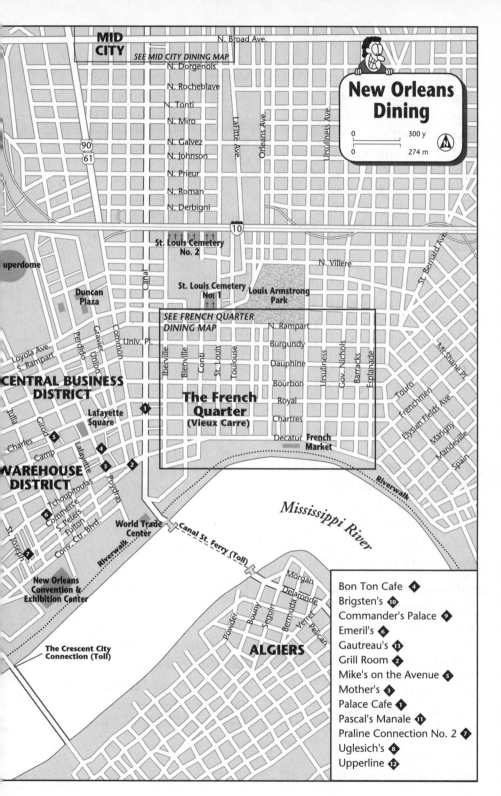

New Orleans Dining

0   300 y
0   274 m

MID CITY

SEE MID CITY DINING MAP

N. Broad Ave.
N. Dorgenois
N. Rocheblave
N. Tonti
N. Miro
N. Galvez
N. Johnson
N. Prieur
N. Roman
N. Derbigni

LaFitte Ave.
Orleans Ave.
Ursullines Ave.

90
61

10

St. Louis Cemetery No. 2

uperdome

Duncan Plaza

St. Louis Cemetery No. 1

N. Villere

Louis Armstrong Park

N. Bernard Ave.

SEE FRENCH QUARTER DINING MAP

Loyola Ave.
S. Rampart

CENTRAL BUSINESS DISTRICT

Gravier
Common
Perdido
Union
Univ. Pl.

N. Rampart
Burgundy
Dauphine
Bourbon
Royal
Chartres

Iberville
Bienville
Conti
St. Louis
Toulouse

Ursullines
Gov. Nichols
Barracks
Esplanade

Touro
Frenchmen
Elysian Fields Ave.

McShane Pl.

The French Quarter
(Vieux Carre)

Lafayette Square

Charles
Julia
Girod
Camp
Lafayette
Poydras

Decatur **French Market**

Marigny
Mandeville
Spain

WAREHOUSE DISTRICT

Tchoupitoulas
Commerce
S. Peters
Fulton
Conv.-Ctr. Blvd.

World Trade Center

Riverwalk

1
5
4
3
2
6
7

St. Joseph

New Orleans Convention & Exhibition Center

Canal St. Ferry (Toll)

Mississippi River

Riverwalk

The Crescent City Connection (Toll)

Morgan
Delaronde
Bouny
Powder
Seguin
Bermuda
Verret
Pelican

ALGIERS

Bon Ton Cafe **4**
Brigsten's **10**
Commander's Palace **9**
Emeril's **6**
Gautreau's **13**
Grill Room **2**
Mike's on the Avenue **5**
Mother's **3**
Palace Cafe **1**
Pascal's Manale **11**
Praline Connection No. 2 **7**
Uglesich's **8**
Upperline **12**

141

continued

Emeril's (Warehouse District, $$$)

Gabrielle (Mid City, $$$)

Gumbo Shop (French Quarter, $)

Lucky Cheng's (French Quarter, $$)

Mother's (Central Business District, $)

Mr. B's (French Quarter, $$$)

Nola (French Quarter, $$$)

Palace Cafe (French Quarter, $$$)

Palm Court Café (French Quarter, $$)

Petunias (French Quarter, $$)

Ralph & Kacoo's (French Quarter, $$)

Remoulade (French Quarter, $)

Tujaque's (French Quarter, $$$)

Upperline (Uptown, $$)

Crepes

Petunias (French Quarter, $$)

French

Antoine's (French Quarter, $$$)

Brennan's (French Quarter, $$$$)

Broussard's (French Quarter, $$$$)

Christian's (Mid City, $$$)

Gabrielle (Mid City, $$$)

Galatoire's (French Quarter, $$$)

Louis XVI (French Quarter, $$$$)

Peristyle (French Quarter, $$$)

International/Eclectic

Bayona (French Quarter, $$$)

Bella Luna (French Quarter, $$$)

Grill Room (Central Business District, $$$$$)

Mike's on the Avenue (Warehouse District, $$$)

Upperline (Uptown, $$)

Italian

Bacco (French Quarter, $$$)

Irene's Cuisine (French Quarter, $$)

Maximo's (French Quarter, $$)

Pascal's Manale (Uptown, $$$)

Peristyle (French Quarter, $$$)

Sandwiches/Hamburgers

Café Maspero (French Quarter, $)

Clover Grill (French Quarter, $)

Mother's (Central Business District, $)

Napoleon House (French Quarter, $)

Poppy's Bar and Grill (French Quarter, $)

Seafood

Café Maspero (French Quarter, $)

Mike Anderson's (French Quarter, $$)

Pascal's Manale (Uptown, $$$)

Ralph & Kacoo's (French Quarter, $$)

Red Fish Grill (French Quarter, $$)

Rib Room (French Quarter, $$$$$)

Uglesich's (Warehouse District, $)

Short Order

Clover Grill (French Quarter, $)

Mother's (Central Business District, $)

Poppy's Bar and Grill (French Quarter, $)

Soul Food

Praline Connection No. 1 (Faubourg Marigny, $$)

Praline Connection No. 2 (Warehouse District, $$)

Steaks

Chart House (French Quarter, $$$$)

Pascal's Manale (Uptown, $$$)

Rib Room (French Quarter, $$$$$)

Ruth's Chris Steak House (Mid City, $$$$$)

My Favorite New Orleans Restaurants

Antoine's

$$$. French Quarter. CLASSIC FRENCH/CREOLE.

A New Orleans classic run by the same family for 150 years, the legendary Antoine's is famous as the birthplace of oysters Rockefeller (with a green topping whose ingredients are still top secret) and as the focus of Frances Keyes's book *Dinner at Antoine's*. Its 15 separate dining areas run the gamut from plain to opulent; ask for the front dining room if you want a non-smoking area.

713 St. Louis St. (half a block from Bourbon St.). An easy walk from anywhere in the French Quarter. ☎ *504/581-4422. You should make reservations a week in advance for the weekend.* **Main courses:** *$17.50–$50 (most under $25). AE, DC, MC, V.* **Open:** *Lunch and dinner Mon–Sat. Jackets required after 5pm, but casual wear is acceptable for lunch. Wheelchair accessible.*

Arnaud's

$$$. French Quarter. CREOLE.

Another classic New Orleans restaurant, with a history nearly as rich (but more complicated) as Antoine's, Arnaud's arguably may have more dependable food. Its lovingly restored turn-of-the-century townhouse, complete with flickering gas lights and antique ceiling fans, provides a lovely setting for an elegant meal with very formal service. Specialties include shrimp Creole and trout meuniére. Jazz is played nightly in the Le Richelieu Room. Check out the **Germaine Wells Mardi Gras Museum** upstairs.

813 Bienville (at the corner of Bourbon), an easy walk from anywhere in the French Quarter or Central Business District. ☎ *504/ 523-5433. You should make reservations a week or more in advance for the weekend.* **Main courses:** *$18–$25. AE, DC, MC, V.* **Open:** *Lunch Mon–Fri; dinner daily; Sun jazz brunch. Dress code is casual for lunch, with shorts allowed. Dinner requires a jacket for men. Wheelchair accessible.*

Bacco

$$$. French Quarter. ITALIAN/CREOLE.

One of the newest in the seemingly endless line of Brennan family restaurants, Bacco returns to its Creole roots while still maintaining an Italian flair. The menu is seasonal, but some regulars are the Creole Italian gumbo (made with roasted goose, Italian sausage, and tasso) and the hickory-grilled pork chop wrapped with apple-smoked bacon.

Best Bets for a Romantic Interlude

Bayona (French Quarter, $$$)
Bella Luna (French Quarter, $$$)
Brigtsen's (Riverbend, $$)
Broussard's (French Quarter, $$$$)
Chart House (French Quarter, $$$$)
Christian's (Mid City, $$$)
Commander's Palace (Garden District, $$$$)
Gabrielle (Mid City, $$$)
Gautreau's (Uptown, $$)
Maximo's (French Quarter, $$)

310 Chartres St. (2 blocks from Bourbon St., 2½ blocks from Canal, and 2½ blocks from Jackson Square). ☎ *504/522-2426. You should make reservations a couple of days in advance for the weekend. **Main courses:** $17.50–$21.50; 3-course meals $22–$32. AE, DC, MC, V. **Open:** Breakfast Mon–Sat; dinner daily; Sun brunch. Shorts and T-shirts are allowed. Wheelchair accessible.*

Bayona
$$$. French Quarter. INTERNATIONAL.
Chef Susan Spicer of Bayona has a flair for creating unconventional dishes. Dishes such as grilled duck breast with pepper-jelly glaze and Parmesan-crusted rabbit with a lemon-sage sauce are truly superb. The Creole cottage's warm and homey atmosphere and intimate courtyard provide the perfect background for a romantic evening.

430 Dauphine (1 block from Bourbon, but take a cab—it's safer). ☎ *504/ 525-4455. Reservations required at least a month in advance for dinner, a week ahead for lunch. **Main courses:** $14–$23. AE, CB, DC, DISC, MC, V. **Open:** Lunch Mon–Fri; dinner Mon–Sat. A low step and small rest room may be problems for people with disabilities.*

Bella Luna
$$$. French Quarter. ECLECTIC/CONTINENTAL.
I always wonder about a restaurant with an Italian name and a German chef, but somehow it all comes together wonderfully in this romantic setting overlooking the Mississippi River. The menu is an eclectic mix of Southwestern, German, Italian, and Louisiana cuisine. Try the smoked shrimp, fettuccine with Parmesan, or quesadillas with shrimp and top it off with some Key lime pie or banana bread pudding.

914 N. Peters (1 block from Jackson Square). ☎ *504/529-1583. You should make reservations at least a week in advance. **Main courses:** $15–$25. All major credit cards accepted. **Open:** Dinner daily. Casual dress is allowed. The restaurant is wheelchair accessible, but the rest rooms are down a half-flight of stairs.*

Bon Ton Cafe
$$$$. Warehouse District. CAJUN.
One of the first real Cajun restaurants in New Orleans, the Bon Ton Cafe has been a favorite of many New Orleanians for over 40 years (though service can sometimes be erratic). Try any of the fried seafood, gumbo, jambalaya, turtle soup, or crawfish dishes. Checkered tablecloths and potted flowers provide the setting for simple but good Cajun food.

401 Magazine (only 4 blocks from Canal St., but take a taxi at night). ☎ *504/ 524-3386. Reservations recommended for dinner. **Main courses:** $21–$26 (fixed price dinners available). AE, DC, MC, V. **Open:** Lunch and dinner Mon–Fri. Casual dress. Wheelchair accessible, but seating for people with disabilities is limited.*

Best Bets for Kids

Bon Ton Cafe (Warehouse District, $$$$)
Clover Grill (French Quarter, $)
Commander's Palace (Garden District, $$$$)
Court of Two Sisters (French Quarter, $$$$)
Galatoire's (French Quarter, $$$)
Gumbo Shop (French Quarter, $)
Pascal's Manale (Uptown, $$$)
Petunias (French Quarter, $$)
Poppy's Bar and Grill (French Quarter, $)
Praline Connection No. 1 (Faubourg Marigny, $$)
Praline Connection No. 2 (Warehouse District, $$)
Ralph & Kacoo's (French Quarter, $$)
Remoulade (French Quarter, $)
Ruth's Chris Steak House (Mid City, $$$$$)

Brennan's
$$$$. French Quarter. FRENCH/CREOLE.

Since 1946, generations of locals and tourists alike have eaten millions of servings of eggs Benedict, eggs Hussarde, and trout Nancy for breakfast, often dropping as much as $50 a person in the process and making "Breakfast at Brennan's" famous the world over. The $35 breakfast includes appetizer, entree, dessert, and coffee; try the turtle soup for starters and top it all off with bananas Foster.

417 Royal St. (1 block from Bourbon).
☎ *504/525-9711. You should make reservations a week in advance for the weekend and a few days ahead for lunch or brunch.* **Main courses:** *dinner $15–$35. AE, CB, DC, DISC, MC, V.* **Open:** *Brunch and dinner daily; lunch Mon–Fri. Jacket required for men at dinner. Wheelchair accessible.*

Best Bets for
Deep-Fried Food

Praline Connection
Mother's
Gumbo Shop
Mike Anderson's
Ralph & Kacoo's

Brigtsen's
$$. Riverbend. CAJUN/CREOLE.

In a small converted shotgun cottage in the romantic Riverbend area, just feet from the Mississippi River levee, Frank Brigsten prepares magnificent cuisine on a small six-burner stove. The menu changes daily, but the food rarely fails, and the place stays crowded with local foodies. Recent raves included the roast duck and a double veal chop with oysters—and the fish is *always* a good bet. Recent desserts include café au lait crème brûlée, homemade lemonade ice cream, homemade mint chocolate chip ice cream (with fresh mint!), and fresh raspberries with a crème fraîche-based sauce.

723 Dante (take the St. Charles Streetcar and walk 3 blocks; take a taxi at night). ☎ ***504/861-7610.*** *Reservations recommended a week or two in advance.* **Main courses:** *$14–$28 (early bird specials available—full meal for $15). AE, DC, MC, V.* **Open:** *Dinner Tue–Sat. Casual dress. Steps may prove a challenge for people with disabilities.*

Broussard's
$$$$. French Quarter. FRENCH/CREOLE.
Signature dishes such as oysters Broussard and duck Normandy have earned Broussard's an excellent and well-deserved reputation—though the place is a bit overpriced if you ask me. The quiet and elegant atmosphere is quite a contrast to the noise of Bourbon Street just a few feet away. If you can afford the menu, there's a great courtyard for atmosphere and romance.

819 Conti (½ block from Bourbon). ☎ ***504/581-3866.*** *Reservations strongly recommended.* **Main courses:** *$20–$34 (dinner for two can easily be $100). AE, CB, DC, DISC, MC, V.* **Open:** *Dinner daily. Casual dress. Wheelchair accessible.*

Café Maspero
$. French Quarter. SANDWICHES/SEAFOOD.
Don't confuse this restaurant with Maspero's Slave Exchange a few blocks away. Though Café Maspero doesn't serve po boys, it does serve some of the biggest and best deli-style sandwiches in town. Just about everything on the menu comes with French fries, and the wine selection is good as well.

601 Decatur (2 short blocks from Jackson Square and 3 blocks from Bourbon). ☎ ***504/523-6250.*** *Reservations are not accepted, and the lines can be long at times, but they usually move fast.* **Main courses:** *$5–$9.* **Open:** *11:00am–11:00pm Sun–Thurs (till midnight Fri–Sat). No dress code. Wheelchair accessible, but the crowded tables and narrow doorways make maneuvering a challenge.*

Chart House
$$$$. French Quarter. STEAKS/SEAFOOD.
If the complex, sauce-laden meals from all the Cajun, Creole, and Italian restaurants in the Quarter leave you hankering for a simple steak, head to the Chart House, which offers romantic balcony seating overlooking Jackson Square. (If the kids are along, though, the dining room is probably a better choice.)

801 Chartres St. (at the corner of St. Ann, 2 blocks from Bourbon and 1 block from Decatur). ☎ ***504/523-2015.*** *You should make your reservations two to three days in advance.* **Main courses:** *$22–$36. AE, CB, DC, DISC, MC, V.* **Open:** *Dinner daily. Casual dress. Wheelchair accessible.*

146

Christian's
$$$. Mid City. FRENCH/CREOLE.
If you like your churches with tables instead of pews and paintings by
European masters instead of religious icons, you'll enjoy Christian's. For
appetizers, the oysters en brochette (oysters and crispy bacon fried in a batter
and served with a *buerre noir*—butter that is heated until it is a rich brown
color and flavored with vinegar, wine, parsley, and lemon juice) are fantastic,
as is the crawfish Carolyn (crawfish in a spicy cream sauce with brandy and
Parmesan cheese). For the main course, I recommend the duck with apricot
glaze or the veal chop Madeira (served with mushrooms and a Madeira-
flavored *demiglace*—a rich gravy made from beef stock). For dessert, try the
chocolate espresso torte (flourless chocolate cake flavored with Grand
Marnier and Kahlua in a raspberry sauce).

3835 Iberville (3 miles from the Quarter—take a taxi). ☎ *504/482-4924. Make
reservations a week in advance.* **Main courses: $15–$25. AE, CB, DC, MC, V.**
Open: *Lunch Tues–Fri; dinner Tues–Sat. Jacket and tie strongly recommended for
men. Steps and closely packed tables make it problematic for people with wheelchairs.*

Best Bets for an Aristocratic Meal

Antoine's (French Quarter, $$$)
Arnaud's (French Quarter, $$$)
Bacco (French Quarter, $$$)
Broussard's (French Quarter, $$$$)
Christian's (Mid City, $$$)
Commander's Palace (Garden District, $$$$)
Emeril's (Warehouse District, $$$)
Grill Room (Central Business District, $$$$$)
Louis XVI (French Quarter, $$$$)
Mike's on the Avenue (Warehouse District, $$$)
Mr. B's (French Quarter, $$$)
Nola (French Quarter, $$$)
Palace Cafe (French Quarter, $$$)
Rib Room (French Quarter, $$$$$)
Ruth's Chris Steak House (Mid City, $$$$$)

Clover Grill
*$. French Quarter. SANDWICHES/SHORT ORDER/
BREAKFAST.*
The menu calls this place "The Happiest Grill On Earth," and goes on to say,
"we're here to serve people and make them feel prettier than they are."

A delightful, gay-friendly, 24-hour diner where the staff competes with that menu for fun, the place serves breakfast around-the-clock, and the juicy burgers may be the best in town (cooked under a hubcap, no less). Burgers begin at $3.19, club sandwiches at $4.99, and platters (chicken fried steak, catfish Charlene, or grilled chicken breast) are $5.29. They also serve fabulous shakes, malts, and lots of coffee. If you behave yourself, you might even get to meet Ruthie the Duck Lady (a local celebrity who used to roller skate through the Quarter followed by her pet ducks).

900 Bourbon St. (just follow the drunks). ☎ ***504/523-0904.*** *Reservations are useless. Prices vary, but nothing on the menu is more than $6.29. AE, MC, V.* ***Open:*** *24 hours. No dress code. Steps and small spaces make this place a challenge for people with disabilities.*

Commander's Palace
$$$$. Garden District. CREOLE.

About three years ago, the James Beard Association named Commander's the best restaurant in the country. That's worth repeating: They named it the best restaurant *in the whole country.* It's not just the food; it's the whole package: the 1880 Victorian house setting, the gorgeous dining rooms, and the attentive and helpful wait staff. Each night features a multicourse prix fixe menu for around $35—it's a bargain. The turtle soup is famous, but other standouts include the boned Mississippi roasted quail stuffed with Creole crawfish sausage and served with sauté of corn and jalepeño with reduced port and quail glaze. The staff will tell you to try the bread pudding soufflé for dessert. Trust them.

1403 Washington (take the St. Charles Streetcar and walk 2 blocks along Washington Ave. toward the river; take a taxi at night). ☎ ***504/899-8221.*** *You should make reservations a week in advance.* ***Main courses:*** *Full brunch from $20, main courses from $22, and full dinner from $29 (a là carte prices higher). AE, CB, DC, DISC, MC, V.* ***Open:*** *Lunch Mon–Fri; dinner daily; brunch on Sat–Sun. Men must wear a jacket and tie for dinner. Wheelchairs will need to navigate over one step.*

Best Things That Taste Like Chicken

Ralph & Kacoo's alligator
Pascal's Manale's turtle soup
Brennan's turtle soup
Bon Ton Cafe's turtle soup
Commander's Palace turtle soup

Court of Two Sisters
$$$$. French Quarter. CREOLE.

Set in a historic building with an elegant courtyard and two gurgling fountains, the atmosphere is better than the food. Go for the history or the ambiance, but stick with something simple and relatively inexpensive, such as the shrimp remoulade. The restaurant can accommodate about 600 or so, and casual dress is allowed, though many diners will be dressed more formally.

613 Royal St. (1 block from Bourbon). ☎ *504/522-7261. Reservations are accepted but are not usually required.* **Main courses:** *$15.50–$35 (fixed-price meal available for $37); brunch $21. AE, CB, DC, DISC, MC, V. Open for breakfast, lunch, and dinner daily. Shorts and T-shirts are allowed. Wheelchair accessible.*

Emeril's
$$$. Warehouse District. CREOLE/NEW AMERICAN.
At chef Emeril Lagasse's restaurant, even the ketchup and bread are homemade. If you like fish, try the pan-roasted salmon with herbs and mustard, served with goat cheese; if you enjoy fowl, try the roasted quail. No matter what you have for an entree, don't miss the banana cream pie with caramel sauce (the best in the world!) or the chocolate Grand Marnier soufflé. Although the food is great, it's difficult to hold a conversation here over the noise, and the service can be inconsistent if not downright rude.

800 Tchoupitoulas (8 blocks from Canal—take a taxi). ☎ *504/528-9393. Make reservations a week or so in advance.* **Main courses:** *$14–$32. AE, CB, DISC, MC, V.* **Open:** *Lunch Mon–Fri; dinner Mon–Sat. Casual dress. Wheelchair accessible.*

G & E Courtyard Grill
$$. French Quarter. NEW AMERICAN.
What brings most people back to the G & E Courtyard Grill is not the food but rather the candlelit courtyard, the splashing fountain, and the flames of the grill with its rotisserie full of chicken. The food isn't bad, but it's a bit inconsistent (as the service can be, too). Try the grilled salmon or the shrimp cakes with homemade goat cheese if you will, but you've got to have a piece of the German chocolate cake.

1113 Decatur St. (3½ blocks from Jackson Square). ☎ *504/528-9376. Make reservations two to three days in advance.* **Main courses:** *$12.50–$30. AE, CB, DC, DISC, MC, V.* **Open:** *Lunch Fri–Sun; dinner daily. Rest rooms are not wheelchair accessible.*

Gabrielle
$$$. Mid City. FRENCH/CREOLE/CAJUN.
This small and intimate restaurant reminds me of a sidewalk cafe in Paris and provides the setting for an ever-changing menu that has lately become one of the city's standouts. The gumbos, homemade sausages, rabbit, duck, and any of the desserts made from fresh berries are likely to please. It's a bit out of the way, but worth the trek.

3201 Esplanade (2½ miles from the Quarter—take a taxi). ☎ *504/948-6233. You should make reservations about a week in advance.* **Main courses:** *$14.50–$24. AE, CB, DC, DISC, MC, V.* **Open:** *Dinner Tue–Sat; lunch on Fridays only from Oct–May. Casual dress. The restaurant is wheelchair accessible, but the rest room is not.*

149

Galatoire's
$$$. French Quarter. FRENCH.

One of the classiest New Orleans restaurants, Galatoire's is where generations of families and businessmen have waited in line like everyone else because Galatoire's does not take reservations. In *A Streetcar Named Desire*, Stella took Blanche here to escape Stanley's poker game. Long considered one of the best restaurants in town, Galatoire's is the center of an ongoing debate: is it still the best, or is it living on its rep? Those in the know say to order the trout almondine without sauce.

Twenty-Four-Hour Eats

Clover Grill (French Quarter, $)
Poppy's Bar and Grill (French Quarter, $)

209 Bourbon (located in the second block of Bourbon, it's an easy walk from anywhere in the Quarter or the Central Business District). ☎ *504/525-2021. Reservations not accepted.* **Main courses:** *$14–$22. AE, MC, V.* **Open:** *Lunch and dinner Tue–Sun. Men must wear jackets for dinner and on Sunday. The restaurant is wheelchair accessible, but the rest rooms could be a problem.*

Gautreau's
$$. Uptown. CONTEMPORARY LOUISIANA.

Gautreau's may be in an old converted neighborhood drugstore, but the candlelight and nostalgic photographs set a more romantic mood. The menu changes every few weeks; I've enjoyed the quail stuffed with pecans and cherries and laced with Chambard (a raspberry liqueur). For dessert, try the *tarte tatin* (apples and sun-dried cherries with a strawberry sorbet) if it's available.

1728 Soniat (take the St. Charles Streetcar and walk 2½ blocks away from the river; take a taxi at night). ☎ *504/899-7397. You should make reservations a week or two in advance.* **Main courses:** *$11–$23. AE, CB, DC, DISC, MC, V.* **Open:** *Dinner Mon–Sat. A few steps make the small rest rooms inaccessible to wheelchairs.*

Grill Room
$$$$$. Central Business District. INTERNATIONAL.

With a combination of excellent food, ambiance, service, and comfort, the Grill Room offers an unforgettable dining experience at an unforgettable price, of course. Try the chilled oysters with frozen champagne ginger *migonette* (champagne seasoned with ginger, which has been frozen into a sorbet) or Chinese smoked lobster. Wine starts at a mere $20 a bottle, levels off at $2,300 for an 1898 Chateau Lafitte, and then skyrockets to $18,500 for a double magnum (four bottles) of 1961 Chateau Petrus.

300 Gravier (one block from Canal). ☎ *504/522-1992. You should make reservations a week or two in advance.* **Main courses:** *$30–$39 (3-course lunch specials $19.50). AE, DC, DISC, MC, V.* **Open:** *Breakfast, lunch, and dinner Mon–Sat; brunches Sat–Sun. Men must wear jackets for dinner. Wheelchair accessible.*

Kids Gumbo Shop
$. French Quarter. CREOLE.

An adequate "in a pinch" alternative for Creole dishes such as red beans and rice, gumbo, crawfish étouffée, jambalaya, and shrimp Creole. Murals of the French Market adorn the walls of the dining room, and there's also seating on the patio (which is also the smoking section). The praline parfait is an interesting dessert.

630 St. Peter (1½ blocks from Bourbon). ☎ *504/525-1486. Reservations are not required, but you may wait 10–15 minutes when they're busy.* **Main courses:** *$6–$15. AE, CB, DC, DISC, MC, V.* **Open:** *Lunch and dinner daily. T-shirts and shorts are allowed. A small dining room makes wheelchair passage difficult.*

Irene's Cuisine
$$. French Quarter. ITALIAN/FRENCH PROVINCIAL.

One of the best meals I've ever eaten was at Irene's, and I'm not alone—it seems that most agree about this small restaurant located in the corner of a garage. My wife and I love the rack of lamb served with a port wine sauce, French fried shoestring yams, and spinach. Other good bets are Irene's chicken à la Siciliana and the grilled fish of the day.

539 St. Philip (3 short blocks from Jackson Square and 1 from Decatur). ☎ *504/ 529-8811. Reservations not accepted (go early to avoid a wait).* **Main courses:** *$10.50–$19. AE, MC, V.* **Open:** *Dinner daily. Wheelchair accessible.*

K-Paul's Louisiana Kitchen
$$$. French Quarter. CAJUN.

Chef Paul Prudhomme started all the hoopla about Cajun cooking from this place, and it's still among the best. Known for its blackened redfish and Cajun martini, K-Paul's also specializes in fiery gumbo, chicken and rabbit from its own farm, and Cajun popcorn (fried crawfish tails). The menu changes daily and features a variety of extra-hot interpretations of the Cajun tradition. If they're available, try the bronzed swordfish with "Crawfish Hot Fanny Sauce" or the eggplant pirogue filled with seafood and smothered with "Garlic Slam-Bam Sauce." Try the sweet potato pecan pie with chantilly cream for dessert.

416 Chartres St., between Conti and St. Louis. ☎ *504/524-7394. Reservations suggested for upstairs dining room only; otherwise you have to wait in a sometimes hour-long line.* **Main courses:** *Lunch $7–$14; dinner $21–$30. AE, CB, DC, MC, V.* **Open:** *Lunch and dinner Mon–Sat.*

Louis XVI
$$$$. French Quarter. FRENCH.

One of the premier dining experiences in New Orleans, Louis XVI serves meticulously prepared French food with meticulous attention to detail and utmost care and respect for the diner. The room is subdued and romantic (don't expect over-the-top Louis XVI decor), and the cuisine is rich with sauces and traditional flavors. This is dining at its most formal. Plus, bartender Arlie seems to be everyone's best pal.

Best Bets for Fried Green Tomatoes

Uglesich's
Upperline

730 Bienville (½ block from Bourbon St.). ☎ *504/581-7000. You should make reservations a week in advance. **Main courses:** $18–$34. AE, CB, DC, MC, V. **Open:** Breakfast and dinner daily. Wheelchair accessible.*

Lucky Cheng's
$$. French Quarter. ASIAN/CREOLE.

All you need to know is that Lucky Cheng's is not referred to around town as "that amazing Asian/Creole place," but rather "that drag queen place." Let's just say the sassy wait staff is fabulous. In my book (and this is my book), the best dish is the crispy roast duck accented with plum sauce and scallions, served with a scallion crepe and dirty rice (rice dressing).

720 St. Louis (½ block from Bourbon). ☎ *504/529-2045. You should make reservations two to three days in advance. **Main courses:** $14–$17. AE, DISC, MC, V. **Open:** Lunch and dinner Tue–Sun. Wheelchair accessible.*

Maximo's
$$. French Quarter. ITALIAN.

The budget-minded will like Maximo's reasonably priced selection of pastas, and those in the mood for romance will love the balcony. Downstairs, booths provide a comfortable (if somewhat noisy) atmosphere for sampling veal scallopine with a nice bottle of wine. You can keep an eye on the action in the open kitchen if you prefer.

1117 Decatur St. (4 blocks from Jackson Square). ☎ *504/586-8883. You should make reservations a week in advance. **Main courses:** $9–$24. AE, DISC, MC, V. **Open:** Dinner daily. Wheelchair accessible.*

Mike Anderson's
$$. French Quarter. SEAFOOD.

If you're having fun on Bourbon Street and get a hankering for seafood, pop into Mike Anderson's, where the lunch specials change daily. You can get your seafood any way you want it: Fried, broiled, baked, or even raw. They also serve étouffée and jambalaya. Raw oysters are only 25¢ each when they're in season.

215 Bourbon St. (2 blocks from Canal St.). ☎ **504/524-3884.** *Reservations not accepted (expect to wait 15 minutes or longer for a table).* **Main courses:** *$10–$18. AE, DISC, MC, V.* **Open:** *Lunch and dinner daily.*

Mike's on the Avenue
$$$. Uptown. NEW AMERICAN/INTERNATIONAL.
Mike's is popular with a yuppie and artsy crowd, but the noise level may scare many people away. If you want to escape the noise, ask to be seated in the rear dining room. Mike's Chinese dumplings filled with shrimp, ginger, and scallions with a Szechwan tahini sauce is a favorite. I also like the desserts, including butterscotch Napoleon, crème brûlée, and chocolate mousse.

628 St. Charles (take the St. Charles Streetcar or a taxi). ☎ **504/523-1709.** *You should make reservations at least two to three days in advance.* **Main courses:** *$16–$30. AE, DC, DISC, MC, V.* **Open:** *Breakfast, lunch, and dinner Mon–Fri; breakfast and dinner Sat–Sun. A small step is the only barrier to people with disabilities.*

Mother's
$. Central Business District. SANDWICHES/CREOLE/SHORT ORDER/BREAKFAST.
A couple of years ago, New Orleans was named "Fattest City in the U.S." by researchers looking at Americans' eating habits, and no restaurant in town beamed more happily at this label than Mother's, whose overstuffed, mountain-sized po boys have added many a pound to many a patron over the years. There's long lines and zero atmosphere, but who cares when faced with a Ferdi special—a giant roll filled with baked ham, roast beef, gravy, and other bits of beef debris? They serve food other than po boys, but that's what New Orleans goes for (and you should, too).

401 Poydras (easy walk from anywhere in the Quarter or Central Business District). ☎ **504/523-9656.** *Reservations not accepted.* **Menu selections:** *$3–$16.50. No credit cards.* **Open:** *Breakfast, lunch, and dinner daily. Wheelchair accessible.*

Best Desserts

Ralph & Kacoo's satin pie
Clover Grill's lemon ice box pie and shakes
Commander's Palace's chocolate Diane
Brennan's bananas Foster
Emeril's banana cream pie with caramel sauce
Petunias' dessert crepes
Mr. B's chocolate molten "up" cake

Mr. B's
$$$. French Quarter. CONTEMPORARY CREOLE.
Mr. B's is another restaurant run by the ubiquitous Brennan family, so you know the food is *fine*—skip K-Paul's and come here for delicious basic traditional food. The crab cakes are as good as they get, the andouille is superb

(order anything it comes with), the gumbo hearty, and the Cajun BBQ shrimp are large and plump, swimming in a rich, spicy butter sauce that's practically obscene. A jazz brunch is served from 10:30am to 3:00pm on Sunday.

201 Royal St. (1 block away from Bourbon or Canal St.). ☎ *504/523-2078. Reservations recommended.* **Main courses:** *$15.50–$22. AE, DC, MC, V.* **Open:** *Lunch Mon–Sat; dinner daily.*

Napoleon House
$. French Quarter. SANDWICHES.
Part of this restaurant was built in 1797 with the hope of rescuing Napoleon Bonaparte from his island exile and providing him with a place of refuge in New Orleans. These days, ambiance is the name of the game at the Napoleon House. Known more as a bar where classical music fills the air, the Napoleon House offers a limited selection of sandwiches and pastries to munch on while you people-watch in the dimly lit space. Their warm muffuletta sandwich (round Italian bread filled with cold cuts, cheese, and olive salad) is probably the best in town.

500 Chartres (2 blocks from both Bourbon St. and Jackson Square). ☎ *504/ 524-9752. Reservations required only for large parties.* **Menu selections:** *$4.25–$10.* **Open:** *Mon–Sat 11:00am–1:00am; Sun 11:00am–7:00pm. AE, MC, V. Wheelchair accessible.*

Nola
$$$. French Quarter. CREOLE/NEW AMERICAN.
This modern two-story building with a glass-enclosed elevator is the cheaper and more casual of chef Emeril Lagasse's two restaurants, but the same problems Emeril's has surface here: fine food is marred by the staff's often horrible attitude and sometimes painfully slow service. Unique entrees such as Caribbean-style grilled free-range chicken (with a brown sugar-cayenne rub served with sweet potato casserole, guacamole, and fried tortilla threads) and cedar-plank fish fill the menu.

534 St. Louis (2½ blocks from Bourbon). ☎ *504/522-6652. You should make reservations at least two to three days in advance.* **Main courses:** *$16–$24. AE, DC, DISC, MC, V.* **Open:** *Lunch and dinner Mon–Sat; dinner only on Sun. Wheelchair accessible.*

Palace Cafe
$$$. French Quarter.
CONTEMPORARY CREOLE.
If it was good enough for President Clinton, it should be good enough for you and me, right? But in a city known for its superb restaurants, this place somehow seems to fall short. Call it "Commander's Palace Lite," with all that implies. The bright spot is the dessert menu, featuring white chocolate bread

pudding and Napoleon pastry served with strawberries. Noise can be a problem here.

605 Canal St. (an easy walk from anywhere in the Quarter). ☎ *504/523-1661. You should make reservations a week in advance.* **Main courses:** *$8.75–$25 (average is $19). AE, DC, MC, V.* **Open:** *Lunch and dinner Mon–Sat; brunch (10:30am–2:30pm) and dinner Sun. Wheelchair accessible.*

Palm Court Café
$$. French Quarter. CREOLE.
Known more for its jazz than its food (see chapter 19), the Palm Court still manages to provide a good meal while you enjoy excellent entertainment. If you stick to traditional fare such as grilled fish, shrimp Creole, or red beans and rice, you won't go wrong. The place is usually crowded, and service can be slow, but the great jazz should keep you from noticing.

> **Best Bets for Live Entertainment with Your Meal**
>
> Arnaud's (French Quarter, $$$)
> Bacco (French Quarter, $$$)
> Brennan's (French Quarter, $$$$)
> Court of Two Sisters (French Quarter, $$$$)
> Lucky Cheng's (French Quarter, $$)
> Palm Court Café (French Quarter, $$)

1204 Decatur St. (5 blocks from Jackson Square and a safe walk). ☎ *504/ 525-0200. Reservations strongly recommended.* **Main courses:** *$10–$17, 4-course special $14. AE, DISC, MC, V.* **Open:** *Dinner Wed–Sun. Wheelchair accessible.*

Kids Pascal's Manale
$$$. Uptown. ITALIAN/SEAFOOD/STEAKS.
A bit out of the way but worth the trip, Pascal's is well-known for its barbecued shrimp—which aren't barbecued at all but rather served in a spicy butter sauce that will have you swabbing your plate with bread to get every last drop. It also serves a famous turtle soup, delicious pasta Alfredo, good gumbo, and great *osso bucco* (Italian stew made of braised veal shanks). Their mushrooms stuffed with crab meat are what keeps my mouth watering, though.

1838 Napoleon Ave. (take the St. Charles Streetcar to Napoleon and walk 3 blocks away from the river—take a taxi at night). ☎ *504/895-4877. You should make reservations a week in advance, but waits are often inevitable, anyway.* **Main courses:** *$14–$22. AE, CB, DC, DISC, MC, V.* **Open:** *Lunch and dinner Mon–Fri; dinner only on Sat and Sun (closed Sun Memorial Day weekend through Labor Day).*

Peristyle

$$$. French Quarter. FRENCH/ITALIAN/NEW AMERICAN.

The former home of Marti's, Tennessee Williams's favorite restaurant (he would sit on the balcony and play poker), the relatively new Peristyle has quickly become a New Orleans foodie favorite. The duck a l'orange wins raves, and how can you resist seared foie gras with a cranberry preserve reduction?

1041 Dumaine (3 blocks from Bourbon St.—take a taxi for safety). ☎ *504/ 593-9535. You should make reservations a week or two in advance.* **Main courses:** *$18.50–$22.50. MC, V.* **Open:** *Lunch Fri; dinner Tue–Sat.*

Kids Petunias

$$. French Quarter. CAJUN/CREOLE/CREPES/BREAKFAST.

Petunias bills its 14-inch crepes as the world's largest, and who can argue? Go ahead, have an all-crepe meal, starting with crepes stuffed with shrimp, crab ratatouille, and Swiss cheese, and then for dessert try the St. Louis flambé, which is a crepe stuffed with vanilla ice cream and fresh pecans, topped with both bananas Foster (bananas sautéed in butter and banana liqueur, topped with rum, flamed, and then served over vanilla ice cream) and cherries jubilee.

817 St. Louis (½ block from Bourbon St.). ☎ *504/522-6440. Reservations are not required, but are recommended.* **Main courses:** *Dinner $10–$19; Breakfast from $5; lunch from $6. AE, CB, DC, DISC, MC, V.* **Open:** *Breakfast, lunch, and dinner daily.*

Kids Poppy's Bar and Grill

$. French Quarter. SANDWICHES/SHORT ORDER/ BREAKFAST.

From the folks who brought you the Clover Grill, here's its "sister grill," Poppy. It has the same fabulous attitude ("dancing in the aisles only"), same 24-hour schedule, and the same fabulous shakes, burgers, and other diner fare. Poppy does have her own special qualities, including the steak and eggs platter for $9, biscuits and gravy for $3, plus cocktails from $3.25, and a 20-ounce beer for $2.

717 St. Peter (½ block from Bourbon St., across from Pat O'Brien's). ☎ *504/ 524-3287. Reservations not accepted. Prices vary. AE, MC, V.* **Open:** *24 hours a day. Wheelchair accessible.*

Port of Call

$$. French Quarter. HAMBURGERS.

Locals generally agree that this little dive bar has the best burgers in town. They certainly are huge—each weighs in at a half-pound, and that's without condiments or the baked potato that accompanies each order. Steaks are another specialty. It's busy most all the time, but especially late at night. Attentive service is not a strong point here.

838 Esplanade (take a taxi for safety).
☎ *504/523-0120. Reservations are not*
accepted. **Menu items:** *$6–$19. AE, MC, V.*
Open: *Sun–Thurs 11am–1am; Fri–Sat*
11am–3am.

 ## Praline Connection No. 1
$$. Faubourg Marigny.
SOUL FOOD.
This restaurant does an adequate job of
introducing home-style soul food to the
general public. Gumbo, fried okra, maca-
roni and cheese, candied yams, cooked
greens (collard, mustard, or spinach), rice
and beans (red, white, green, lima, or crow-
der peas), meat loaf, fried chicken, seafood,
sweet potato pie, and pralines form the
backbone of the menu.

> ### Best Bets for Sunday Brunch
>
> Arnaud's (French Quarter, $$$)
> Commander's Palace (Garden
> District, $$$$)
> Court of Two Sisters (French
> Quarter, $$$$)
> Mr. B's (French Quarter, $$$)
> Palace Cafe (French Quarter,
> $$$)

542 Frenchmen (just outside the Quarter, about 8 blocks from Jackson Square; take
a taxi at night for safety). ☎ *504/943-3934. Reservations not accepted or needed.*
Main courses: *$7–$15 (most under $10). AE, DC, DISC, MC, V.* **Open:** *Lunch*
and dinner daily. Wheelchair accessible.

 ## Praline Connection No. 2
$$. Warehouse District. SOUL FOOD.
Essentially the same as Praline Connection No. 1, Praline Connection No. 2
has a larger dining room and a large gospel and blues performance hall.

907 S. Peters (if you're at the convention center, it's only a couple of blocks; from
the Quarter, take a taxi). ☎ *504/523-3973. Reservations not accepted.* **Main**
courses: *$4–$14 (most under $10). AE, DC, DISC, MC, V.* **Open:** *Lunch and*
dinner daily. Wheelchair accessible.

 ## Ralph & Kacoo's
$$. French Quarter. CREOLE/SEAFOOD.
It's the hush puppies (fried, ground corn mush—they taste better than they
sound) that have me coming back to this place time and time again—the
well-prepared and plain fried seafood and dishes such as trout Ruby (stuffed
with crab meat and topped with shrimp in a hollandaise sauce) are just an
added bonus. This restaurant is a solid, dependable (if not adventuresome)
choice for seafood. A full-sized replica of a fishing boat serves as a bar for
drinks and raw oysters.

519 Toulouse St. (2½ blocks from Bourbon St. and around the corner from Jackson
Square). ☎ *504/522-5226. Reservations not required, but be prepared to wait a*
while on the weekends. **Main courses:** *$9–$19. AE, DISC, MC, V.* **Open:** *Lunch*
and dinner daily.

Red Fish Grill

$$. French Quarter. SEAFOOD.

Though the ambiance here is too noisy and avant-garde for my taste, the gumbo is some of the best I've ever eaten, the sweet potato catfish served with an andouille cream sauce is as unique as it is good, and the desserts are absolutely sinful. This restaurant is another one owned by those Brennans. I've heard they're opening a jazz club adjoining the restaurant, so stay tuned.

115 Bourbon (½ block from Canal St.). ☎ **504/598-1200.** *Reservations not necessary, but recommended.* **Main courses:** *$12–$18. AE, DC, MC, V. Open: Dinner daily; lunch Mon–Sat; brunch Sun 10am–3pm. Wheelchair accessible.*

Best Bread Pudding

Commander's Palace's bread pudding soufflé
Palace Cafe's white chocolate bread pudding

Remoulade

$. French Quarter. CREOLE/AMERICAN.

Your budget won't permit a trip to Arnaud's? Try their less formal offshoot, where a full meal can be had for the price of an Arnaud's entree. Check out the shrimp Arnaud, boudin (rice sausage), jambalaya, or shrimp and eggplant casserole. Located right on Bourbon Street, this place is noisy and slightly reminiscent of modern-day fast food, so children will feel right at home.

309 Bourbon (2 blocks from Canal St.). ☎ **504/523-0377.** *Reservations accepted, but not usually needed.* **Main courses:** *$4–$13. AE, CB, MC, V.* **Open:** *Lunch and dinner daily. Wheelchair accessible.*

Extra! Extra!

As this book went to print, I learned that a branch of **Smith and Wollensky** (New York's quintessential steak house, according to *Gourmet* magazine) is slated to open here in April of 1998. September '97's *Preservation In Print* magazine reported that the restaurant will take up the entirety of the 1000 block of Poydras (5 blocks from the Superdome, 10 blocks from the river, and 4 blocks from Canal Street).

Rib Room

$$$$$. French Quarter. STEAKS/SEAFOOD.

The colors, texture, and ambiance of the Rib Room remind me of a conservative British men's club, though its quiet elegance and low lighting is ripe for romance as well. The specialty, prime rib, is slow-roasted on a rotisserie over an open flame at the back of the restaurant. Personally, I come for the spit-roasted lamb. Spit-roasted jumbo shrimp and other seafood dishes round out the menu, and breakfast is also served.

621 St. Louis (1 block from Bourbon in the Omni Royal Orleans Hotel). ☎ *504/ 529-7045. Reservations recommended. **Main courses:** $24–$35. AE, CB, DC, DISC, MC, V. **Open:** Breakfast, lunch, and dinner daily. Wheelchair accessible.*

_{Kids} Ruth's Chris Steak House
$$$$$. Mid City. STEAKS.

Ruth's Chris Steak House is not in the Quarter or even nearby, but the serious steak lover will make the trek for one of the best steak houses around. The USDA prime, aged, corn-fattened, white-faced Hereford beef is sliced an inch and a half thick and broiled to order in an 1800-degree broiler, and then served on a sizzling platter. If you're not a steak lover and were just dragged along, the restaurant serves live lobster, shrimp, and fish as well.

711 N. Broad (take a taxi). ☎ *504/486-0810. Reservations recommended. **Main courses:** $19–$55. AE, DC, MC, V. **Open:** Lunch and dinner Sun–Fri; dinner only on Sat. Wheelchair accessible.*

Tujaque's
$$$. French Quarter. CREOLE.

Pronounced *two-jacks,* this is the second-oldest restaurant in New Orleans (it opened in 1856). Tujaque's is simple, traditional, and not for everyone. Instead of having a printed menu, the waiters recite the limited but changing selections each day, including their signature beef brisket with horseradish sauce (VERY spicy) and shrimp remoulade (with a spicy mustard sauce).

823 Decatur (1 short block from Jackson Square). ☎ *504/525-8676. Reservations not required, but are recommended, especially on the weekend. **Main courses:** 6-course meal with choice of 3 entrees (no choice for the other courses) for $23–$30 (2- to 5-course lunches are $9–$15). AE, DISC, MC, V. **Open:** Lunch daily; dinner Mon–Sat. Wheelchair accessible.*

Best Barbeque Specials

Pascal's Manale's BBQ Shrimp
Mr. B's BBQ Shrimp
Mother's Ferdi Special

Uglesich's
$. Central Business District/Warehouse District. SEAFOOD.

It's dangerous to call any one place "the best in New Orleans," but it's mighty tempting to make an exception for "Ugly's," a tiny, crowded, greasy neighborhood place that serves some of the most divine seafood dishes in town. With choices such as fried green tomatoes with shrimp remoulade, shrimp on a fried cake of grits, and voodoo shrimp (in a peppery butter sauce), not only will it all be worth the possibly long wait, but you might well come back for more the next day. Uglesich's is only open for lunch.

1238 Barrone St. (take the St. Charles Streetcar and walk a couple blocks west from Erato St.). ☎ *504/523-8571. Reservations not accepted, but expect a line anywhere around lunch time.* **Main courses:** *$6–$13.75. No credit cards.* **Open:** *Mon–Fri 9am–4pm, and occasionally on Sat.*

Upperline
$$. Uptown/University. ECLECTIC/CREOLE.
Located in a small but charming and pretty house in a largely residential area, Upperline is more low-key than high-profile places like Emeril's, but in its own way, it's every bit as inventive. It's a good choice for imaginative food at reasonable prices (reasonable at least by fancy restaurant standards). Standbys include their fried green tomatoes with shrimp remoulade sauce and duck with a wine sauce that tingles. If you're lucky, they'll be doing one of their special menus, such as the All-Garlic selection.

1413 Upperline (take the St. Charles Streetcar to the Upperline Ave. stop). ☎ *504/ 891-9822. Reservations required.* **Main courses:** *$9–$17.50. AE, DC, MC, V.* **Open:** *Dinner Wed–Sat; lunch and dinner on Sun.*

Light Bites & Munchies

There are two main reasons to snack: (1) You want more food, and (2) You want quick and easy food. Chapters 10 and 11 told you where to have a nice dinner and a great lunch, but we all know that the three basic meals are only a springboard to more eating—particularly when you're on vacation and even more so when you're vacationing in New Orleans.

If life were ideal and there were more than 24 hours in a day, you'd be able to dine like a true New Orleanian at every one of your vacation meals—and by that I mean you'd linger over your meal for hours at a time. Unfortunately, your time is probably limited, and there will probably be days when you'll just have to just grab a quick gumbo and *run*. For those times when the perfect end to a seven-course gourmet dinner is taking a walk around the corner for a sack of beignets or a po boy, here's a quick chapter devoted to quick food.

Food Between Two Slices of Bread

Sure, food between bread is typically known as a sandwich, but that word just doesn't cut it when referring to a half-pound Port of Call burger or a gigantic Central Grocery muffuletta.

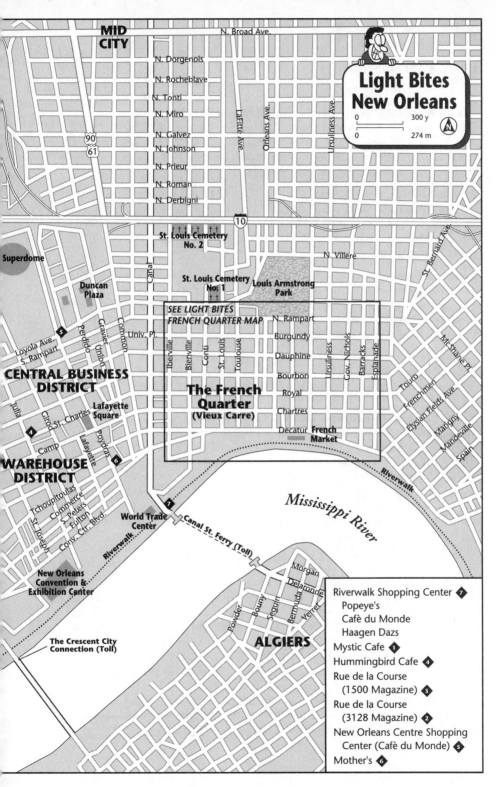

Whazza Muffuletta?

Muffulettas (say muff-*ah*-let-as) are large, really large, sandwiches on round Italian bread filled with Italian cold cuts and cheese and slathered with olive salad dressing. It may not sound all that special, but boy are they delicious. They're also filling, to say the least. One person cannot (or at least, should not) eat a whole one. A half makes a great meal; a quarter makes a nice, filling snack. Arguments rage about who makes the best one. Join in the fun by taste-testing and deciding for yourself.

Central Grocery (923 Decatur St., ☎ 504/523-1620) probably invented the muffuletta and makes the most likely winner; if you have just one muff, have it here. Don't be surprised if you stand in a long line of like-minded folks. Best of all, if you get hooked (and you may), the Grocery will ship them to your home.

Progress Grocery (915 Decatur St., ☎ 504/525-6627), right next door to Central Grocery, makes another popular muffuletta. As at Central Grocery, you can pick up other deli items and many New Orleans spices here as well. At either of these places, you can take your sandwich and go across the street to eat it by the side of the Mississippi.

Napoleon House (500 Chartres St., ☎ 504/524-9752) is the only place in town that heats its muffulettas. Some locals swear by this, but others find it blasphemous. Start with them cold and work your way to hot.

How 'Bout a Po Boy for This Po Boy?

The po boy sandwich, named for the idea that it was the only thing a "po' boy" could afford, is the "other" signature sandwich of New Orleans (after the muffuletta). It's made with a long, skinny loaf of bread that can contain anything from roast beef and gravy to ham and cheese to fried fish, shrimp, soft-shell crabs, or oysters. **Mother's** (401 Poydras St., ☎ 504/523-9656; see review in chapter 11) serves up a fine po boy in a raucous, crowded atmosphere, and the **Napoleon House** (see review in chapter 15) does a pretty good job with 'em, too. The most popular po boy spot in the Quarter, though, is **Johnny's Po-Boys** (511 St. Louis, ☎ 504/524-8129).

Flip Me a Burger, Mac, & Make It the Real Kind

A real burger is thick and juicy, with a slightly toasted bun and all the trimmings. Although locals almost universally agree that the half-pound burger at **Port of Call** (838 Esplanade, ☎ 504/523-0120) is the best in town, I'll take a bold stance here and throw the vote to the **Clover Grill** (900 Bourbon St., ☎ 504/523-0904). Its burgers are smaller (a third of a pound) and are cooked under a hubcap, supposedly to seal in the juices. It seems to work. Clover's "sister" grill, **Poppy's Bar and Grill** (717 St. Peter, a half-block from Bourbon St., across from Pat O'Brien's, ☎ 504/524-3287), does the same thing, but somehow the Clover Grill's burgers seem just slightly better.

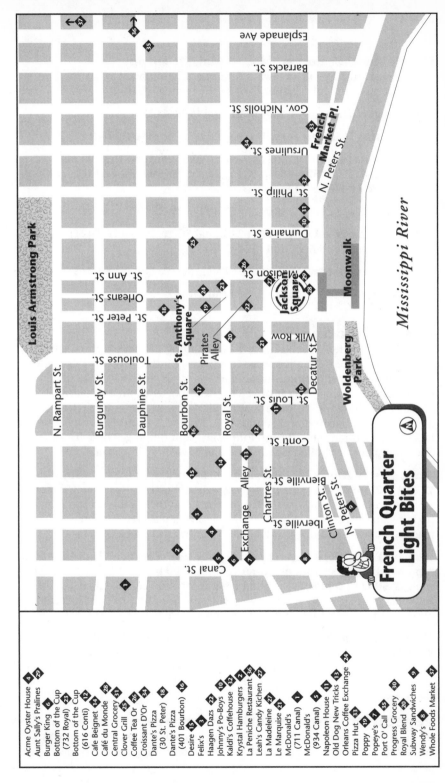

French Quarter Light Bites

Mississippi River

Louis Armstrong Park

Moonwalk

Woldenberg Park

Jackson Square

St. Anthony's Square

French Market Pl.

Esplanade Ave
Barracks St.
Gov. Nicholls St.
Ursulines St.
St. Philip St.
Dumaine St.
St. Ann St.
Orleans St.
St. Peter St.
Toulouse St.
Bourbon St.
Royal St.
Exchange Alley
Chartres St.
Bienville St.
Iberville St.
Canal St.
Madison St.
Pirates Alley
Wilk Row
Decatur St.
St. Louis St.
Conti St.
Clinton St.
N. Peters St.
N. Rampart St.
Burgundy St.
Dauphine St.

Acme Oyster House	**4**
Aunt Sally's Pralines	**29**
Burger King	**6**
Bottom of the Cup (732 Royal)	**23**
Bottom of the Cup (616 Conti)	**12**
Café Beignet	**14**
Café du Monde	**28**
Central Grocery	**31**
Clover Grill	**25**
Coffee Tea Or	**34**
Croissant D'Or		
Dante's Pizza (30 St. Peter)	**18**
Dante's Pizza (401 Bourbon)	**16**
Desire		
Felix's	**3**
Haagen Dazs	**22**
Johnny's Po-Boys	**10**
Kaldi's Coffeehouse	**32**
Krystal Hamburgers	**2**
La Peniche Restaurant	**36**
Leah's Candy Kitchen	**27**
La Madeleine	**27**
Le Marquise	**21**
McDonald's (711 Canal)	**1**
McDonald's (934 Canal)	**5**
Napoleon House	**11**
Old Dog New Tricks	**43**
Orleans Coffee Exchange	**24**
Pizza Hut	**33**
Poppy	**19**
Popeye's	**7**
Port O' Call	**45**
Progress Grocery	**30**
Royal Blend	**20**
Subway Sandwiches	**9**
Wendy's	**8**
Whole Foods Market	**37**

165

Flip Me Another Burger, Mac, & Make It Snappy

If you're in a rush, you can always find one of your favorite fast food restaurants—they're particularly abundant in the French Quarter:

➤ **Burger King.** 623 Canal St. ☎ **504/524-4147**

➤ **Krystal Hamburgers.** 116 Bourbon St. ☎ **504/523-4030**

➤ **McDonald's.** 711 Canal St. (with side entrance in the 100 block of Royal) ☎ **504/525-4560;** 934 Canal St. ☎ **504/524-3116;** Audubon Zoo ☎ **504/865-7116**

➤ **Pizza Hut.** 1118 Decatur St., ☎ **504/529-3233** for delivery

➤ **Popeye's Fried Chicken.** 621 Canal St. ☎ **504/561-1021;** Riverwalk Shopping Center, ☎ **504/524-3564**

➤ **Subway Sandwiches.** 237 N. Peters St., ☎ **504/568-0169**

➤ **Wendy's.** 509 Canal St. ☎ **504/561-0087**

Oyster Shooting

Consider the oyster, as M.F.K. Fisher said. Among its many virtues is that sometimes it's the right alternative to a heavy, multicourse meal. If you've never tried oyster shooting—slurping a raw oyster right out of its shell (preferably dressed with a bit of ketchup and horseradish) and letting it slide, virtually unchewed, right down your gullet—this is the time to try it. You might like it, disgusting as it sounds. The following oyster bars also serve oysters fried and often have shrimp for peeling and dipping. These bars should also offer plenty of boiled crawfish when crawfish is in season.

Acme Oyster House (724 Iberville, a half-block from Bourbon Street, ☎ **504/522-5973**) has some *serious* oysters. Have them your way (to borrow a phrase): raw, fried, or overstuffed po boys. Top them off with some bread pudding and wash it all down with a beer like a real New Orleanian. The place is crowded and noisy as a good oyster bar should be.

Close by, **Felix's Restaurant and Oyster Bar** (739 Iberville, a half-block from Bourbon Street with an entrance in the 200 block of Bourbon Street as well, ☎ **504/522-4440**) is another great oyster choice. Like its neighbor, Felix's is often crowded and noisy and all the more fun for it. It specializes in oysters and fried seafood, but it also offers Creole dishes.

The **Desire Oyster Bar** (300 Bourbon St., ☎ **504/586-0300**), part of the Royal Sonesta Hotel and right on the corner of Bourbon and Bienville, is a bit less authentic than the other two listings and a little too shiny and clean for some. The location helps keep it hopping, though.

Vegetarian Ports in a Deep-Fat Storm

If you're a veggie-type person in New Orleans, all I can say is "poor you." You'll quickly notice that green stuff doesn't take priority in this town, and that if anything can be cooked with animal fat, it is. Even the red beans and rice (*especially* the red beans and rice) often hides ham and sausage. Nevertheless, a few places in town will take you in and feed you.

Old Dog New Trick (307 Exchange Alley, ☎ **504/522-4569**), a tiny cafe tucked away on an equally tiny alley in the Quarter, calls itself "vegan friendly," and though it does have dishes with cheese (and some with tuna), the cooks can make them without. The sandwiches, salads, and stuffed pitas here have been voted best vegetarian in town by *Gambit* readers.

Mystic Cafe (3226 Magazine St., ☎ **504/891-1992**) is technically Mediterranean, so there's meat in some dishes, but most are butter-free and can be made without sugar on request. Vegetarians and the heart-conscious will find plenty to chose from among the whole-grain, high-quality options.

Whole Foods Market (3135 Esplanade Ave., ☎ **504/943-1626**) is perfect for a carrot fix, conveniently located outside the race track where Jazz Fest (known for its high-fat food) is held. A local favorite for organic produce and vegetarian specialties, the Whole Foods Market serves something healthy for every meal of the day, and you can get all items to go.

Bet You Didn't Know

Kombo is the Indian word for *filé* (the dried and ground leaves of the sassafras tree), and *gomba* (or *gombo*) is an African word for okra—hence the name "gumbo" for a thick and hearty cross between a stew and a soup usually made with filé, okra, or sometimes both.

Street Food

Lucky Dog carts have been a tradition in New Orleans since 1948 and were made famous by the Pulitzer Prize–winning book *Confederacy of Dunces*. Basically, lucky dogs are hot dogs, and you can find the carts that sell them (unmistakable since they look like giant hot dogs) on street corners throughout the French Quarter and Central Business District. During special events, they spread out to other locations throughout the city. For less than $5, you can get a regular or foot-long hot dog or sausage dressed with the works (including chili). Some carts sell cold drinks as well. Sacred tradition or ptomaine poisoning waiting to happen? You decide!

Late-Night Snacks

Although Café du Monde (see following section), Clover Grill, and Poppy's Grill (see previous section) are all well-located, delicious, and reliable post-club-hopping, I've-got-the-3am-munchies spots, some other choices are available.

Hummingbird Cafe (804 St. Charles Ave., ☎ **504/561-9229**) is the place to go for your middle-of-the-night red beans and rice cravings (they have other filling options, too). It's a funky place that's also a popular hangout.

167

After a hard night of frolicking, the down-home snacks and meals at **La Peniche Restaurant** (1940 Dauphine St., ☎ 504/943-1460) hit the spot. Try the biscuits, red beans and rice, fried chicken, or po boys. The desserts are all homemade. During one recent 4:30am visit, a woman spontaneously broke into an aria. Applause followed.

Camellia Grill (626 S. Carrollton Ave., ☎ 504/866-9573) is not really a breakfast place, but because it's open until the wee hours most nights, you can have those famous pecan waffles or an enormous omelet on your way back from club-going.

Coffee, Tea, & Me

New Orleans isn't exactly the coffee capital of the Western World, but there are a few great places you can go to get a jolt of the blessed bean.

Café du Monde (800 Decatur St. at Jackson Square, ☎ 504/525-4544) has been selling café au lait and beignets (see listing in following section) since 1862. Order a café au lait, which is strong New Orleans coffee flavored with chicory to make it less bitter and mixed with an equal portion of scalded milk. Café du Monde is open 24 hours and is *the* place for premiere people-watching, as its many tables are clustered under an awning right on the edge of Decatur Street, overlooking the scene at Jackson Square.

Kaldi's Coffeehouse (941 Decatur St., ☎ 504/586-8989) is where the local alternative youths and folkies come to brood over their journals and swig all kinds of coffee drinks. The menu is quite long and features everything from the traditional to the trendy (mocha drinks and whatnot) to the vaguely healthy (they have a blended drink made with soy milk that's surprisingly tasty). Poetry readings and folk music sometimes happen at night.

Pizza by the Slice

Pizza ain't exactly home-grown New Orleans fare, but if you get a hankering, **Dante's Pizza** serves it up by the slice. It has two locations: 730 St. Peter St. (☎ 504/523-2683) and 401 Bourbon St. (☎ 504/561-8670).

People actually go to the **Bottom of the Cup Tearoom** for psychic readings, as the place has a rep for pretty "accurate" psychics, but you can have tea, too—and yes, you can also have your tea leaves read when you're done. They have two locations: 732 Royal St. (☎ 504/523-1204) and 616 Conti (☎ 504/524-1997).

Rue de la Course is your basic bohemian coffeehouse, with cool, friendly college kids and locals lingering over the paper. You can buy loose-leaf tea and coffee by the pound here, as well as some periodicals. There are two locations: 1500 Magazine St. (☎ 504/529-1455) and 3128 Magazine St. (☎ 504/899-0242).

Other decent choices on the java front are **Coffee Tea Or** (630 St. Ann, ☎ 504/522-0830), **Orleans Coffee Exchange** (712 Orleans, ☎ 504/522-5710), and the **Royal Blend Coffee & Tea House** (623 Royal St., ☎ 504/523-2716).

The Sweet Stuff

The time comes when all good people succumb to a craving for things either rolled in sugar or boiled in fat—and sometimes both. Here's some options that'll make your sweet tooth sing.

Beignets for You, Beignays for Me

I've never met a beignet I didn't like. Pronounced "ben-yays," what they are is pieces of dough fried fresh and covered with lots of powdered sugar. Novices will be tempted to shake some of the sugar off: Don't—it melts from the heat of the fresh beignet and is blissful. You might want even more. *Hint:* Don't wear black when eating beignets unless you want to look like a reverse dalmatian.

Café du Monde (800 Decatur St. at Jackson Square, ☎ 504/525-4544) is the king of beignets. At three for about a buck, they're a heck of a deal, and you can get 'em at any hour, because the place is open 24 hours a day every day but Christmas. Café du Monde also has locations at the **Riverwalk Shopping Center** (1 Poydras, ☎ 504/587-0841) and the **New Orleans Centre Shopping Center** (1400 Poydras, by the Superdome, ☎ 504/587-0842), though these locations are not open 24 hours.

It's so tempting to say "why bother?" when discussing any beignet joint other than Café du Monde, but **Cafe Beignet** (334-B Royal St., ☎ 504/524-5530) is a nice coffeehouse-type place in its own right. It's hard to compete with the other's atmosphere and tradition, but think of all the calories you'll burn walking between the two to make a comparison.

French Pastries

Does your stomach want to pretend that it's back in French Colonial days? Then drop by one of these spots for a pastry.

La Marquise (625 Chartres St., ☎ 504/524-0420) is a great place for a leisurely breakfast or an afternoon break. It has coffee, soft drinks, all sorts of delicious pastries, sandwiches, and an indoor seating area as well as the outdoor patio. If it's full or if you prefer, take your pastry to Jackson Square, which is only a half-block away.

Croissant D'Or (617 Ursulines St., ☎ 504/524-4663) is only a few blocks away from La Marquise and is where the pastries for both locations are baked fresh daily. The seating arrangement and menu is the same except this place also serves soup.

La Madeleine (547 St. Ann at Jackson Square, ☎ 504/568-0073) serves delectable French pastries as well as quiches, soups, salads, and other light menu items. It has only indoor seating, although it's located right on Jackson Square, so you can take your selection outdoors if you like.

I Scream, You Scream
Ice cream carts are located throughout the French Quarter, most notably at Jackson Square, and there's a **Haagen Dazs Ice Cream Parlor** at 621 St. Peter St. (a half-block from Jackson Square; ☎ **504/523-4001**). They have a few tables both inside and on the sidewalk, but most of their business is carryout. They have a second location at the Riverwalk Shopping Center (1 Poydras, ☎ **504/523-3566**). If you want something really special though, **Angelo Brocato's** (214 N. Carrollton Ave., ☎ **504/486-1465**) makes Italian ice cream (*not* gelato) that's so creamy and rich, you won't be able to go back to the ordinary commercial varieties. The place is delightful.

I Want Candy
Pralines, a confection made with brown sugar and pecans, is the one word you need to know when it comes to home-grown New Orleans–style sugary snacks. Make sure you try some. **Aunt Sally's Pralines** (810 Decatur St., ☎ **504/524-5107**) allows you to watch the famous local candy being made, and **Laura's Candies** (600 Conti St., ☎ **504/525-3880**) not only has the ubiquitous pralines, but also delicious fudge and golf-ball-size truffles in all sorts of extraordinary flavors. **Leah's Candy Kitchen** (714 St. Louis St., ☎ **504/523-5662**) wins some votes for the best pralines around. Heck, since they're open later (till 10pm), they must win the late-night candy cravings vote by default.

Part 5

Ready, Set, Go! Exploring New Orleans

Now that you have a place to hang your hat and food in your stomach, you're ready to do what you went to all this trouble for in the first place: See the city. The following chapters will help you decide what attractions you want to see and help you figure out how you're going to see them. There are so many things to see in New Orleans that you'll have to prioritize the "top sights" by tailoring your list to your specific interests. Beyond the major sights, there are bucketloads of lesser-known places to explore.

Then, of course, there's shopping. New Orleans is a great place to indulge in some serious credit-card binging, whether you want to browse in its high-toned department stores, dig through the past in the antique shops, or look for some Cajun music to bring home in the music stores. In chapter 16, I'll run through the biggest and best shops and suggest some places to go for specialty items.

In chapters 17 and 18, I'll give you help planning your days so you don't waste a lot of time. First, I'll give you six great itineraries that take in a lot of the major sights, and then I'll offer some constructive help in shaping your own itineraries, allowing plenty of leeway so that your trip doesn't become too regimented.

Chapter 13

Should I Just Take a Guided Tour?

In This Chapter

➤ Orientation tours

➤ Special interest tours

➤ Riverboat cruises

Guided tours can give you an entertaining overview of the city (or of a specific part of it, such as the French Quarter or Garden District); however, there's the goofy-tourists-in-a-bus factor to consider. Deciding whether to go on a guided tour basically comes down to this issue: Are you the intrepid type who thinks nothing of setting off into the unknown with your guidebook and a sun hat, or do you want to do your exploring with a little extra security, structure, and comfort? If you're the Lawrence of Arabia type, then a tour probably isn't for you, but if you feel better seeing the sights in the company of a licensed professional, then a guided tour will mean at least a few hours in which you don't have to do anything more than look and listen.

If you think, though, that a tour's going to teach you anything deep and meaningful about the city rather than just show it to you, I've got some bad news: This is show biz, baby. When you step on the bus (or carriage, or riverboat), you become an audience, and New Orleans becomes light comedy, with current and historical locals as the actors, the streets as the set, and your tour guide as the master of ceremonies. You'll get history, intrigue, drama, comedy, and innuendo, and you can bet all your questions will be answered, but be sure to take it all with a grain of salt—tour guides tend to be charming and can appear amazingly well-informed, but they're not exactly history Ph.Ds.

All that said, tours can be a lot of fun—like settling down for a couple hours of prime-time TV—and are perfect for that afternoon when you're balancing your aching feet against the urge to get out and see some sights. Guided tours fall into two main categories: general orientation tours and specialty tours. This chapter tells you what you can expect from both types.

Here's the Church & Here's the Steeple: Orientation Tours

General orientation tours will give you a run-down on what's old, what's new, what's borrowed, and especially what's blue (as in "rhythm and") and are particularly good if you have limited time. A half-hour carriage tour can give you the condensed version of New Orleans history, show you where the clubs are, tell you about the architecture, and point out the attractions. Walking tours or bus tours take longer and will give you a little more information. If your guide is good, you'll walk away feeling like you're a part of things.

Bus Tours

If the idea of seeing the sights without leaving the air-conditioning is your idea of heaven, then a bus tour is definitely in your future. You can see the whole city or a specific part of it, head outside town to visit the plantations, or take one of these tours in combination with walking tours, riverboat cruises, swamp tours, and nightclub tours. Tours are narrated by licensed guides, and buses are variously equipped with bathrooms, TVs/VCRs, cellular phones, stereo sound, and equipment for travelers with disabilities. (Not all buses have all amenities, so be sure to ask ahead if something's particularly important to you.)

New Orleans Tours (☎ **504/592-0560** or www.new.orleans.com) is one of the oldest and most reliable tour companies. They offer city and neighborhood tours as well as riverboat cruises, combination tours, plantation tours, swamp tours, walking tours, jazz tours, and nightlife tours.

You might want to check out these tour companies as well:

➤ **Custom Bus Charters** (☎ **504/528-1865**)

➤ **DixieLand Tours** (☎ **800/489-8747** or 504/833-1991)

➤ **Gray Line** (☎ **800/535-7786** or 504/587-0861)

➤ **Hotard** (☎ **800/553-4895** or 504/832-9247, e-mail charters@hotard.com)

Walking Tours

The French Quarter is the oldest and most interesting part of New Orleans and is thus, naturally, the main tourist destination. Large buses are *verboten* here (though smaller buses and vans are allowed), so your feet are your best option for getting around.

The best way to enjoy the French Quarter is to just walk around and explore on your own. You'll see street entertainers, be able to poke your head in all the cute shops you find, and follow your nose into all the nooks and crannies. In chapter 17, I'll give you several itineraries for walking tours you can take on your own, but if you'd rather have someone along to tell you what you're seeing, contact **Friends of the Cabildo** (☎ 504/523-3939), a non-profit group of volunteers that give two-hour walking tours of the French Quarter.

Because the French Quarter and other parts of New Orleans are considered a part of the Jean Lafitte National Park, the **National Park Service** also gives tours. Stop by the Visitor's Information Center at 419 Decatur St. or call ☎ 504/589-2636 for information.

Dollars & Sense

You can rent a bike and do your own tour around New Orleans, using the information given in this and other books. **Olympic Bike Rentals** (☎ 504/523-1314) and **Bicycle Michael's** (☎ 504/945-9505) are two good bets for rentals.

Carriage Tours

If you read my biographical information at the front of this book, you know that I used to be a carriage driver. I loved meeting new people and telling them a little about each of the major sights we passed, answering people's questions about other sights and restaurants, and giving them an overview of New Orleans history. Riding in a carriage is a more personal experience than riding around in a bus with 50 or 60 nameless passengers. In 30 minutes, a good carriage driver can show you the highlights of the Quarter; give him or her an hour, and you'll feel like a native.

Every carriage, as well as its mule and driver, is unique. Some of the carriages have flowers or other decorations, and some of the mules (and many of the drivers) have hats or other ornaments. You could always spot me by the black vest, bow tie, and top hat I wore. Every driver's area of expertise also varies. Some are licensed tour guides, though most are not. Some are historians, some have eaten their way through the city, and others know where every bar is. One driver may give you a history lesson, another might regale you with ghost stories or tell you jokes, and another might just drive you around. Talk to the driver for a minute and try to gauge his personality before getting in the rig. If the match seems wrong, move on to the next carriage.

Only 30 carriages are licensed to do business on a regular basis in town (though others are used for special events), and all of these are owned by four companies. You can find most of the carriages lined up along Decatur Street at Jackson Square and at carriage stands at Royal and St. Louis, Bourbon and Conti, or Bourbon and Toulouse. You can also find carriages cruising throughout the Quarter like taxis or parked on a corner waiting for a fare. You can also call to have one pick you up, though you may have to pay more.

There are two types of carriages to choose from: the large hard-topped, bus-like models in which you share the ride with whomever comes along, and the smaller convertible models that you hire individually for your party. In general, the large carriages cost only $8 per adult and $4 for children, but you must sit in the carriage and wait until the minimum number of passengers board (you may wind up sitting a long time if business is slow). The smaller carriages are $10 each with a $40 minimum (once the minimum is satisfied, extra children are only $5). Tours should last 30 minutes; if they're appreciably shorter, the driver is giving you what is known as a "zip tour." You should complain to his boss. If he won't tell you who his boss is, note the number of the carriage (located on its side or back) along with the name of the company and the driver's name if you know it. Complain to the company or the **Taxicab Bureau** (☎ 504/565-6272).

As I said, you'll probably catch a carriage right on the street, but if you want to be picked up, you can call one of the following licensed carriage companies:

➤ **Royal Carriages** (☎ **504/943-8820** during office hours). For pickup at your hotel or other location or for emergency service, call ☎ **504/ 495-8273** (days) or **504/236-7020** (nights).

➤ **Good Old Days Buggies** (☎ **504/523-0804**)

➤ **Mid City Carriages** (☎ **504/581-4415**)

➤ **Old Quarter Tours** (☎ **504/944-0446**)

See chapter 9 for additional information on the carriage trade.

Specialty Tours

So what would make your trip to New Orleans really special? How about taking a tour that covers the highlights of Anne Rice's vampire world or a tour that shows you the jazz hot spots? How about a tour of the outlying plantations or a swamp tour that lets you feed marshmallows to alligators? If any of these options ring your bell, then you're a prime candidate for a specialty tour.

Black History Tours

African American Heritage Tours (☎ **504/288-3478**) delve into the history of Africans and African Americans in New Orleans. Tours include trips to Xavier University (the first Black Catholic university in the U.S.) and plantations, as well as a narrative on historic sites such as Liberty Bank, which was founded by blacks.

Jazz Tours for Serious Hepcats

John McCusker of **John McCusker's Jazz Tours** (☎ **504/282-3583**) is a photographer for the *Times-Picayune* newspaper and a well-known local jazz historian. Every Saturday morning he gives a bargain-priced ($25), $2\frac{1}{2}$-hour van tour that traces the history of New Orleans jazz. You'll see the spots where jazz was born, where it matured, and where performers like Louis Armstrong were born or played their music.

Bet You Didn't Know

A Monsieur Peychaud, who presided over the bar at 437 Rue Royale in the early 19th century, took to serving small drinks in egg cups called *couquetiers* in French. Americans took to the drinks, but never quite learned to pronounce the word, rendering it instead as *cocktail*.

Vampire Tours & Other Spooky Trips

Magic Walking Tours (☎ 504/588-9693), owned by Richard Rochester, was a "Frommer's Favorite" in both 1996 and 1997 and has long been a favorite of mine as well. He or one of his tour guides gives cemetery tours. They also take visitors on a vampire hunt. If you're lucky, you might get to carry the mallet and wooden stake.

Haunted History Tours (☎ 504/897-2030), owned by Sidney Smith, offers vampire tours and tours of the cemeteries. A guy called Chaz does the vampire tours of the Quarter and let me tell you, if there are any true vampires in New Orleans, Chaz must be one. You'll love his tours, but don't forget the garlic and cross.

Anne Rice's New Orleans Tours (☎ 504/899-1400) is owned by Ms. Rice, but don't expect her to guide one personally. Her company gives tours of those sections of New Orleans that play a part in her best-selling vampire books, as well as of the Garden District in general. Call ☎ 888/RICE-ANNE for tour information or check out www.annerice.com on the Web.

Where the Bodies Are Buried: Cemetery Tours

Save Our Cemeteries (☎ 504/525-3377) is a non-profit organization that is credited with doing more to restore and maintain New Orleans cemeteries than anyone else. Many of the cemeteries are not safe unless you're with an organized group such as this. I highly recommend them.

Semi-retired native New Orleanian **Fred Hatfield** (☎ 504/891-4862) has spent his whole life in the neighborhood of Lafayette No. 1 cemetery, and as any good neighbor would, he's done extensive research on who is buried there. His tours of Lafayette No. 1 and St. Louis No. 1 cemeteries take about 45 to 60 minutes and cost $6. He's usually home, so give him a call.

Born on the Bayou: Swamp Tours

The really isolated swamp areas lie three hours outside of the city, but there's also plenty of swampland within the metro area worth exploring. **Dr. Paul Wagner** (☎ 504/691-1769) is a well-known swamp ecologist and a national conservationist who gives excellent swamp tours, though not on a fixed schedule. If he's not available, he can probably recommend another guide. His tours cost $20 per person. Some other operators to try are **Honey Island Swamp Tours** (☎ 504/242-5877), **Cypress Swamp Tours** (☎ 504/581-4501), and **Jean Lafitte Swamp Tours** (☎ 504/689-4186).

There are also several tour companies operating in the Atchafalaya Basin, a vast swamp between Baton Rouge and Lafayette (about 2 ½ hours west of New Orleans). These include **McGee's Landing** (☎ 318/228-2384), **Angelle's Swamp Tours** (☎ 318/667-6135), and **Errol Verret's Swamp Tours** (☎ 318/394-7145).

Antiquing Tours
Macon Riddle of **Macon Riddle's Antique Tours** (☎ 504/899-3027 or e-mail hillrid@aol.com) is as enthusiastic about New Orleans antiquing as she is knowledgeable and will take you for an exciting tour of the city's antique districts.

Rollin' on the River: Riverboat Cruises
As you'd expect, riverboat cruises are extremely popular in New Orleans. Think Mark Twain. Think Huck Finn watching the riverboats from his raft. Think the riverboat gamblers in every other 1930s Hollywood movie. Today gambling cruises in the downtown area are a thing of the past, but New Orleans still has dinner and dancing cruises, harbor cruises, river cruises, and combination cruises where you also visit the Audubon Zoo or Chalmette Battlefield. Both stern and side paddlers are in use, and some riverboats are still steam powered; others are diesel. Companies and boats offering riverboat tours include **Creole Queen Paddle Wheel Tours** (☎ 504/529-4567), the **New Orleans Steamboat Co.** (☎ 504/586-8777), and the *John James Audubon* (☎ 504/586-8777). See chapter 19 for specific information on gambling cruises in the greater New Orleans area.

The Top Sights
A to Z

➤ Attractions indexes by location and type

➤ Full write-ups of all the top attractions in town

➤ Your personal Greatest Hits list and a worksheet for making your choices

New Orleans isn't a manufactured tourist attraction. It doesn't have big theme parks with lots of whirling rides and flashing lights to draw you in, and nobody's standing at the city limits with a megaphone shouting "Step right up, ladies and gentlemen, see the amazing..." Instead, New Orleans' appeal lies in smaller things: in how its people live, what they eat, in its music, in its melting-pot culture, and in its historic buildings.

This chapter starts off with indexes that list all the top sights by location and by type (museums, parks, cemeteries, and so on), so that, for instance, when you come out of the Aquarium of the Americas and say "What else is there to do around here?" you can turn to the French Quarter listing and find the nearest other big attraction. Following the indexes is an alphabetical list of the major attractions that I think you'll be interested in. I'll note with a "kid" icon (Kids) the sights I think your children will like (and point out the places you might not want to take the kids), note the attractions that are accessible to people with disabilities, and give you easy directions to the sights that are a little bit hard to find.

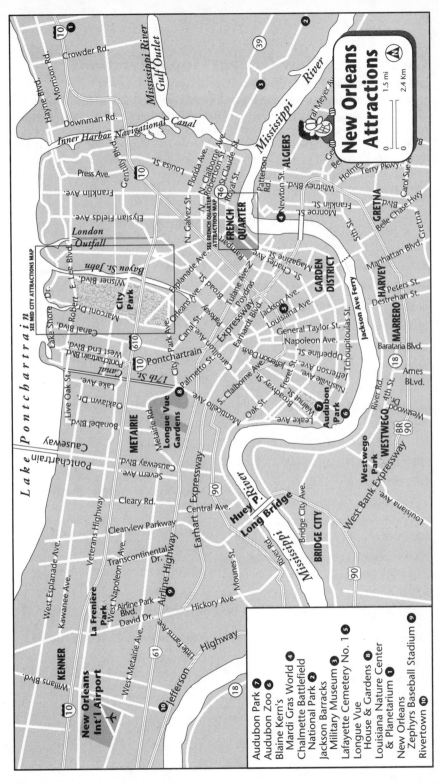

New Orleans Attractions

0 1.5 mi

0 2.4 Km

Crowder Rd.

Mississippi River Gulf Outlet

Mississippi River

Morrison Rd.

Hayne Blvd.

Downman Rd.

Inner Harbor Navigational Canal

Press Ave.

Louisa St.

Florida Ave.

N. Claiborne Ave.

Robertson St.

Royal St.

St. Claude Ave.

ALGIERS

Patterson Rd.

Newton Blvd.

Whitney Blvd.

Gen. Meyer Ave.

GRETNA

Terry Pkwy.

Belle Chase Hwy.

Gretna Blvd.

Carol Sue Ave.

Franklin Ave.

Elysian Fields Ave.

FRENCH QUARTER

Rampart

Monroe St.

Franklin St.

5th St.

Holmes

Manhattan Blvd.

HARVEY

Peters St.

Destrehan St.

London Outfall

Bayou St. John

Wisner Blvd.

City Park

Esplanade Ave.

N. Galvez St.

Broad St.

Tulane Ave.

Orleans Ave.

GARDEN DISTRICT

St. Charles Ave.

Magazine St.

SEE FRENCH QUARTER ATTRACTIONS MAP

SEE MID CITY ATTRACTIONS MAP

Canal Blvd.

E. Lee Blvd.

Marconi Dr.

Robert E.

Lake Shore Dr.

Canal St.

EXPRESSWAY

Canal St.

City Park Ave.

Carrollton Ave.

Jackson Ave.

Louisiana Ave.

Poydras

Earhardt Blvd.

Jefferson Davis Pkwy.

General Taylor St.

Napoleon Ave.

Upperline St.

Tchoupitoulas St.

Jackson Ave Ferry

BARRERO

MARRERO

Baratria Blvd.

West End Blvd.

Pontchartrain Blvd.

Pontchartrain

17th St. Canal

Lake Ave.

Oaklawn Dr.

Live Oak St.

Bonabel Blvd.

Palmetto St.

Monticello Ave.

S. Claiborne Ave.

Nashville Ave.

Jefferson Ave.

Broadway St.

Freret St.

Walnut St.

Oak St.

Leake Ave.

Audubon Park

River Rd.

4th St.

Westwood Dr.

WESTWEGO

WESTWEGO

Ames Blvd.

Louisiana Ave.

Lake Pontchartrain

Causeway

Metairie Rd.

METAIRIE

Longue Vue Gardens

Severn Ave.

Causeway Blvd.

Cleary Rd.

Earhart Expressway

Central Ave.

Huey P. Long Bridge

Bridge City Ave.

BRIDGE CITY

West-Bank Expressway

BR 90

Veterans Highway

West Esplanade Ave.

Kawanee Ave.

La Freniere Park

West Napoleon Ave.

Clearview Parkway

Transcontinental Dr.

Airline Highway

West Airline Park Blvd.

David Dr.

Hickory Ave.

Mounes St.

River Rd.

Mississippi River

Highway

Little Farms Ave.

West Metairie Ave.

Jefferson

KENNER

Willans Blvd.

New Orleans Int'l Airport

Legend

Audubon Park **7**
Audubon Zoo **6**
Blaine Kern's
Mardi Gras World **4**
Chalmette Battlefield
National Park **2**
Jackson Barracks
Military Museum **3**
Lafayette Cemetery No. 1 **5**
Longue Vue
House & Gardens **8**
Louisiana Nature Center
& Planetarium **1**
New Orleans
Zephyrs Baseball Stadium **9**
Rivertown **10**

179

Quick Picks: New Orleans' Top Attractions at a Glance

Here's an interesting question: What should you do if you're in the mood to visit an historic house in the French Quarter? Well, instead of making you read through every single listing until you come across the perfect place, I've created the following list of attractions indexed by neighborhood and type of attraction. Once you've found what you're looking for, you can jump right to it in the alphabetical listing of the top sights in New Orleans later in this chapter.

The Top Sights by Neighborhood

French Quarter

Aquarium of the Americas

Beauregard-Keyes House

Black Music Hall of Fame

Bourbon Street

French Market

Gallier House

Germaine Wells Mardi Gras Museum

Hermann-Grima House

Historic New Orleans Collection

Jackson Square

Moonwalk

New Orleans Historic Voodoo Museum

New Orleans Pharmacy Museum

Old U.S. Mint

Presbytere

Central Business District/ Warehouse District

Confederate Museum

D-Day Museum

Louisiana Children's Museum

St. Charles Streetcar

World Trade Center

Algiers

(via the Canal St. ferry)

Blaine Kern's Mardi Gras World

Garden District/Uptown

Audubon Park

Audubon Zoo

Lafayette Cemetery No. 1

Mid City/Metairie/Kenner

City Park

Longue Vue House and Gardens

Metairie Cemetery

New Orleans Museum of Art

Pitot House

Rivertown

New Orleans East/Chalmette

Chalmette Battlefield

Jackson Barracks Military Museum

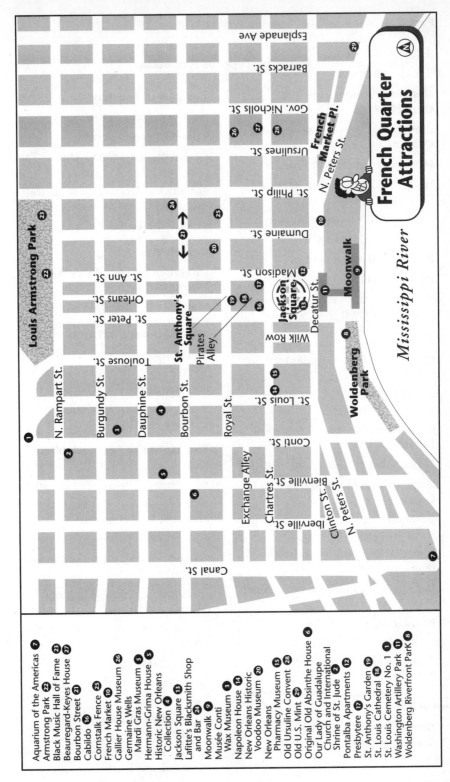

French Quarter Attractions

Mississippi River

Esplanade Ave
Barracks St.
Gov. Nicholls St.
Ursulines St.
St. Philip St.
Dumaine St.
St. Ann St.
Orleans St.
St. Peter St.
Toulouse St.
Conti St.
Bienville St.
Iberville St.
Canal St.

N. Rampart St.
Burgundy St.
Dauphine St.
Bourbon St.
Royal St.
Chartres St.
Exchange Alley
Clinton St.
N. Peters St.
Decatur St.
French Market Pl.
N. Peters St.

Louis Armstrong Park
St. Anthony's Square
Pirates Alley
Jackson Square
Wilk Row
Moonwalk
Woldenberg Park
French Market Pl.

Madison St.

Aquarium of the Americas 7
Armstrong Park 22
Black Music Hall of Fame 23
Beauregard-Keyes House 27
Bourbon Street 21
Cabildo 16
Cornstalk Fence 25
French Market 10
Gallier House Museum 26
Germaine Wells
Mardi Gras Museum 5
Hermann-Grima House 5
Historic New Orleans
Collection 4
Jackson Square 13
Lafitte's Blacksmith Shop
and Bar 24
Moonwalk 9
Musée Conti
Wax Museum 3
Napoleon House 14
New Orleans Historic
Voodoo Museum 20
New Orleans
Pharmacy Museum 15
Old Ursuline Convent 28
Old U.S. Mint 29
Original Old Absinthe House 6
Our Lady of Guadalupe
Church and International
Shrine of St. Jude 2
Pontalba Apartments 12
Presbytere 17
St. Anthony's Garden 19
St. Louis Cathedral 18
St. Louis Cemetery No. 1 1
Washington Artillery Park 11
Woldenberg Riverfront Park 8

Index by Type of Attraction

Historic Attractions and Churches

Beauregard-Keyes House (French Quarter)

French Market (French Quarter)

Hermann-Grima House (French Quarter)

Old U.S. Mint (French Quarter)

Pitot House (Mid City)

Presbytere (French Quarter)

Rivertown (Kenner)

St. Charles Streetcar (Central Business District)

Museums

Black Music Hall of Fame (French Quarter)

Blaine Kern's Mardi Gras World (Algiers)

Confederate Museum (Warehouse District)

D-Day Museum (Warehouse District)

Gallier House Museum (French Quarter)

Germain-Wells Mardi Gras Museum (French Quarter)

Historic New Orleans Collection (French Quarter)

Jackson Barracks Military Museum (New Orleans East)

Louisiana Children's Museum (Warehouse District)

New Orleans Historic Voodoo Museum (French Quarter)

New Orleans Museum of Art (Mid City)

New Orleans Pharmacy Museum (French Quarter)

Parks and Gardens

Audubon Park (Uptown)

Audubon Zoo (Uptown)

Chalmette Battlefield National Park (Chalmette)

Longue Vue House and Gardens (Metairie)

Moonwalk (French Quarter)

Cemeteries

Lafayette Cemetery No. 1 (Garden District)

Metairie Cemetery (Metairie)

Miscellaneous Attractions

Aquarium of the Americas (French Quarter)

Bourbon Street (French Quarter)

World Trade Center (Central Business District)

Top Sights to See with Your Kids

Aquarium of the Americas (French Quarter)

Audubon Park (Uptown)

Audubon Zoo (Uptown)

Blaine Kern's Mardi Gras Museum (Algiers)

Louisiana Children's Museum (Warehouse District)

Chalmette Battlefield National Park (Chalmette)

City Park (Mid City)

Confederate Museum (Warehouse District)

D-Day Museum (Warehouse District)

Jackson Barracks Military Museum (New Orleans East)

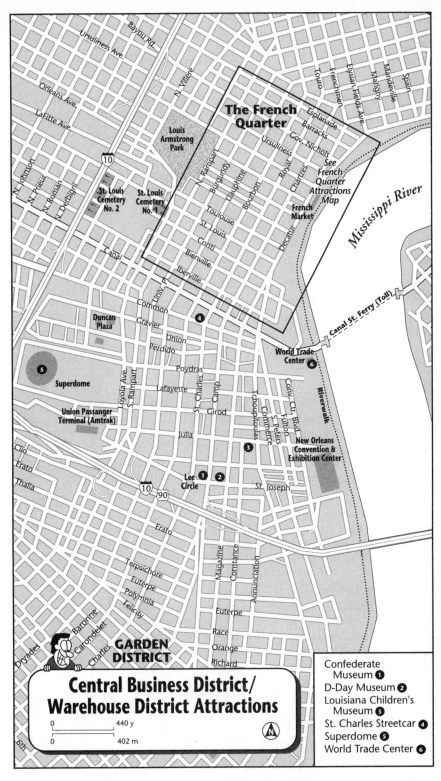

The French Quarter

See French Quarter Attractions Map

Louis Armstrong Park

St. Louis Cemetery No. 2

St. Louis Cemetery No. 1

French Market

Mississippi River

Canal St. Ferry (Toll)

Duncan Plaza

World Trade Center ❻

Superdome ❺

Riverwalk

Union Passanger Terminal (Amtrak)

New Orleans Convention & Exhibition Center

Lee Circle ❶ ❷

❸

St. Joseph

GARDEN DISTRICT

Central Business District/ Warehouse District Attractions

0 ___ 440 y
0 ___ 402 m

Confederate Museum ❶
D-Day Museum ❷
Louisiana Children's Museum ❸
St. Charles Streetcar ❹
Superdome ❺
World Trade Center ❻

Louisiana Children's Museum
(Warehouse District)

New Orleans Historic Voodoo
Museum (French Quarter)

New Orleans Museum of Art (Mid
City)

New Orleans Pharmacy Museum
(French Quarter)

Old U.S. Mint (French Quarter)

Presbytere (French Quarter)

Rivertown (Kenner)

St. Charles Streetcar (Central
Business District)

World Trade Center (Central
Business District)

**Top Spot to Stroll with Your
Main Squeeze**

Moonwalk (French Quarter)

The Top Sights

Aquarium of the Americas
French Quarter.

Question: How many aquariums in the United States have flesh-eating piranhas on display? Answer: only one—this one. One of the 10 best aquariums in the United States, the Aquarium of the Americas also has resident penguins (which are fed daily at 1pm and 4pm) and sharks (fed by divers on Tuesdays, Thursdays, and Saturdays at 1pm). Allow one to two hours to tour the aquarium; films shown in the adjoining IMAX theater vary in length and require extra time. Volunteers in blue or green shirts will answer questions (ask for my friend Janet). For $26.50 adults ($13.25 children), you can also purchase a combination ticket that includes admission to both the aquarium and the Audubon Zoo, with a riverboat ride on the sternwheeler *John James Audubon* taking you between the two. Trips depart from the Riverwalk (in front of the aquarium) at 10am, noon, 2pm, and 4pm.

One Canal St. (at the Mississippi River, a few blocks from Bourbon St.). ☎ *800/ 774-7394 or 504/581-4629. Sun–Thur 9:30am–6pm, Fri–Sat 9:30am–7pm. IMAX shows hourly 10am–6pm. Admission $10.50 adults; $8 seniors; $5 children 12 and under. Separate charge for IMAX shows; discounted combination tickets available. Wheelchair accessible.*

Audubon Park
Uptown.

Right across the street from Loyola and Tulane universities, nestled between St. Charles and Magazine streets is one of the prettiest and most peaceful spots in New Orleans, Audubon Park. This 340-acre park contains a public golf course, tennis courts, riding and jogging paths, hundreds of centuries-old live oaks, and resident populations of squirrels and birds. It's a great place to have a picnic, contemplate the nature of the universe, and regain your sense of sanity and faith in human nature—but don't stay after dark. Allow 30 to 60 minutes for a visit.

6500 St. Charles Ave. (take the St. Charles Streetcar and get off in front). ☎ *504/ 581-4629. Daily 6am–10pm. Admission is free. Wheelchair accessible.*

Mid City
Attractions

0   220 y

0   201 m

City Park ❹
Fair Grounds ❷
Metairie Cemetery ❺
New Orleans Museum of Art ❸
Pitot House ❶

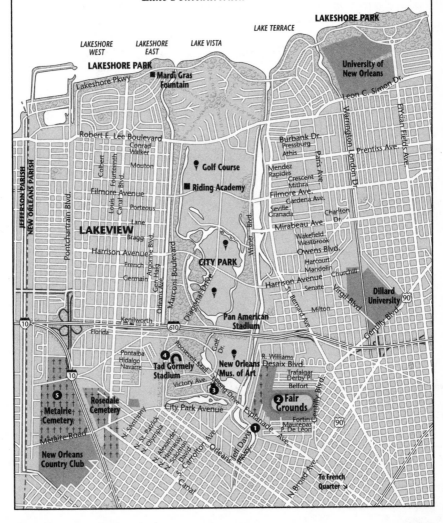

Lake Pontchartrain

LAKESHORE PARK

LAKE TERRACE

LAKESHORE
WEST

LAKESHORE
EAST

LAKE VISTA

LAKESHORE PARK

University of
New Orleans

Lakeshore Pkwy.

■ Mardi Gras
Fountain

Leon C. Simon Dr.

Robert E. Lee Boulevard

Conrad
Walker

Burbank Dr.
Pressburg
Athis

Warrington London Dr.

Prentiss Ave.

Elysian Fields Ave.

Colbert

Mouton

Paris Ave.

♟ Golf Course

Mendez
Rapides
Crescent
Mithra

Filmore Avenue

Louis
XIV

Canal Blvd.

Fourteenth

Porteous

■ Riding Academy

Filmore Ave.
Gardena Ave.
Seville
Granada

Charlton
Dr.

Lane

Mirabeau Ave.

Wisner Blvd.

Wakefield
Westbrook

Bragg

LAKEVIEW

Harrison Avenue

CITY PARK

Owens Blvd.

French

Gen. Haig

Argonne Blvd.

Marconi Boulevard

Harcourt
Mandolin
Churchill

Germain

Diagonal Drive

Harrison Avenue
Senate

Dillard
University

Kenilworth

Pan American
Stadium

Bernard Ave.

Virgil Blvd.

Milton

Gentilly Blvd.

Florida

Pontalba
Hidalgo
Navarre

Roosevelt Mall

Golf Dr.

Lelong Drive

R. Williams
Desaix Blvd.

❹ Tad Gormely
Stadium

New Orleans
Mus. of Art ❸

Trafalgar
Derby Pl.
Belfort

Victory Ave.

Gentilly Blvd.

❺ Metairie
Cemetery

Rosedale
Cemetery

City Park Avenue

❷ Fair
Grounds

Fortin
Maurepas
De Leon

Metairie Road

N. St. Anthony

N. St. Patrick

N. Olympia

N. Alexander

N. Hennessy

N. Solomon

N. David

N. Carrollton Ave.

Jeff Davis Pkwy.

Orleans

Esplanade Ave.

❶

N. Broad Ave.

Gentilly Blvd.

New Orleans
Country Club

Canal

To French
Quarter ↘

JEFFERSON PARISH
NEW ORLEANS PARISH

Pontchartrain Blvd.

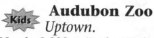

Audubon Zoo
Uptown.

Nearly 2,000 animals—including a white alligator and a white Bengal tiger—make their home among the carefully constructed lagoons, waterfalls, and winding pathways of this zoo, located on the banks of the Mississippi River and inside Audubon Park. I never miss the Louisiana Swamp exhibit or the Butterflies in Flight exhibit, where more than 1,000 butterflies flit among the lush colorful plants. A great way to visit is to take the *John James Audubon* riverboat from the aquarium (see the Aquarium of the Americas listing). Allow two to four hours for a visit.

6500 Magazine St. Take the St. Charles Streetcar and get off at the park entrance (6500 St. Charles). A free shuttle through the park runs every 20 minutes. If you prefer, take the Magazine St. bus and get off right at the zoo. ☎ **504/581-4629.** *Daily 9:30am–5pm (hours vary in the summer). Admission $8 adults; $4 seniors and children 2–12. Wheelchair accessible.*

Beauregard-Keyes House
French Quarter.

A lovely house in its own right—with Doric columns, twin staircases, and "raised cottage" architecture—the main appeal of this place is its historical associations. Built in 1826 by Joseph Le Carpentier—grandfather of America's first world chess champion, Paul Morphy, who was born to Le Carpentier's daughter in 1837—it served as a boardinghouse during the Civil War; was home to Confederate general Pierre Gustave Toutant Beauregard after the war; and was the place where Frances Parkinson Keyes wrote many of her novels, including her most famous, *Dinner at Antoine's*. The beautiful garden adjoining the house is wheelchair accessible, but the house is not. Allow 45 to 75 minutes.

1113 Chartres St. (2 blocks from Bourbon St.). ☎ **504/523-7257.** *Hourly tours Mon–Sat 10am–3pm. Admission $4 adults; $3 seniors and students; $1.50 children 12 and under.*

Extra! Extra!

The **Black Music Hall of Fame** in the French Quarter was just getting its act together as this book went to press and still didn't have a permanent home, any permanent exhibits, or even a phone number—but they're working on it. By the time you buy this book they may be up and running, so if you'd like more information, call the **Mayor's Music and Entertainment Committee** at ☎ **504/565-8104.**

Blaine Kern's Mardi Gras World
Algiers.

It may not be Mardi Gras when you come, but you can still catch the flavor of it by visiting Blaine Kern's Mardi Gras World and watching the Mardi Gras floats being made and decorated. You can watch a Mardi Gras film, dress up in a Mardi Gras costume and have your picture taken, or even participate in a mini-parade. Allow about two hours to get here, take the tour, and get back to the Quarter.

223 Newton St., Algiers Point. (Take the Canal St. Ferry from the Quarter. It's free to pedestrians, and a van will meet you, take you to the site, and bring you back.) ☎ *504/362-8211 or 504/361-7821. Daily 9:30am–4:30pm (closed some holidays). Admission $8.50 adults; $6.50 seniors; $4 children 3–12. Wheelchair accessible.*

Bourbon Street
French Quarter.

Walking along the 100 to 1000 section of Bourbon Street, with its wide open, anything-goes attitude and its barkers, buggy drivers, and scam artists competing for your attention, you may think you're on a carnival midway, but you're not; where you are is New Orleans Party Central. In the evening, people are everywhere, the street is blocked off for pedestrians only, all the bars are open and operating full blast, and you'll hear loud and raucous music coming from most every doorway and catch the smell of Cajun and Creole food wafting on the air. Liquor is served 24 hours a day here, but during the daylight hours, Bourbon Street is relaxed and sometimes looks almost deserted, with only restaurants, T-shirt and souvenir shops, and a few bars open. Depending on the ages of your children and your definition of family values, you may want your kids to see Bourbon Street only in daylight—or you may not want them to see it at all. Allow about one hour.

Tourist Traps

Don't fall for the "two for one drink" or "three for one drink" offers. Yes, they'll give you more than one drink for the price of one, but they give the drinks to you all at one time, and the price for one drink is usually outrageous.

 ### Chalmette Battlefield National Park
Chalmette.

The cold and misty morning of January 8, 1815, found General Andrew Jackson with a ragtag band of a few hundred regular soldiers and about 3,000 poorly trained and ill-supplied men, among them local militia, riflemen from

Kentucky and Tennessee, two regiments of free blacks, slaves, and even some of Jean Lafitte's pirates, facing more than twice their number of well-trained and well-supplied British regular soldiers. Yet when the smoke cleared, the British had lost more than 2,000 men, and the Americans only suffered 65 wounded and six or seven dead. Ironically, this battle, the Battle of New Orleans (the last major battle of the War of 1812 and one of the most important in U.S. history), took place after the war was officially over—word just hadn't reached anyone yet. The National Cemetery is also the final resting place of 14,000 Union soldiers who died during the Civil War. Allow at least one hour in the park, plus 30 to 60 minutes to get there and back.

8606 W. Saint Bernard Hwy., Chalmette, LA (about 7 miles down river from New Orleans). No public transportation is available. A taxi from the French Quarter will cost about $15 each way for 1 or 2 people (add 75¢ for each additional person). ☎ 504/589-4430. Daily 8:30am–4:30pm. Admission is free.

City Park
Mid City.

New Orleans' City Park is the fifth largest urban park in the country and shelters within its 1,500 acres the largest collection of mature live oaks in the world, including the McDonogh Oak, which dates back approximately 1,000 years. Other trees of note include the "Dueling Oaks" (only one of which survives), which were the scene of numerous duels, both before and after duels were outlawed in 1890. The park receives nearly 10 million visitors a year. Allow one hour or more for the park and at least one hour more if you choose to visit the **New Orleans Museum of Art (☎ 504/488-2631;** see later in this chapter), located on the park grounds.

Also in the park are the **Carousel Gardens (☎ 504/483-9356)**, home to one of the few remaining antique carved wooden carousels in the country. There are two miniature trains that take riders on a 2½-mile trip through the park as well as a small Ferris wheel and a wading pool. Admission is $1 (ride tickets separate), and children under two are free. **Storyland (☎ 504/483-9382)** has 26 larger-than-life storybook exhibits for children. Admission is $1.50 (children under two are free). The **Botanical Garden (☎ 504/483-9386)** is 10 acres of gardens, ponds, fountains, and sculptures, plus a horticultural library and a gift shop. Admission is $3 (children under 12 free with parent). Other features of the park include:

➤ Four **18-hole public golf courses** with lessons by PGA pros, electric carts, rentals, pro shop, and restaurant (☎ 504/483-9396), plus a **100-tee driving range (☎ 504/483-9394)**

➤ **Softball center (☎ 504/482-4888)**

➤ **Canoes and pedal boats (☎ 504/483-9371)** for the eight miles of lagoons

➤ **36 tennis courts (☎ 504/483-9383)**

188

➤ **Fishing** (☎ **504/483-9371**) in the park's lagoons for bass, catfish, and perch

➤ **Horseback rides, lessons, and pony rides** (☎ **504/483-9398**)

City Park is located all the way up Esplanade Ave. out of the French Quarter. For information, call ☎ *504/482-4888. Take the Esplanade bus from the French Quarter and get off at the park. The park opens when the sun rises and closes when it sets. Wheelchair accessible.*

Confederate Museum

Kids *Warehouse District.*

Since 1891, this museum—the oldest in Louisiana—has displayed memorabilia from the Civil War, including battle flags, uniforms, guns, swords, photographs, and personal effects of Gen. P. G. T. Beauregard, Gen. Robert E. Lee, and Confederate president Jefferson Davis. The museum also has an excellent display of pictures tracing Louisiana's part in the Civil War. It's a dignified, eloquent, and moving display that will fascinate anyone with an interest in American history. Allow 30 to 60 minutes.

900 Camp St. (take the St. Charles Trolley to Lee Circle and walk one block to Camp St). ☎ *504/523-4522. Mon–Sat 10am–4pm. Admission $4 adults; $2 children under 16.*

Extra! Extra!

The **New Orleans' D-Day Museum** is currently under construction at the corner of Magazine and Howard streets in the Warehouse District and is expected to open in the fall of 1999. When it's finished, it will offer numerous exhibits concerning this historic event. Call ☎ **504/527-6012** for information.

French Market

French Quarter.

Since the early 1700s, this area along the river has been used for trade, and with its shops, flea market, and farmer's market, it's still a dandy place to shop for souvenirs, gifts, and your recommended daily allowance of fresh produce. Wind up your trek with some beignets (New Orleans doughnuts) at Café du Monde, located right in the market. Allow 30 to 60 minutes.

The French Market stretches along Decatur and N. Peters streets from St. Ann to Barracks. Most shops are open 10am–6pm daily. The Farmer's Market and Café du Monde are open 24 hours. No admission. Wheelchair accessible.

Gallier House Museum

French Quarter.

In 1857, a working bathroom and hot and cold running water made this one of the most modern buildings around. It was the home of noted architect James Gallier and is said to have been the model for a home in Anne Rice's vampire books. Take a guided tour and get a great look at mid-19th century New Orleans life. Allow one hour.

21132 Royal St. (one block from Bourbon St.). ☎ 504/525-5661. Open Mon–Sat 10am–3:30pm. Admission $5 adults; $4 seniors; $3 children 8–18.

Germaine Wells Mardi Gras Museum
French Quarter.
Atop Arnaud's restaurant is a museum housing the Mardi Gras gowns worn by former Arnaud's owner Wells between 1910 and 1960. Allow 15 to 20 minutes.

813 Bienville St. (½ block from Bourbon St.). ☎ 504/523-5433. Mon–Fri 11:30am–2:30pm and 6–10pm (Fri until 10:30pm), Sat 6–10:30pm, Sun 10am–2:30pm and 6–10pm. Admission is free.

Hermann-Grima House
French Quarter.
If you think cooking is a chore now, check out this 1832 building with its operational period kitchen. Something's always cooking here on Thursdays from May through October, so drop in and see how they did it way back then. During December, the house is decked out "Creole-style" for Christmas, and during the rest of the year, the house depicts funeral customs of the time. Tours include the house and stable. Allow 30 to 60 minutes.

820 St. Louis (½ block from Bourbon St.). ☎ 504/525-5661. Mon–Sat 10am–3:30pm. Admission is free. Wheelchair accessible, but call ahead so the workers can put out the portable ramp.

Historic New Orleans Collection
French Quarter.
This complex of buildings (one of which was built in 1794) houses art, maps, and original documents from Louisiana's past and is one of the very best places to go if you want the lowdown on the evolution of New Orleans. The research center, located in a beautifully restored courthouse and police station at 410 Chartres St., is a treasure trove of research materials. The exhibits change periodically. Allow 30 to 60 minutes.

533 Royal St. (one block from Bourbon St.). ☎ 504/523-4662. Tue–Sat 10am–4:45pm. Admission is free. Guided tours cost $4 and are given at 10am, 11am, 2pm, and 3pm. Wheelchair accessible.

Kids Jackson Barracks
Holy Cross.
Both Gen. Robert E. Lee and Gen. Ulysses S. Grant served here prior to the Civil War, and now the place has been turned into a great museum of military history. Your kids will love the guns, artillery pieces, uniforms, flags, and other military hardware. It's a few miles downriver, but it's on the way to Chalmette Battlefield, so you might as well drop in. Allow 60 to 90 minutes, including time to get there from the Quarter.

6300 St. Claude Ave. (take the St. Claude bus and get off in front of the museum). ☎ **504/271-6262, ext. 242.** *Mon–Fri 7:30am–4pm. Admission is free. Wheelchair accessible.*

Free (or Practically Free) Stuff to See & Do

➤ Explore the French Quarter on foot (French Quarter)

➤ Ride the St. Charles Streetcar (Central Business District)

➤ Ride the Canal St. free ferry (Central Business District)

➤ Take a walk along the Moonwalk (French Quarter)

➤ Visit Audubon Park (Uptown)

➤ Visit City Park (Mid City)

Jackson Square
French Quarter.

This place is where it all began. Jackson Square was the city's town square, place of execution, and military parade ground. Four small statues (one in each corner) are called the Four Seasons and are the oldest outdoor statues in New Orleans—that is, if you don't count the ones in the cemeteries. The statue in the middle of the square is of Andrew Jackson, hero of the Battle of New Orleans.

Beautiful landscaping, trees, benches, and a fountain make this square one of the more popular public places in the city. Artists set up shop on the sidewalk just outside the iron fence while mules stand patiently along Decatur Street waiting for their drivers to load the carriages for tours of the Quarter. Tarot card readers and psychics will tell your future and your past while mimes, clowns, and street musicians entertain you. Street vendors sell ice cream, soft drinks, and other snacks, and there are restaurants located on each corner of the square. Allow 30 to 60 minutes.

The square fronts the 700 block of Decatur St. and is bounded by Chartres St. in the back and by St. Ann and St. Peter along its sides. Hours are seasonal, but they are usually from dawn to dusk. Admission is free.

Lafayette Cemetery No. 1
Garden District.

When Americans began moving into town after the Louisiana Purchase, they weren't accepted by the French Creoles, so they built their own cities upriver from the French Quarter—which was, at the time, the whole of New Orleans. The Garden District was part of one of these cities (Lafayette, which was later

Bet You Didn't Know

You may not notice it with today's interstate highway system and modern bridges, but a 10-mile-wide strip of land to the west of the city is the only way to get to New Orleans without crossing a body of water. If that land were flooded out, the city of New Orleans and the East bank of Jefferson Parish would be an island.

annexed by New Orleans) and Lafayette Cemetery No. 1 was started in 1883 as that city's burial place. Though not as old as St. Louis No. 1, it's still full of large above-ground tombs and is notable for being the family burial place of Anne Rice's fictional vampire Lestat. (This cemetery was featured in the movie version of *Interview with a Vampire* and in many other books and films as well.) Many of the city's cemeteries are not safe, but a friend who lives right next to Lafayette No. 1 and gives tours of the place (see chapter 15) says he's heard of absolutely no incidents in the last 15 years. Allow 30 to 60 minutes.

1400 block of Washington Ave. 7:30am–2:30pm Mon–Fri, 7:30–noon Sat. Free admission. Wheelchair accessible.

Longue Vue House and Gardens
Metairie.

Gorgeous fountains, tranquil ponds, and both natural and formal gardens form the backdrop for this beautiful Greek Revival mansion at the end of an oak-lined drive. Built between the years 1939 and 1942, it was home to philanthropist Edgar Stern and his wife Elizabeth (daughter of Sears and Roebuck magnate Julius Rosenwald), who intended from the start that the house would become a museum after their deaths. The interior features beautiful antiques, Oriental carpets, rice-paper wall coverings, and other lovely touches. Allow one to two hours plus transportation time.

7 Bamboo Rd. Catch the Canal St. bus at any stop on Canal (every other corner) and get off at the cemeteries; take the Metairie Rd. bus, get off at Bamboo Rd., and walk ½ block. ☎ *504/488-5488. Mon–Sat 10am–4pm, Sun 1–5pm. Closed most holidays. Admission $7 adults; $6 seniors; $3 children and students. Wheelchair accessible, though some parts of the garden are wild and might be rough going.*

Louisiana Children's Museum
Warehouse District.

Your children can be chefs in the Kid's Cafe, musicians in the Music Makers exhibit, or television personalities in the WDSU Channel 6 Kids' TV Studio. Hands-on exhibits let them discover the worlds of science and nature, or they can take in a live performance or puppet show in the Times-Picayune Theatre. Allow 30 to 60 minutes.

420 Julia St. (four blocks from the Convention Center). ☎ *504/523-1357. Open Tue–Sat 9:30am–5pm (Mon 9:30am–5pm in Jun–Aug), Sun noon–5pm. Admission $5; children under 1-year-old free. Wheelchair accessible.*

Metairie Cemetery
Metairie.

Metairie is the largest of all New Orleans cemeteries, and though it's the youngest—it was built after the Civil War—it's the most beautiful, with many huge and elaborate graves and monuments. The cemetery is here supposedly because of revenge: At one time a racetrack operated on these grounds, and it's said that a certain New Orleans resident, denied admission to the race-track's exclusive Jockey Club, swore that if he couldn't get in, only the dead would—and then he bought up the land and turned it into a graveyard. Unlike most cemeteries in town, Metairie Cemetery can be toured by auto-mobile (and walked through safely). You can get a cassette-tape tour (with player) free of charge at the office. Allow one hour.

5100 Pontchartrain Blvd. ☎ *504/486-6331. The Canal St. bus will take you from the French Quarter to the cemeteries at the end of Canal St. From there, it's only a block or two to the Metairie Cemetery (ask the driver), but it's several more blocks from the street to the office. It's a big place. Free admission. Wheelchair accessible.*

Moonwalk
French Quarter.

If you want a great view of the Mississippi River or a great place for a roman-tic stroll, Moonwalk is a good bet. Watch the ships go by (New Orleans is the second-busiest port in the world), have a romantic interlude, or just take a leisurely stroll. It's located directly across the street from Jackson Square and was named for Mayor Moon Landrieu, during whose administration it was built. It's open 24 hours a day, but for safety's sake I suggest going before midnight. Allow 10 to 15 minutes.

Jackson Square. ☎ *504/587-0738. Free admission. Wheelchair accessible.*

Bet You Didn't Know

You'd never guess from the bad rep it got from Hollywood, but voodoo is a religion, whose roots lie in an African religion called Vodun (which means "the creator of all things"). Africans brought to the Americas as slaves developed voodoo (and other religions like Macumba, Santería, and Candoble) by com-bining African religious practices with the imagery, iconography, and ritual of Catholicism, which the slaveowners forced on them. Today, it's estimated that nearly 15% of New Orleanians still practice some form of the religion.

New Orleans Historic Voodoo Museum
French Quarter.

This museum, dedicated to voodoo and Marie Laveau (Voodoo Queen of New Orleans from 1796 to 1881), is a dim, atmospheric, and titillating look at the world of zombies and gris-gris. Mysterious artifacts, potions, talismans, and icons peculiar to this blend of African and Christian religions fill the building, and the museum staff will tell you all about them (and maybe even introduce you to the snakes that live out back). Tours depart from the museum to visit Congo Square, Marie Laveau's tomb at St. Louis Cemetery No. 1, and a pharmacy that displays voodoo potions—or you can stick around for the occasional staged voodoo ritual (call for schedules). Allow 30 minutes.

724 Dumaine St. ☎ 504/523-7685. Daily 10am–dusk. Admission $6.50 adults; $5.25 students and seniors. Tours are $12–$18. Wheelchair accessible, though the narrow door may be a tight fit.

New Orleans Museum of Art
Mid City.

The green spaces and ancient oaks of City Park provide a peaceful backdrop to this museum and its 40,000-piece permanent collection of European paintings, sculpture, and decorative glassware. Ever-changing exhibits also display art from North and South America, Asia, and Africa, and traveling international exhibits come through regularly, bringing paintings by Claude Monet, eggs by Fabergé, and who knows what else. NOMA always has special exhibits for kids, and volunteers will sometimes give them lists of objects to find in the museum (like a scavenger hunt), so they end up touring the entire museum instead of just seeing the one or two exhibits they came for. Allow one to two hours, plus transportation.

1 Dreyfous Ave. (take the Esplanade bus and get off in front of the museum). ☎ 504/488-2631, Web site www.noma.org. Tue–Sun 10am–5pm. Admission $6 adults; $5 seniors; $3 children 3–17. Wheelchair accessible.

New Orleans Pharmacy Museum
French Quarter.

In 1823, this museum was the residence and apothecary shop of Louis Dufilho, the first licensed pharmacist in the United States. Your kids will love the voodoo potions, leeches, bone saws, giant syringes, and other medical instruments, and you'll enjoy the Italian marble soda fountain and the beautiful courtyard planted with many of the same herbs used by pharmacists of the time. Allow 15 to 30 minutes.

514 Chartres St. (2 blocks from Bourbon St.). ☎ 504/565-8027. Tue–Sun 10am–5pm. Admission $2 adults; $1 seniors and students; children under 12 free. Wheelchair accessible.

Old U.S. Mint
French Quarter.

This huge Greek Revival building has a history—from 1837 to 1909, money was minted here for both the United States and the Confederacy, and during the Civil War, the Union used it as a prison—but it's what goes on there now that's the really interesting part. Two large exhibitions—one on New Orleans jazz and one on the city's Mardi Gras celebrations—take up most of the building. The jazz collection features a comprehensive collection of pictures, musical instruments—including Louis Armstrong's first cornet—and other artifacts that trace the development of the jazz tradition and New Orleans' place in that history. Across the hall there's a stunning array of Mardi Gras momentos from New Orleans and other communities across Louisiana—from ornate costumes to a street scene complete with maskers and a parade float. You might need to be a jazz fan to appreciate the first exhibit, but all you need are eyes to take in the other. Allow one hour.

400 Esplanade. ☎ *504/568-6968. Tue–Sun 9am–5pm. Admission $4 adults; $3 seniors and students; children 12 and under free. Wheelchair accessible.*

Pitot House
Mid City.

Built on a different site in the late 1700s, this house was purchased in 1810 and subsequently moved to its present location. Curator Myrna Bergeron will be glad to show you around this excellent example of an 18th century West Indies–style plantation home. Allow one to two hours, plus transportation time.

1440 Moss St. (near City Park). ☎ *504/ 482-0312. Wed–Sat 10am–3pm. Admission $5 adults; $2 seniors; $2 children under 12. The first floor is wheelchair accessible, but the second floor is not.*

Extra! Extra!

The proverb says "See Naples and die." G.A. Sala's view of things is that you should see Canal St., New Orleans, and then try to live as much longer as ever you can.

Presbytere
French Quarter.

This building was begun as a home for the Spanish clergy, but it took many years to finish and wound up being used as a courthouse instead. Today, it's a branch of the Louisiana state museum and houses historic paintings by Louisiana artists, history exhibits, and artifacts from the Civil War (including a submarine). There are frequent rotating exhibits. Allow 45 to 60 minutes.

751 Chartres St. (on Jackson Square). ☎ *504/568-6968. Open Tue–Sun 9am–5pm. Admission $4 adults; $3 seniors and students; children 12 and under free. Wheelchair accessible.*

 Rivertown
Kenner.

About 10 miles northwest of the French Quarter is the city of Kenner, which has built a nice little tourist area along the banks of the Mississippi River. The **Louisiana Toy Train Museum** at 519 Williams Blvd. (☎ **504/468-7223**) is a favorite with kids for its six working train layouts, and kids also love the planetarium and observatory at the **Freeport McMoRan Daily Living Science Center** (☎ **504/468-7229**), located at 409 Williams Blvd. There are shows at 2pm Tuesday through Friday, with three shows on the weekend. You can view the night sky from 7:30 to 10:30pm Thursday through Saturday.

Kids will also enjoy the mimes, magic, puppet shows, and stories of the **Children's Castle** (☎ **504/468-7231**), located at 501 Williams Blvd., and kids and sports fans will enjoy the **Rivertown Saints Hall of Fame Museum** at 409 Williams Blvd. (☎ **504/468-6617**), where you can view memorabilia and film clips of the NFL team.

At the **Louisiana Wildlife and Fisheries Museum,** 303 Williams Blvd. (☎ **504/468-7232**), you can see many animals and a small aquarium and hear people in period costume talk about how everyday life was lived from 1750 to 1850. If you didn't come during Mardi Gras, didn't visit Mardi Gras World, or just can't get enough, there's the **Mardi Gras Museum of Jefferson Parish** at 407 Williams Blvd. (☎ **504/468-7258**).

All of the museums are located within a 3-block area and are an easy walk from each other. They're all open from 9am–5pm Tue–Sat and from 1pm–5pm Sun, except the football museum, which is closed Sunday. Admission to each is $3 for adults; $2 for seniors and children under 12. A multiticket pass is also available at $10 for adults; $5 for seniors and kids (pass doesn't include the Children's Castle). All museums are wheelchair accessible.

St. Charles Streetcar
Central Business District.

The oldest continually operating streetcar system in the world, the St. Charles Streetcar was begun in 1835 as a mule-drawn railway and electrified in 1893. In addition to being an historic attraction, it's also a functioning part of the New Orleans public transportation system. The streetcar travels from Canal Street, passes through the Garden District and Uptown neighborhoods (past many beautiful homes), turns onto Carrollton Avenue in the Riverbend area, and continues to S. Claiborne Avenue before making the return trip.

*The round trip is about 15 miles and takes about 1½ to 2 hours. The cost is $1 each way (exact change is required), but a VisiTour pass entitling you to unlimited rides on streetcars or buses is available at a cost of $4 for 1 day or $8 for 3 days— ask at your hotel for the nearest VisiTour pass vendor or call ☎ **504/248-3900**. You can catch the streetcar at St. Charles and Common (1 block from Canal), Canal and Carondelet, or every two blocks along its route.*

World Trade Center
Kids *Central Business District.*

If you don't get dizzy easily, take the World Trade Center's outside elevator for a breathtaking view as you ascend to the 31st floor. When you get to the top, you'll have a panoramic view of the city and the surrounding area from the observation deck. *Note:* As we go to press the elevators have been temporarily closed.

2 Canal St. ☎ *504/529-1601. Daily 9am–5pm. Admission $2 adults; $1 children 6–12; children under 6 are free. High-powered telescopes are available for a few minutes at a cost of 25¢. There's also a revolving cocktail lounge on the 33rd floor, but children aren't allowed (see chapter 20). Wheelchair accessible*

Worksheet: Your Must-See Attractions

Enter the attractions you most would like to visit to see how they'll fit into your schedule. Then use the date book below to plan your itinerary.

Attraction and location	Amount of time you expect to spend there	Best day and time to go

Chapter 15

More Fun
Stuff to Do

In This Chapter

➤ More sights and activities for history buffs, cemetery enthusiasts, and people who like to mix a little food and drink with their sightseeing

➤ Pilgrimage sites for Anne Rice fans

➤ Spots for sports—the Superdome, Zephyrs Baseball Stadium, and more

➤ More parks and gardens for outdoors types

➤ Day trips out to Cajun country and the plantations

If you have something that particularly fascinates you, then the sights listed in the last chapter may only have only scratched the surface. Here's some stuff that's buried a little lower.

If You're Interested in History

 ### The Cabildo
French Quarter.
Built in 1795 as the Spanish seat of government, the Cabildo is where the Louisiana Purchase was turned over to the United States in 1803. The great exhibits of how people lived in early Louisiana will entertain you and help you to better understand the way people live now. Allow at least one hour.

701 Chartres St. at the corner of St. Ann St. on Jackson Square (2 blocks from Bourbon St.). ☎ *504/568-6968. Tue–Sun 9am–5pm. Admission $4 adults; $3 seniors and students; children 12 and under free. Wheelchair accessible, though the elevator is small.*

Old Ursuline Convent
French Quarter.

If you're interested in history in general and religious history in particular, take a tour of the oldest surviving building in the Mississippi Valley (erected 1745 through 1752) and learn about early colonial New Orleans. The Ursuline nuns had the country's first school for girls only (blacks, Indians, and whites) on the site until 1824; in 1831, the state assembly used the convent as a meeting place; and today the convent houses a Catholic archive with documents that go back to 1718. End your tour with a look at the beautiful stained and painted glass windows in the adjoining church—one depicts the Battle of New Orleans with the Virgin Mary looking on. Allow 60 to 75 minutes.

1112 Chartres St. (2 blocks from Bourbon St.). ☎ *504/529-3040. Hourly tours are given Tue–Fri 10am–3pm and Sat–Sun 11:15am–2pm. Admission $5 adults; $4 seniors and students; children under 8 free.*

Our Lady of Guadalupe Church and International Shrine of St. Jude
French Quarter.

The oldest church in New Orleans, Our Lady was erected in 1826 across the street from St. Louis Cemetery No. 1 as a convenient place to hold funerals for yellow fever victims and those who died of similar diseases. Known as the Mortuary Chapel, it also serves as a shrine to both St. Jude (saint of impossible causes) and St. Expedite. Legend has it that a saint's statue arrived at the church in a crate with no identifying marks save for the word "expedite" stamped on the outside. The name stuck, and petitioners began directing their prayers his way. The church may not want to admit it, but St. Expedite has also been revered as a voodoo saint for many years. Allow 15 minutes.

411 N. Rampart St. (3 blocks from Bourbon St.). ☎ *504/525-1551. Daily 7am–7pm. Admission is free. Wheelchair accessible.*

Pontalba Apartments
French Quarter.

Originally individual townhouses, the beautifully restored Pontalba Apartments were built in 1849 at the behest of the Baroness Pontalba as the showplace of the old Creole section of New Orleans. The private courtyard, servants' quarters, and huge rooms with their high ceilings, marble fireplaces, and authentic period furniture will give you a fascinating look at the lifestyles of the rich and famous, 19th-century-style.

751 Chartres St. (on Jackson Square). ☎ *504/568-6968. Open Tue–Sun 9am–5pm. Admission $4 adults; $3 seniors and students; children 12 and under free.*

Kids St. Louis Cathedral
French Quarter.

The oldest continuously operating cathedral in the U.S. dates from 1794, although the church was largely rebuilt in the 1850s. Long the spiritual center of New Orleans, the first church on the site was destroyed by a hurricane in 1722 and the second by the great fire of 1788, in which 856 buildings were destroyed. Be sure to check out the beautiful stained glass windows and mural depicting the life of King Louis IX, the cathedral's patron saint.

721 Chartres St. (at Jackson Square). ☎ 504/525-9585. Tours are given Mon–Sat 9am–5pm and Sun 2–5pm. Admission and tours are free, but donations are requested. Wheelchair accessible.

If You're into Sports

Superdome
Central Business District.
One of the largest buildings in the world, the Superdome allows 77,000 people to watch the New Orleans Saints football team and over 100,000 to attend concerts in climate-controlled comfort. If you go to an event, don't worry about not being able to see—there are no posts anywhere to obstruct your view, and giant television screens provide instant replays as well as other entertainment. Hour-long guided tours of the place leave hourly from Gate A between 10am and 4pm, except when there's an event scheduled.

1500 Poydras. Take the Poydras bus and get off in front. ☎ 504/587-3808 or 504/587-3810. Tours $6 adults; $5 seniors; $4 children 5–10; children under 5 are free. Wheelchair accessible.

New Orleans Zephyrs Baseball Stadium
East Jefferson.
New Orleans doesn't have a major league team, but it does have the Zephyrs, the AAA-class farm team of the Houston Astros. If you'd like to attend a game, call the following number.

6000 Airline Hwy., East Jefferson (approximately 9 miles from the French Quarter, on the way to the airport). Take the Airline bus and get off by the stadium. Call ☎ 504/734-5155 for game times and admission.

Fair Grounds Race Course
Mid City.
One of the oldest racetracks in the country, the Fair Grounds course has seen such visitors as Generals Ulysses S. Grant and George Custer, Pat Garrett, and Frank James (brother of Jesse), who was a betting commissioner here in the early part of the century. The season begins each year on Thanksgiving Day and ends in late March.

1751 Gentilly Blvd., Mid City (approximately 10 minutes by car from the Central Business District and the French Quarter). ☎ 504/944-5515, Web site www.fgno.com.

If You're into Wax

〔Kids〕 Musée Conti Wax Museum
French Quarter.

Sure, wax museums are goofy, but kids generally like them, and this museum is one of the better ones around. My bet is that your kids will get a bigger kick out of the Haunted Dungeon than they will out of the Louisiana legends display. I mean, how can Andrew Jackson, Marie Laveau, Napoleon Bonaparte, and the Mardi Gras Indians compete with s-c-a-r-y monsters and scenes from famous horror stories? Allow 30 minutes.

917 Conti St., near the corner of Burgundy. ☎ *504/525-2605. Daily 10am–5pm. Admission $6 adults; $5.50 seniors; $4.50 children 4–17; children under 4 free. Wheelchair accessible.*

A Corny Photo Op

Cornstalk Fence Hotel
French Quarter.

Another take on the "If you build it, they will come" phenomenon, the people who live at this house made a cornfield out of cast iron and erected it as a fence in front of their house (now a hotel). Stalks of corn comprise the fence itself, while pumpkins lounge at the bottom and corn tassels decorate the top. The fence is so detailed that you can see the individual kernels on the ears and the morning glory vines intertwined throughout. For years the stalks, pumpkins, and morning glories have been painted green with the kernels and tassels in yellow, but at one time the morning glory flowers were painted blue. Just about everyone who comes here wants a picture standing in front of the fence. Allow five minutes.

915 Royal St. (1 block from Bourbon St.). ☎ *504/525-1515. The hotel is not open for tours, but the fence is always open—so to speak. Wheelchair accessible.*

See a Sight, Drink a Beer, Eat a Meal

Lafitte's Blacksmith Shop
French Quarter.

Records say this building has been around since 1772 (although many insist that it's much older), and legend says that the pirate Jean Lafitte used it as a blind for his illegal activities. It's been a bar since 1944 and was a haunt of Tennessee Williams. Kids aren't allowed inside, but the open doorway allows an excellent view of the interior. Allow five minutes unless you're going to stay and have a drink.

941 Bourbon St. ☎ *504/523-0066. Daily 11:30–4am. No cover charge. Part of it is not accessible to wheelchairs.*

Dollars & Sense

Why pay big money to hear music? You can find some of the best performers in town playing on the street for tips. They move around and don't always have a particular schedule, but if you keep your ears open, you can find them. When Royal Street is blocked to cars during the day, many musicians set up shop in the middle of the street. Many also play in front of the Cabildo at the back of Jackson Square. At night, you can find them on street corners, mostly on Royal Street. In my opinion, Grandpa and Stoney B. are the absolute best. You can sometimes find them at the corner of Royal and St. Louis, across the street from the Rib Room.

Napoleon House
French Quarter.
The home of Mayor Nicholas Girod was offered to Napoleon Bonaparte as a place of refuge in hopes he would be rescued and brought to New Orleans. Napoleon died before this dubious scheme ever got off the ground, but the building's been trading on its near miss with glory ever since and in recent decades has become a favorite spot of bohemian locals. Today this bar and cafe enjoys a dark and quiet atmosphere, with classical music playing in the background and waiters that don't hound you every other minute. Allow five minutes unless you're going to eat and/or drink.

500 Chartres St. (at the corner of Chartres and St. Louis, 2 blocks from Bourbon St. and Jackson Square). ☎ *504/524-9752. Mon–Thur 11am–midnight (Fri–Sat till 1am), Sun 11am–7pm. No admission. Wheelchair accessible.*

Original Old Absinthe House
French Quarter.
Legend says this 1806 building was one of the places Andrew Jackson and the Lafitte brothers met to plan the Battle of New Orleans. Later it became famous for dispensing absinthe, an addictive drink that's illegal today. The place is still a bar, though now they serve anisette instead—which tastes like absinthe but doesn't cause brain damage, so you can sip away, enjoy the atmosphere, and pretend you're doing something wicked. Allow five minutes to look around, more if you're going to drink. Two restaurants—**Tony Moran's** and **Pasta E Vino**—are located right on the premises. (In case you get hungry after your drink.)

240 Bourbon St. ☎ *504/523-3181. Daily 9:30am–2am. Admission is free, but it is a bar, so children aren't allowed. Wheelchair accessible.*

Bet You Didn't Know

The **Lake Pontchartrain Causeway,** which connects the metro area of New Orleans with the north shore of Lake Pontchartrain, is the longest bridge in the world, stretching more than 23 miles across the lake. The toll is $1.50 each way, but you can turn around and come back for free at several locations along the way. Allow 15 to 20 minutes to drive out to one of the turnarounds and come back.

If You're the Park & Garden Type

Armstrong Park
French Quarter.
At one time this section of real estate was known as Congo Square and was the only place slaves were allowed to congregate. Converted to a park and dedicated to Louis Armstrong, it now features peaceful lagoons, stately sycamores, and rolling grassy knolls and is home to the Municipal Auditorium and the Theatre for the Performing Arts. The entrance is located at the corner of St. Ann and Rampart streets just outside of the Quarter in the Faubourg Treme neighborhood. Though the area is safe in the daytime, I wouldn't venture there at night unless there's an event going on. Hours are seasonal. Allow 30 to 60 minutes. The park is wheelchair accessible.

Louisiana Nature Center and Planetarium
New Orleans East.
Eighty-six acres of native Louisiana forest provide an urban home for local flora and fauna; a wheelchair-friendly raised wooden walkway and three miles of public trails let you wander through on your own or on guided tours (given every day except Monday). Your kids will love both the planetarium presentations and the laser rock shows on the weekend. Films and special activities such as canoeing, bird watching, and arts and crafts round out the activities. Allow one to two hours, plus transportation time.

5601 Read Blvd., in the Joe Brown Memorial Park. Catch the Lake Forest Express bus at Canal and Basin (2 blocks from French Quarter), get off at Lake Forest Blvd. and Nature Center Dr., walk 3 to 4 blocks. ☎ 504/246-9381. Tue–Fri 9am–5pm, Sat 10am–5pm, Sun noon–5pm. Admission $4 adults; $3 seniors; $2 children. Call ☎ 504/246-7827 for planetarium hours and admission. Wheelchair accessible.

St. Anthony's Garden

French Quarter.

Located directly behind St. Louis Cathedral, the garden is named for Pere (father) Antoine, a popular rector who served New Orleans in the late 18th and early 19th centuries. Legend has it that many duels were fought here in the past, but the main attraction now is at night, when the spotlight illuminates the statue of Christ and casts a huge shadow against the back of the church. The garden is not open, but you can easily view it from Royal Street, Pirates' Alley, or Pere Antoine's Alley along the sides. The garden is in the 700 block of Royal Street, and you can see the shadow from anywhere along Orleans Street. The corner of Bourbon Street and Orleans Street is where many people discover the shadow when walking along Bourbon at night—no reports of how many people have given up drinking as a result.

Washington Artillery Park

French Quarter.

Along with Jackson Square, this small park has long been popular with tourists and as a gathering point for young people (when I came here in the 1960s, it was a hippie hangout; more recently it was the stomping ground for a group of kids known as "gutter punks"). The steps leading to the top of the levee double as seats for a small amphitheater, where street performers often put on their acts for tips. The area has recently been taken over by the Audubon Institute, which also operates the aquarium and zoo. They've relandscaped it, cleaned it up, reopened the public restrooms, opened a tourist information center and a small newsstand, and hired security for the area, all of which has once again made the park a vibrant part of the French Quarter.

Just west of the French Market, along the riverfront. ☎ *504/587-0738 or 504/529-5284. Free admission. Wheelchair accessible.*

 Woldenberg Riverfront Park

French Quarter.

This park with all of its open space, green grass, trees, and shrubs along the Mississippi River is a great place for an afternoon break. Let your the kids play, pretend to be Tom Sawyer or Huck Finn, or watch the river and the many ships. At night, it's a great place for a romantic stroll.

Riverfront behind the 500 block of Decatur St. ☎ *504/581-4629. Dawn–10pm. Admission is free. Wheelchair accessible.*

Where the Bodies Are Buried (More of Them)

St. Louis Cemetery No. 1

French Quarter.

Dating from the late 1700s, this "city of the dead" has large tombs, monuments, and smaller unmarked niches that resemble baker's ovens. Those of you with wicked imaginations will love this place—especially the tomb of voodoo queen Marie Laveau, where people still leave gifts in homage. Due to crime in the area, you should only visit with a group of people or on an organized tour—and, naturally, only during daylight.

400 block of Basin St. (4 blocks from Bourbon St.). ☎ ***504/482-5065.*** *Mon–Sat 9am–3pm, Sun 9am–noon. Admission is free, but organized tours are not. Call* ***Save Our Cemeteries*** *at* ☎ ***504/588-9357*** *for tour information. Wheelchair accessible for the most part, but some spots may be a problem.*

If You're an Anne Rice Fan

Think Anne Rice and what pictures come to mind? Dissolute vampires wandering around New Orleans cemeteries, right? Rice has been so successful in marrying her fiction to the atmosphere and architecture of the city that people come from far and wide to see her home, the places written about in her books, and the places she frequents. In this section, I'll run through some of the major Rice sites for you.

Extra! Extra!

There's more to New Orleans' literary world than Anne Rice vampire novels, of course. For a riotously funny take on the city, pick up John Kennedy Toole's *A Confederacy of Dunces;* if you want an older perspective, try George Washington Cable's 1879 *Old Creole Days.* Other books set in and about the city include Walker Percy's *The Moviegoer,* Frances Parkinson Keyes's *Dinner at Antoine's,* and Shirley Ann Grau's *The Keepers of the House.* And then of course there's Tennessee Williams's classic play *A Streetcar Named Desire.* You remember: STELLA!!!!!!!

A Rice Primer

Anne Rice was born in New Orleans on October 4, 1941, and spent the formative years of her childhood there before moving to Texas at age 16 and then to California after marrying her husband, Stan. Her *Interview with the Vampire* was published in 1976, and a slew of other vampire works followed (as well as a series of steamy romance novels published under the pen names A. N. Roquelaure and Anne Rampling). In the 1980s, Rice apparently decided that sunny California just didn't square with her dark, romantic image, so she and her husband and son moved back to New Orleans.

Since that return, Rice has been slowly taking over the city—or so it sometimes seems. She's been buying up property, starting a tour company (more on that below), marketing her own brand of wine, and making her presence felt by, among other things, acting as a one-woman preservation league against certain developers who raise her dander. If you're a devotee, this is a good time to put on that dark eye makeup you packed and start skulking in the shadows. I promise I'll have you back before the sunrise...

French Quarter Rice Recipes

Asking if Anne Rice writes about the French Quarter is like asking if Tolstoy wrote about Russia. Are you kidding? The old section of town? All that romantic history? All those creole balls? All those ruffled shirts? It's vampire country for sure. Here are some prime Rice sites:

➤ **Boyer Antiques and Doll Shop** (241 Chartres St.) is the shop in the *Interview with the Vampire* movie where the young Claudia admires a doll and then deals with the patronizing shopkeeper in typical vampire fashion. (See listing in chapter 16.)

➤ **Hotel Monteleone** (214 Royal St.) was Aaron Lightner's house in the vampire chronicles.

➤ **Omni Royal Orleans Hotel** (621 St. Louis St.) was where Katheryn and Julien Mayfair stayed in *The Witching Hour.*

➤ **Jackson Square** is where Claudia ponders Lestat's fate in *Interview* and also where Raglan James meets Lestat in *The Tale of the Body Thief.*

➤ In the *Interview* movie, **Madame John's Legacy** (632 Dumaine St.) is the house from which the caskets are being carried as Brad Pitt describes Lestat and Claudia going out on the town: "Together, they finished off whole families."

➤ Quite a few of the *Interview* movie's exterior shots were filmed along the **700–900 section of Royal St.** Imagine it covered with mud, and you may be able to picture the way it looked after the set decorators got done with it.

➤ **Café du Monde** (800 Decatur St.) is apparently as popular with vampires as it is with everybody else: Lestat visits here in *The Tale of the Body Thief,* and Michael and Rowan dine here in *The Witching Hour.*

➤ The **Gallier House Museum** (1132 Royal St.; see chapter 14) is said by Rice scholars to be the model for the vampire Lestat's house on Rue Royal in *Interview.*

➤ A few blocks north of the French Quarter at the intersection of Esplanade and Claiborne avenues, the **Marsoudet-Caruso House** (1519 Esplanade Ave.) is where Louis finds Lestat hiding at the end of the *Interview* movie.

➤ South of the French Quarter along the Mississippi, the **Jackson Barracks** area was used for numerous exterior shots in the *Interview* movie, including the scene where Louis and Claudia run for their ship after setting Lestat on fire.

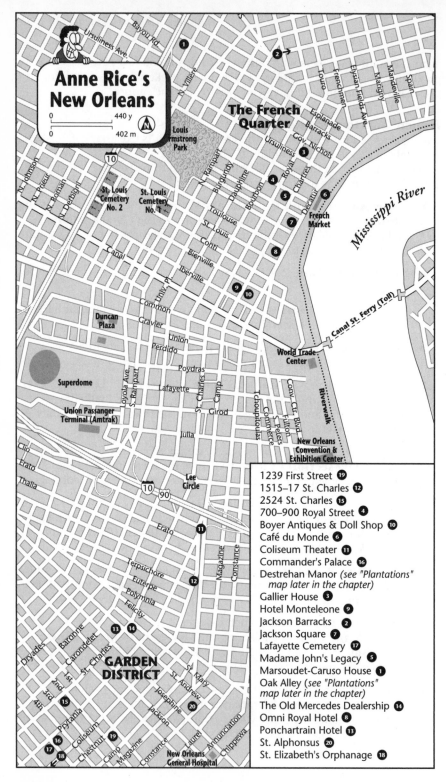

Anne Rice's New Orleans

0 — 440 y
0 — 402 m

The French Quarter

Bayou Rd
Ursulines Ave.
N. Villere
❶
❷→
Touro
Frenchmen
Elysian Fields Ave.
Mandeville
Margny
Spain

Louis Armstrong Park
Esplanade
Barracks
Gov. Nichols
Ursulines
Rampart
Burgundy
Dauphine
Bourbon
Royal
Chartres
Decatur
❸
❹
❺
❻
French Market

St. Louis Cemetery No. 2
St. Louis Cemetery No. 1
Toulouse
St. Louis
Conti
Bienville
Iberville
N. Johnson
N. Prieur
N. Roman
N. Derbigny

Mississippi River

Canal
Univ. Pl.
Common
Gravier
Union
Perdido
❽
❾ ❿

Duncan Plaza

Canal St. Ferry (Toll)

World Trade Center

Superdome
Loyola Ave.
S. Rampart
Poydras
Lafayette
St. Charles
Camp
Tchoupitoulas
Conv. Ctr. Blvd.
Fulton
Commerce
S. Peters
Girod
Union Passanger Terminal (Amtrak)
Julia
Riverwalk

Clio
Erato
Thalia
Lee Circle
10
90

New Orleans Convention & Exhibition Center

Erato
❶❶
Terpsichore
Euterpe
Polymnia
Felicity
Magazine
Constance
❶❷

Dryades
Baronne
Carondelet
St. Charles
❶❸ ❶❹
GARDEN DISTRICT
St. Mary
St. Andrew
Josephine
Jackson
❷⓿
Annunciation
Chippewa
Laurel
3rd
4th
❶❺
Prytania
Coliseum
Chestnut
Camp
Magazine
Constance
❶❾
❶❻
❶❼ ❶❽
New Orleans General Hospital

1239 First Street ❶❾
1515–17 St. Charles ❶❷
2524 St. Charles ❶❺
700–900 Royal Street ❹
Boyer Antiques & Doll Shop ❿
Café du Monde ❻
Coliseum Theater ❶❶
Commander's Palace ❶❻
Destrehan Manor *(see "Plantations" map later in the chapter)*
Gallier House ❸
Hotel Monteleone ❾
Jackson Barracks ❷
Jackson Square ❼
Lafayette Cemetery ❶❼
Madame John's Legacy ❺
Marsoudet-Caruso House ❶
Oak Alley *(see "Plantations" map later in the chapter)*
The Old Mercedes Dealership ❶❹
Omni Royal Hotel ❽
Ponchartrain Hotel ❶❸
St. Alphonsus ❷⓿
St. Elizabeth's Orphanage ❶❽

Bet You Didn't Know

Anne Rice: author, gothic romance icon, and now wine merchant? It looks that way. In the last couple of years, Rice has teamed up with California wine-maker Bryan Babcock to produce Cuvée Lestat, her own blood-red vino. Their first effort was Cuvée Lestat Syrah, followed by a chardonnay and then a claret. Each $35 bottle comes looking appropriately dark and scary, with a painting by Rice's husband adorning the label. If you're curious, you can order all three from **Babcock Vineyards** at ☎ **805/736-1455,** fax 805/736-3886. (More info is available on Rice's Web page, **www.annerice.com.**)

Honey, There's a Vampire in the Garden

Garden *District,* that is. Rice and her husband own a number of properties here, and both these and other neighborhood landmarks figure prominently in her books, as well as in the *Interview* movie.

➤ **Lafayette Cemetery** is the appropriately creepy roaming ground for Lestat and Claudia in *Interview* and is the Mayfairs' graveyard in *The Witching Hour.* **Commander's Palace,** across the street, was a favorite of the Mayfair family.

➤ The impressive **St. Elizabeth's Orphanage** (1314 Napoleon Ave.) was built in 1865, served as an orphanage and boarding school until 1989, and was bought by the Rice family in the early 1990s as a residence. It houses Anne's doll collection, a chapel, and a gallery of Stan's paintings.

➤ The Greek Revival cottage at **2524 St. Charles Ave.** was Rice's childhood home and is featured in her novel *Violin.*

➤ The historic property at **1239 First St.** is Anne Rice's primary residence. Don't knock on the door—that would be rude.

➤ The vampire Lestat saw his reflection in the window of **The Old Mercedes Dealership** (2001 St. Charles Ave.) and disappeared from the world. Now the place is a post-modern restaurant—**Al Copeland's Straya**—and Rice is *mad.* The battle over appropriate use of the site was played out in full-page ads in the local newspaper.

➤ Readers will know the small **St. Alphonsus Church** (2029 Constance St.) as a setting in *The Witching Hour,* but it was also Anne's family's church when they lived in New Orleans—her parents married here, and she was baptized and received communion here. Now she owns the place and used it to kick off a book-signing tour in 1996.

➤ In the film version of *Interview,* the **Coliseum Theater** at 1233 Coliseum St. is where Louis sees *Tequila Sunrise.*

➤ Care to have a *bite* at the **Cafe Lestat?** You might soon be able to. In 1997, Rice purchased the old Happy Hour movie theater on Magazine Street (at St. Andrew). The site appears briefly in *The Vampire Lestat,* but Rice intends to integrate it more fully into her world by opening the long-rumored **Cafe Lestat** there. No news on when it'll be unveiled. Stay tuned...

Rice Plantations

Dripping Spanish moss, creeping humidity, white-pillared mansions—where else would a vampire go for a weekend in the country? Both **Destrehan Manor** and **Oak Alley Plantation,** 30 to 45 minutes upriver from New Orleans along the Mississippi, were used as locations in the *Interview with the Vampire* movie. Some Rice readers think Oak Alley was the model for Pointe du Lac in the book; others believe that Pointe was based on the **Pitot House.** (See listings elsewhere in this chapter for travel info to the plantations; see listing in chapter 14 for the Pitot House.)

Touring with the Vampire

➤ **Anne Rice's New Orleans Tours** (☎ 888/SEE-RICE or 504/ 592-0560; Web site **www.annerice.com**) offers guided tours featuring sites and attractions around the city that relate to her life and/or her work.

➤ **Anne Rice's French Quarter Tour** begins in the lush courtyard of the New Orleans Pharmacy Museum, then visits Maspero's Slave Exchange, Pirates' Alley, Jackson Square, St. Louis Cathedral, the Ursuline Convent, and Gallatin Street—the infamous Port of Missing Men. The tour concludes at Gallier House, of which tours are available at a discounted price. The two-hour tours run Tuesday through Saturday at 10am and Sunday at 2pm and cost $20 for adults and $12 for children 6 to 12.

➤ **Anne Rice's Garden District Tour** visits her childhood home on St. Charles, the grounds of her current home on First St., and Lafayette Cemetery. Tours leave at 10am and 1:30pm and cost $20 for adults and $12 for children 6 to 12.

➤ **Inside the World of Anne Rice** is a five-hour bus tour of the St. Charles home, St. Alphonsus and St. Mary's churches, Lafayette Cemetery, St. Elizabeth's Orphanage, and the First Street home and includes lunch at Commander's Palace. Tours run Wednesday and Friday at 10am and cost $80 for adults and $42 for children 6 to 12.

➤ **Anne's Lost New Orleans** is a three-hour bus tour that visits Destrehan Manor and Pitot House. Tours run Thursday and Saturday, with hotel pickup starting at 1pm. The cost is $45 for adults and $25 for children 6 to 12.

210

➤ Private tours of Rice's **St. Elizabeth's Orphanage,** with its doll collection and gallery of Stan Rice oil paintings, are available Monday through Saturday by special arrangement for $15 per person. Call ☎ **504/899-6450.**

If You're Searching for Cajun Country

New Orleans itself is not considered Cajun country. You'll have to make the three-hour journey from the city to Lafayette to experience some true Cajun culture. Lafayette (167 miles west of New Orleans) is a straight shot from New Orleans on Interstate 10 west. The **Lafayette Parish Convention and Visitor's Commission Center** (☎ **800/346-1958**) offers a wealth of information on what's doing in Lafayette.

The Cajuns are descendants of French colonists (Acadians) from Nova Scotia, who settled in this area in the 18th century. The swampy land they found was low-lying and boggy with a few bayous and lakes mixed in. (What's a bayou? It's something less than a river, but more than a creek, with little or no current.) A visit to Lafayette will introduce you to the culture—the food, music, and lifestyle—that developed over the past 300 years as the relatively isolated Acadians adapted to their surroundings.

Passing a Good Time: What to Do in Cajun Country

Acadian Village

Acadian Village is a reconstructed Cajun bayou community. There's a footpath you can use to explore the banks of the bayou and the houses that have been set up alongside it. Take a peek inside for a glimpse of Cajun furniture. The gift shop sells Cajun handicrafts and books.

To get there, take I-10 to Exit 97. Go south on La. 93 to Ridge Rd., then take a right followed by a left on West Broussard. ☎ ***800/962-9133** or 318/981-2364. Open daily 10am–5pm. Admission is $6.00 adults; $5.00 seniors; $2.50 children 6–14; under 6 free.*

Vermilionville

On the banks of Bayou Vermilion, sits the village Vermilionville, which re-creates Cajun life as it existed in the 18th and 19th centuries. Costumed staff give demonstrations and craftspeople ply their crafts. Shows feature Cajun music, dancing, and stories. The restaurant serves authentic Cajun grub.

To get here, take I-10 to Exit 103A. Get on the Evangeline Thruway going south and keep going until you get to Surrey St., and then follow the signs. ☎ ***800/ 99-BAYOU** or 318/233-4077. Admission is $8 adults; $6.50 seniors; $5 students; children under 6 free. Closed New Year's and Christmas Day.*

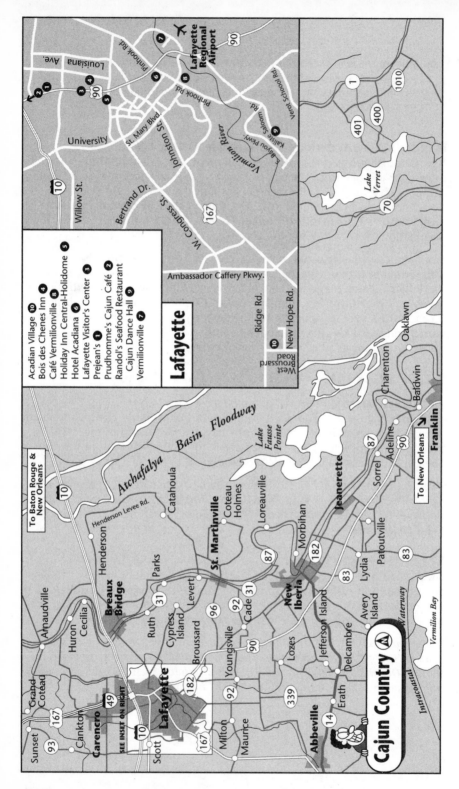

Lafayette

Acadian Village **10**
Bois des Chenes Inn **4**
Café Vermilionville **8**
Holiday Inn Central-Holidome **5**
Hotel Acadiana **6**
Lafayette Visitor's Center **3**
Prejean's **1**
Prudhomme's Cajun Café **2**
Randol's Seafood Restaurant
  Cajun Dance Hall **9**
Vermilionville **7**

Cajun Country

Eating a Good Time: Cajun Cooking

Café Vermilionville $$$

Café Vermilionville serves the best of Louisiana French and Cajun cuisines; you'll find lots of fresh seafood on the menu here. Specialties include salmon au poivre and Louisiana crawfish madness, which is crawfish tails prepared according to the mood of the chef: au gratin, étoufée, crawfish beginet, and fried.

1304 Pinhook Rd. ☎ 318/237-0100. Reservations recommended. Main courses are $18–$35. AE, DC, DISC, MC, V. Mon–Fri lunch and dinner, Sat dinner.

Prejean's $$

Prejean's is the place for nouvelle Cajun cooking. Specialties include boiled crawfish, shrimp, oysters, gumbo, alligator, and steaks. There's live Cajun music at 7pm.

3480 U.S. 167 North. To get here, go on I-49 to U.S. 167 North. Follow the signs— it's next to the Evangeline Downs Racetrack. ☎ 318/896-3247. Main courses $12–$21; children's menu $2–$6. AE, CB, DC, DISC, MC, V. Lunch and dinner daily.

Prudhomme's Cajun Café $$

In an authentic Acadian country home, Enola Prudhomme and her whole family work together preparing Cajun dishes, using the freshest ingredients around. Blackened tuna and eggplant pirogue (eggplant filled with seafood) are just two of her specialties.

4676 NE Evangeline Thruway, near Carencro. To get here, take Exit 103B off I-10. Go north on I-49 to Exit 7 (3 miles past racetrack). The restaurant is located on the right side of Frontage Rd. ☎ 318/896-7964. Main courses are $7–$17. AE, DISC, MC, V. Mon–Sat lunch and dinner.

Randol's Seafood Restaurant Cajun Dance Hall $$

How about a little Cajun music with your seafood? Randol's specializes in both. Between dance numbers, you can enjoy seafood fresh from the bayou—fried, steamed, blackened, or grilled. The house specialty is a seafood platter, which includes a cup of seafood gumbo, fried shrimp, fried oysters, fried catfish, stuffed crab, crawfish étouffée, warm French bread, and coleslaw.

2320 Kaliste Saloom Rd. To get there, take I-10 from New Orleans to the Evangeline Thruway (Exit 103A), and then follow the Thruway to Pinhook Rd. Turn right onto Pinhook and follow it to Kaliste Saloom Rd. (right). Randol's will be on your right. ☎ 800/962-2586 or 318/981-7080. Main courses are $8–$16. MC, V. Dinner daily, no lunch served on weekends.

213

Sleeping a Good Time: Lafayette Accommodations

$$. Bois des Chenes Inn

This plantation home-turned-hotel was once the center of a 3,000-acre cattle and sugar plantation. There are only five suites, but each has been lovingly restored and furnished with Louisiana French antiques. The rates include a Louisiana-style breakfast, a bottle of wine, and a tour of the house. The owner, a retired geologist, conducts nature and birding trips into Atchafalya Swamp, as well as guided fishing and hunting trips.

338 N. Sterling, Lafayette, LA 70501. ☎ *318/233-7816.* **Rack rates:** *$100–$130 double. Extra person $20–$30. Rates include breakfast. AE, MC, V. Free parking.*

$$. Holiday Inn Central-Holidome

This place features everything you'd expect from a Holiday Inn and more—superior guest rooms, lounge, coffee shop, indoor pool, whirlpool, sauna, game room, tennis courts, jogging track, a playground, and a gift shop.

2032 NE Evangeline Thruway, Lafayette, LA 70509. ☎ *800/942-4868 or 318/233-6815.* **Rack rates:** *$79 double. AE, CB, DC, DISC.*

$$. Hotel Acadiana

Close to all the sights of Lafayette, the Hotel Acadiana offers great value for your money and all the conveniences you'd expect to find in a large chain hotel. The hotel's restaurant, Bayou Bistro, serves great Cajun food. A complimentary airport shuttle is also provided.

1801 W. Pinhook Rd., Lafayette, LA 70508. To get there, take I-10 West from New Orleans to Exit 103A. Follow the Evangeline Thruway to Pinhook Rd. Go right onto Pinhook, follow Pinhook across the bridge, and you'll see the hotel on your left. ☎ *800/874-4664 or 318/233-8120.* **Rack rates:** *$85 double. AE, DC, DISC, MC, V.*

If You Give a Damn About Plantations

From the 1820s to the beginning of the Civil War, plantation homes flourished in Louisiana. The plantation home was the focal point of a self-sustaining community and generally was located near the riverfront. Today, a few plantations remain within a short distance of New Orleans. Here are a few worth visiting.

Destrehan Manor

The oldest plantation open to the public in the Lower Mississippi Valley, Destrehan Manor, was built in 1787 by a free person of color. Some of the largest live oaks in the country grow here. The restoration of this home, which was sponsored by the American Oil Company, recovered some of the earliest methods of construction. There are guided tours every 20 minutes.

La. 48, Destrehan, LA. To get there, take I-10 west to Exit 220 (I-310 South), stay on I-310 for about 6 miles, exit onto River Rd., turn left at the light. ☎ *504/764-9315. Admission $7 adults; $4 teenagers; $2 children 6–12. Open daily 9am–4pm.*

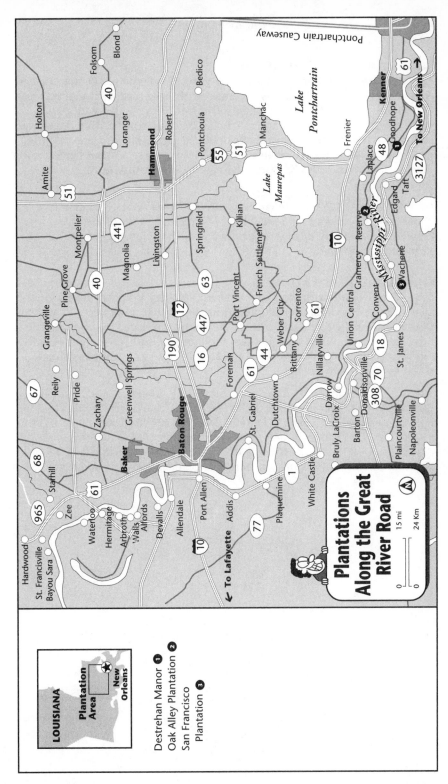

Plantations Along the Great River Road

15 mi
24 Km

Destrehan Manor ❶
Oak Alley Plantation ❷
San Francisco Plantation ❸

LOUISIANA

Plantation Area

New Orleans

215

San Francisco Plantation

An antebellum plantation only by a few years, San Francisco Plantation was completed in 1856. The owners decorated with little regard for money, and their house thus gained the nickname *sans fruscin* (without a cent). The name was later changed to San Francisco. The three-story Gothic house has broad galleries that resemble a ship's double decks and twin stairs that lead to a broad main portal much like one that leads to a steamboat's grand salon. The restoration includes English and French 18th-century furniture and paintings.

La. 44, Reserve, LA 70084. To get there, take I-10 West to U.S. 51 (23 miles). Turn south and continue for 3 miles to ST44, and then go west for 5 miles. ☎ *504/535-2341. Admission $7 adults; $4 children 12–17, $3 children 6–11. Open daily 10am–4pm.*

Oak Alley Plantation

Sixty miles from downtown New Orleans, Oak Alley is known for its long alley of live oaks. Today, a non-profit foundation acts as owner, and authentically costumed guides lead tours of the lovingly restored mansion, which is furnished with a mix of antiques and modern furniture. Overnight accommodations are available at rates of $85 to $115, and an on-site restaurant serves breakfast and lunch.

3645 La. 18, Vacherie, LA. To get there, take I-10 West about 15 miles to I-310. Follow I-310 South for 7 miles to ST18. From ST18, go west for 10 miles to LA3141 Southwest for 1 mile to LA3127. Stay on 3127 Northwest for 15 miles to ST20. Take ST20 Northeast for 3 miles to Vacherie and follow the signs to the plantation. ☎ *800/44-ALLEY or 504/265-2151. Admission $8 adults; $5 students; $3 children 6–12. Mar–Oct, daily 9am–5:30pm; Nov–Feb, daily 9am–5pm.*

Chapter 16

Charge It!
A Shopper's
Guide to
New Orleans

In This Chapter

➤ The lowdown on the major shopping areas

➤ Where to go to find what you want

➤ Where to go when you don't know what you want

➤ Where to find some bargains

➤ When to go

People go a little wacky with the credit cards when they're on vacation. Maybe it's something to do with being away from the responsibilities of house and home; maybe it's something to do with unfamiliar elevations affecting the amount of oxygen that gets to their brains. Whatever the reason, the results are the same: Vacationers shop with a vengeance, determined to get the ultimate momento of their trip, to find items unknown in their local shops, and, sometimes implausibly, to find the same old stuff they can find at home, but at insanely lower prices.

As an international port, New Orleans has access to more imported items than many other American cities, so you can find home furnishings, pottery, kitchen utensils, designer clothes, and whatever else you can name from just about whatever *place* you can name. There's also a glut of fine jewelry here. Much of it is imported, but many places in the city sell locally crafted goods; some of the jewelry shops will seem more like art galleries.

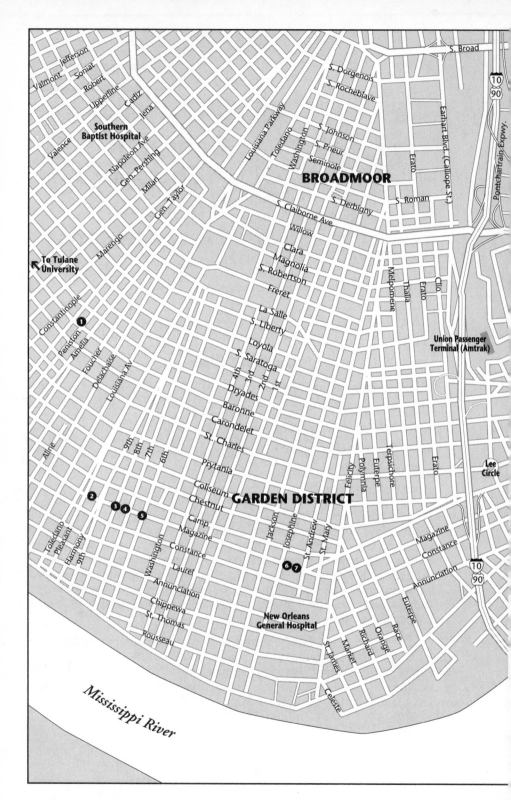

Jefferson
Valmont
Soniat
Robert
Upperline
Cadiz
Jena
Valence

Southern
Baptist Hospital

Napoleon Ave
Gen. Pershing
Milan
Gen. Taylor

Marengo

To Tulane
University

Constantinople
Peniston
Amelia
Foucher
Delachaise
Louisiana Av

Aline

9th
8th
7th
6th

Toledano
Pleasant
Harmony
9th

Washington
Laurel
Annunciation
Chippewa
St. Thomas
Rousseau

Camp
Magazine
Constance

Prytania
Coliseum
Chestnut

GARDEN DISTRICT

St. Charles
Carondelet
Baronne
Dryades
4th
3rd
2nd
1st
S. Saratoga
Loyola
S. Liberty
La Salle
Freret
S. Robertson
Magnolia
Clara
Willow

S. Claiborne Ave

S. Derbigny

BROADMOOR

S. Roman

Seminole
S. Prieur
S. Johnson
Washington
Toledano
Louisiana Parkway
S. Rocheblave
S. Dorgenois

S. Broad

Earhart Blvd. (Calliope St.)

Pontchartrain Expwy.

Erato

Clio
Erato
Thalia
Melpomene

Union Passenger
Terminal (Amtrak)

Lee
Circle

Tchoupitoulas
Euterpe
Polymnia
Felicity

Jackson
Josephine
St. Andrew
St. Mary

Magazine
Constance

Annunciation

New Orleans
General Hospital

St. James
Market
Richard
Orange
Race
Euterpe

Celeste

Magazine

Erato

Mississippi River

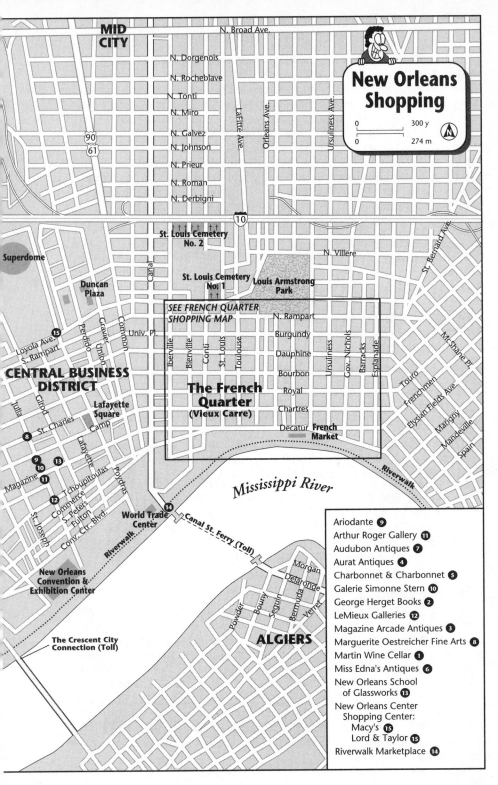

New Orleans Shopping

0 ─────────── 300 y
0 ─────────── 274 m

MID CITY

N. Broad Ave.

N. Dorgenois
N. Rocheblave
N. Tonti
N. Miro
N. Galvez
N. Johnson
N. Prieur
N. Roman
N. Derbigni

LaFitte Ave.
Orleans Ave.
Ursulines Ave.

90
61

St. Louis Cemetery No. 2

Superdome

Duncan Plaza

St. Louis Cemetery No. 1

Louis Armstrong Park

N. Villere

St. Bernard Ave.

SEE FRENCH QUARTER SHOPPING MAP

N. Rampart
Burgundy
Dauphine
Bourbon
Royal
Chartres
Decatur

Univ. Pl.

Loyola Ave.
S. Rampart
Perdido
Gravier
Union
Common

CENTRAL BUSINESS DISTRICT

Iberville
Bienville
Conti
St. Louis
Toulouse

Ursulines
Gov. Nichols
Barracks
Esplanade

McShane Pl.

Julia
Girod
St. Charles
Lafayette Square
Camp
Lafayette

The French Quarter (Vieux Carre)

French Market

Touro
Frenchmen
Elysian Fields Ave.
Marigny
Mandeville
Spain

St. Charles

Magazine
Tchoupitoulas
Commerce
S. Peters
Fulton
St. Joseph
Poydras
Conv. Ctr. Blvd.

Riverwalk

Mississippi River

World Trade Center

Canal St. Ferry (Toll)

New Orleans Convention & Exhibition Center

Morgan
Delaronde
Powder
Boury
Seguin
Bermuda
Verret

The Crescent City Connection (Toll)

ALGIERS

Ariodante **9**
Arthur Roger Gallery **11**
Audubon Antiques **7**
Aurat Antiques **4**
Charbonnet & Charbonnet **5**
Galerie Simonne Stern **10**
George Herget Books **2**
LeMieux Galleries **12**
Magazine Arcade Antiques **3**
Marguerite Oestreicher Fine Arts **8**
Martin Wine Cellar **1**
Miss Edna's Antiques **6**
New Orleans School of Glassworks **13**
New Orleans Center Shopping Center:
  Macy's **15**
  Lord & Taylor **15**
Riverwalk Marketplace **14**

219

Speaking of art galleries (and the like), you'll have no trouble finding antiques and contemporary art in town. New Orleans has always been a place for fine homes and fine furnishings, and as people trade up to the next level, they leave some great antiques for the rest of us. Much of the stuff you'll find in New Orleans came from Europe in the early days; other items were crafted right in the city by internationally known cabinetmakers. Antiquing has become so popular in New Orleans that there are even people who will take you on a personalized guided tour of city shops (see the sidebar titled "Antiquing Tours" later in the chapter). In addition, the **Royal Street Guild (☎ 504/524-1260)**, an association of some of the city's antique dealers, has put together brochures that are available at most hotels.

With or without a brochure, you can easily guide yourself through the world of New Orleans' antique shops just by keeping in mind that Royal Street and Magazine Street are the places to be. As you'll see in the listings in this chapter, these streets are the two strips for antique shops. Generally, the finest, most expensive goods are on Royal Street; any bargain basement prices are probably on Magazine Street. The city's art galleries are clustered in the same areas as the antiques and on Julia Street as well. Over the past 20 years, New Orleans has grown to be an important regional and national market for contemporary fine arts.

In general, just keep these two things in mind:

1. The major shopping areas you'll want to visit in town are the French Quarter, Central Business District, Warehouse District, and along Magazine Street, both in the Garden District and the Uptown areas.

2. Even though I'm going to give you a selection of good shops to start you on your way, the best way to shop in any of these areas is just to meander through and see what you can find.

The hours for most shops are Monday through Saturday from 10am to 5pm. Many shops, however, are open later on Saturday night and Sunday afternoon, especially in the French Quarter, where souvenir shops are likely to remain open until 11pm every day of the week. If you plan to visit a shop at any odd hours, call ahead to make sure the place is open.

The Big Names

As I've said elsewhere in this book, New Orleans is pretty much an island and, because of its unique location, was a fairly insular community for most of its life, nurturing an entirely home-grown crop of big-name stores. During the last half-century, though, it has pretty much joined the rest of mainstream America, and that's unfortunately meant that its stores were eaten alive by the giants. **Maison Blanche,** 901 Canal St. (☎ 504/566-1000), is one of the few local big names still operating, a classic department store with housewares, personal items, clothing, and much more. Once this store took up several floors of its building while the rest was used as office space. Today, it plans to remain open with only one floor; the rest of the building will be converted to a hotel.

220

All local resentment aside, here are the mighty giants:

➤ **Macy's.** New Orleans Centre Shopping Center at 1400 Poydras (☎ **800/743-6229**). Located near the Superdome, this is a place almost everyone is familiar with. They're a department store that sells everything you'd need in clothing, housewares, and personal items, and they stock a good selection of upscale items.

➤ **Lord and Taylor.** New Orleans Centre Shopping Center at 1400 Poydras (☎ **504/581-5673**). This is a great place to go for men's and women's clothing.

➤ **Brooks Brothers.** Canal Place Shopping Center in the 300 block of Canal Street (☎ **504/522-4200**). This is the place your banker grandfather probably bought his shirts (and the place your banker cousin probably still does). They're famous for their suits, shirts, and other men's (and women's) clothing.

➤ **Saks Fifth Avenue.** Canal Place Shopping Center in the 300 block of Canal Street (☎ **504/524-2200**). Saks has a national reputation for offering high-quality fashion, shoes, and accessories for men and women. It carries the work of such designers as Hermès, Chanel, Ferragamo, and Gucci and also offers a personalized shopping service, the Fifth Avenue Club.

➤ **Gucci.** Canal Place Shopping Center in the 300 block of Canal Street (☎ **504/524-5544**). Fancy yourself a regular Marcello Mastroianni, do you? Then head for this famous Italian store, where you'll find all the shoes, leather goods, and other Italian-design items you could want.

Dollars & Sense

If you're just looking for some souvenirs to take home as proof of your trip, there are whole colonies of shops selling snow globes, sunglasses, posters, T-shirts, and the like in the French Quarter. Pick one—they're all about the same.

Prime Hunting Grounds

As I said, the best shopping strategy is to just head to a good shopping area and see what shops catch your eye. In the following section, I tell you what areas are best and give you a few suggestions about where to start your shopping binge.

Bourbon Street

Bourbon Street doesn't have any big stores, but it's *the* place to go for the dozen or so stupid plastic souvenir items you have to bring back for your friends and coworkers. Besides, how many chances do you get to window shop with a big ol' drink in your hand, while listening to some of the best music around blasting out of the bars? Take advantage of the opportunity.

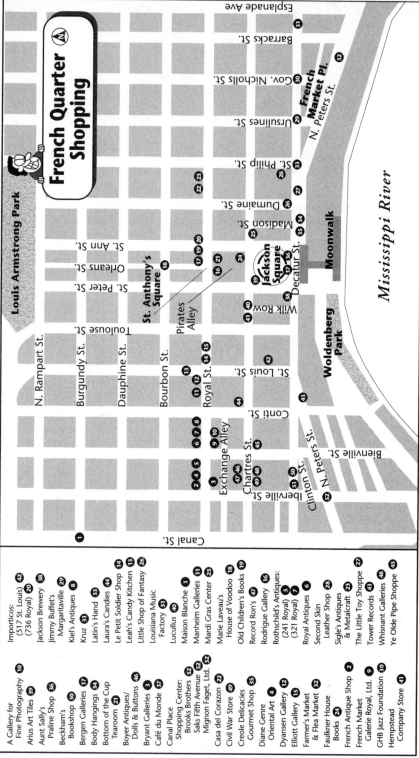

French Quarter Shopping

Louis Armstrong Park

St. Anthony's Square

Jackson Square

Pirates Alley

Wilk Row

Moonwalk

Woldenberg Park

Mississippi River

French Market Pl.

Esplanade Ave
Barracks St.
Gov. Nicholls St.
Ursulines St.
St. Philip St.
Dumaine St.
Madison St.
St. Ann St.
Orleans St.
St. Peter St.
Toulouse St.
N. Rampart St.
Burgundy St.
Dauphine St.
Bourbon St.
Royal St.
St. Louis St.
Conti St.
Exchange Alley
Chartres St.
Iberville St.
Clinton St.
Bienville St.
N. Peters St.
Decatur St.
N. Peters St.
Canal St.

A Gallery for
Fine Photography ⓾
Arius Art Tiles ㊴
Aunt Sally's
Praline Shop ㊱
Beckham's
Bookshop ㊿
Bergen Galleries ⓱
Body Hangings ㉞
Bottom of the Cup
Tearoom ㉑
Boyer Antiques/
Dolls & Buttons ㊺
Bryant Galleries ③
Café du Monde ㊲
Canal Place
Shopping Center:
Brooks Brothers ㊲
Saks Fifth Avenue ㊲
Mignon Faget, Ltd. ㊲
Casa del Corazon ㉒
Civil War Store ㊾
Creole Delicacies
Gourmet Shop ㉟
Diane Genre
Oriental Art ④
Dyansen Gallery ⓬
Elliott Gallery ⓯
Farmer's Market
& Flea Market ㉜
Faulkner House
Books ㉔
French Antique Shop ②
French Market
Galerie Royal, Ltd. ⑨
GHB Jazz Foundation ㉚
Hempstead
Company Store ㊶

Importicos:
(517 St. Louis) ㊷
(736 Royal) ⓴
Jackson Brewery ㊳
Jimmy Buffet's
Margaritaville ㉙
Kiel's Antiques ⑧
Kruz ㊶
Latin's Hand ㉝
Laura's Candies ㊸
Le Petit Soldier Shop ⓮
Leah's Candy Kitchen ⓭
Little Shop of Fantasy ㉖
Louisiana Music
Factory ㊼
Lucullus ㊵
Maison Blanche ①
Manheim Galleries ⓫
Mardi Gras Center ㉕
Marie Laveau's
House of Voodoo ⓲
Old Children's Books ⓳
Record Ron's ㊼
Rodrigue Gallery ⓰
Rothschild's Antiques:
(241 Royal) ⑤
(321 Royal) ⑦
Royal Antiques ⑥
Second Skin
Leather Shop ㉘
Sigle's Antiques
& Metalcraft ㉓
The Little Toy Shoppe ㉗
Tower Records ㊸
Whisnant Galleries ㊽
Ye Olde Pipe Shoppe ㊺

222

Dollars & Sense

The **sales tax** in New Orleans is 9%, so if you're buying anything big and expensive, it might pay to have it shipped to you at home. You'll pay handling charges instead of the sales tax, but the difference might still work out to a big savings.

If you're from outside the country, you can take advantage of **Louisiana Tax-Free Shopping,** whereby merchants who display this program's logo will give you a tax refund voucher that you can then cash in at the airport or by mail. A valid foreign passport and round-trip airline ticket is required to participate. Call ☎ **504/568-5323** for details.

Canal Place

Canal Street used to be the only place to shop in New Orleans, and people would dress up in their Sunday best to go there. As more people moved to the suburbs, though, the stores moved to the shopping malls, and today the Canal Street shopping scene is pretty much confined to the Canal Place Shopping Center, located at the foot of Canal Street (365 Canal St.), where it reaches the Mississippi River. The three-tiered mall has polished marble floors, a landscaped atrium, fountains, and pools and is home to more than 50 shops, many of which are branches of some of this country's most elegant retailers: Brooks Brothers, Bally of Switzerland, Saks Fifth Avenue, Gucci, Williams-Sonoma, and Jaeger. It's open Monday to Wednesday from 10am to 6pm; Friday and Saturday from 10am to 7pm; Thursday from 10am to 8pm; and Sunday from noon to 6pm.

The French Market

Shops within the Market (☎ **504/522-2621**) begin on Decatur Street across from Jackson Square and sell candy, cookware, fashions, crafts, toys, New Orleans memorabilia, and candles. **Café du Monde (☎ 504/525-4544)** is here, and the **Farmer's Market** and **Flea Market (☎ 504/596-3420)** are in the 1200 block of North Peters. **Jimmy Buffet's Margaritaville Souvenir Shop** is at 1100 Decatur (1 French Market Place actually; ☎ **504/ 529-4177**). The rest of the Market is a collection of souvenir shops, candy stores, places to buy Mardi Gras stuff, and small specialty shops. It's open from 10am to 6pm (Café du Monde is open 24 hours).

Jackson Brewery

Just across from Jackson Square at 600–620 Decatur St., the old Jax Brewery (☎ **504/566-7245**) has been transformed into a jumble of 125 shops, cafes, delicatessens, restaurants, and entertainment spots. You'll find fashions here, as well as gourmet and Cajun and Creole foodstuffs, toys, hats, crafts, pipes, posters, and souvenirs. The latest addition is a branch of the theme restaurant **Planet Hollywood** and its attached souvenir shop (☎ **504/522-7826**). Keep in mind that many shops in the Brewery close at 5:30 or 6pm, before the Brewery itself closes. The Brewery is open Sunday to Thursday from 10am to 9pm and Friday to Saturday from 10am to 10pm.

Julia Street

From Camp Street down to the river on Julia Street, you'll find many of the city's best contemporary art galleries lining the street (and some off to the sides). Of course, some of the works are a bit pricey, but there are good deals to be had if you're collecting and lots of fine art to be seen if you're not. Check out **Ariodante** (535 Julia St., ☎ **504/524-3233**) for hand-crafted furniture, glass, ceramics, jewelry, and decorative accessories; the **Arthur Roger Gallery** (432 Julia St., ☎ **504/522-1999**), the **Galerie Simonne Stern** (518 Julia St., ☎ **504/529-1118**), and **Marguerite Oestreicher Fine Arts** (626 Julia St., ☎ **504/581-9253**) for fine arts; and **LeMieux Galleries** (332 Julia St., ☎ **504/522-5988**) for contemporary art and fine crafts from Louisiana and the Gulf Coast.

Magazine Street

This major uptown thoroughfare runs from Canal Street to Audubon Park, with some six miles of more than 140 shops, some in 19th-century brick storefronts, others in quaint, cottage-like buildings. Because the overhead is not as high here as in other parts of the city, you can usually find a bargain or three. Just hop on the Magazine bus and explore. Among the offerings here are antiques, art galleries, boutiques, crafts, and dolls.

Antiquing Tours

If you've got some particular antique in mind, or if you just want a little guidance around the different shops, call **Let's Go Antiquing!** (1412 Fourth St., ☎ **504/899-3027**), a tour service founded by Macon Riddle in the mid-1980s. She'll organize and customize antique shopping tours to fit your needs, pick you up at your hotel, and even make your lunch reservations for you, if you want. If you find what you're looking for and you need to ship it home, she'll even take care of that. It's kind of like having a personal trainer for your antiquing habit.

For antiques, try **Aurat Antiques** (3009 Magazine St., ☎ **504/897-3210**) for Indo-Portuguese and Anglo-Indian colonial furniture as well as Oriental rugs; **Charbonnet & Charbonnet, Inc.** (2929 Magazine St., ☎ **504/891-9948**) for country pine; and **Miss Edna's Antiques** (2035 Magazine St., ☎ **504/524-1897**), **Audubon Antiques** (2025 Magazine St., ☎ **504/581-5704**), and **Magazine Arcade Antiques** (3017 Magazine St., ☎ **504/895-5451**) for a general selection.

For art galleries, try **Berta's and Mina's Antiquities** (4138 Magazine St., ☎ **504/895-6201**) for New Orleans– and Latin America–inspired folk art by Nilo Lanzas; **Casey Willems Pottery** (3919 Magazine St., ☎ **504/899-1174**) and **Shadyside Pottery** (3823 Magazine St., ☎ **504/897-1710**) for pottery made right there in the shops; **The Davis Galleries** (3964 Magazine St., ☎ **504/897-0780**) for Central and West African traditional art; and the **New Orleans School of Glassworks** (727 Magazine St., ☎ **504/529-7277**) for work made on-site by glasswork artists and master printmakers and to see the daily art demonstrations.

New Orleans Centre

New Orleans' newest shopping center, New Orleans Centre, at 1400 Poydras features a glass atrium and includes upscale shops such as Lord and Taylor and Macy's. There are three levels of specialty shops and restaurants. It's open Monday to Saturday from 10am to 8pm and Sunday from noon to 6pm.

Riverwalk Marketplace

This popular shopping development at 1 Poydras St. is an exciting covered mall that runs right along the river from Poydras Street to the Convention Center. In December of 1996, the market was big news around the world when it was struck by a grain freighter that went out of control; a number of shops were damaged, but there were no fatalities, and everything was back in place shortly afterward. Among the 140 specialty shops at this location, you'll find Eddie Bauer, The Limited, The Sharper Image, and Banana Republic, plus several places to eat and periodic free entertainment. It's open Monday to Thursday from 10am to 9pm, Friday and Saturday from 10am to 10pm, and Sunday from 12:30pm to 5:30pm.

Royal Street

Many fine art galleries, antique shops, jewelry shops, perfume shops, candy stores, and shops for coin and stamp collectors line Royal Street. **For antiques,** check out **Diane Genre Oriental Art and Antiques** (233 Royal St., ☎ **504/595-8945**) for East Asian porcelains, 18th-century Japanese woodblock prints, and Chinese and Japanese textiles, scrolls, screens, engravings, and lacquers; the **French Antique Shop** (225 Royal St., ☎ **504/524-9861**) for 18th- and 19th-century French furnishings, chandeliers, mirrors, statues, and marble mantels; **Kiel's Antiques** (325 Royal St., ☎ **504/522-4552**) and **Royal Antiques** (307–309 Royal St., ☎ **504/524-7033**) for 18th- and 19th-century French and English furnishings as well as chandeliers and other decorative items; **Manheim Galleries** (403–409 Royal St., ☎ **504/568-1901**) for Continental, English, and Oriental furnishings; **Rothschild's Antiques** (241 and 321 Royal St., ☎ **504/523-5816** or 504/523-2281) for antique and custom-made jewelry, antique silver, marble mantels, porcelains, and English and French furnishings; and **Sigle's Antiques & Metalcraft** (935 Royal St., ☎ **504/522-7647**), which specializes in the kind of lacy ironwork that drips from French Quarter balconies, some of it converted into household items (such as plant holders).

For art galleries, try the Bergen Galleries (730 Royal St., ☎ **800/ 621-6179** or 504/523-7882) for posters and prints; **Bryant Galleries** (524 Royal St., ☎ **504/525-5584**) for jazz bronzes, glasswork, and graphics; **Elliott Gallery** (540 Royal St., ☎ **504/523-3554**) and **Dyansen Gallery** (433 Royal St., ☎ **504/523-2902**) for contemporary art; and **A Gallery for Fine Photography** (322 Royal St., ☎ **504/568-1313**) for—guess what?—rare photographs and books from the 19th and 20th centuries.

In addition, two galleries specialize in the works of two celebrated Southern artists. At the **Galerie Royale, Ltd.** (312 Royal St., ☎ **504/523-1588**), you can see the works of William Tolliver, an African-American artist from Mississippi who came to painting relatively late in his life and without formal training, but has quickly become an internationally recognized contemporary impressionist painter. (He created the official poster for the 1996 Summer Olympics.) The **Rodrigue Gallery of New Orleans** (721 Royal St., ☎ **504/581-4244**), on the other hand, has gone to the dogs—the blue dogs, that is. Cajun artist George Rodrigue began painting blue portraits of his late dog (a terrier-mix) for a children's book in 1984, and he hasn't stopped since. His work is known internationally, and he's represented in galleries in Munich as well as Yokohama. It's worth a trip to Rodrigue's gallery to see what all the fuss is about.

Bet You Didn't Know

It's said that the symbol for the dollar ($) was first used in New Orleans long before the first U.S. Mint was established. The symbol was first used in a letter (dated September 12, 1778) by Oliver Pollock to George Rogers Clark. The symbol was an "S" superimposed over a "P" and was used to refer to the Spanish peso.

Where to Find That Thingie You Wanted: Specialty Shopping

Are you looking for that perfect mahogany highboy or has your sweet tooth got you thinking about pralines? For those of you who don't have time to browse and want to cut to the chase, this section on speciality shopping will lead you to the shop that carries whatever it may be that you came to New Orleans to buy.

Art & Antiques
In addition to the places listed previously under Magazine Street and Royal Street, check out these others—all, coincidentally, on Chartres Street:

➤ **Boyer Antiques/Dolls & Buttons.** 241 Chartres St. (☎ 504/522-4513). In addition to an assortment of antiques, you'll find a great collection of old dolls, doll houses and furniture, and toys from the 19th and early 20th centuries in this store. Also, Anne Rice fans take note: This doll store is featured in the movie version of *Interview with the Vampire.*

➤ **Civil War Store.** 212 Chartres St. (☎ 504/522-3328). This place stocks a selection of memorabilia from the war between the states.

➤ **Lucullus.** 610 Chartres St. (☎ 504/528-9620). An unusual shop, Lucullus has a great collection of culinary antiques as well as 17th-, 18th-, and 19th-century furnishings to "complement the grand pursuits of cooking, dining, and imbibing."

➤ **Whisnant Galleries.** 222 Chartres St. (☎ 504/524-9766). You'll find all sorts of unusual and unique antique collectibles here, including items from Ethiopia, Russia, Greece, South America, Morocco, and other parts of North Africa, and the Middle East.

Books
The many bookshops in New Orleans should please literary enthusiasts. Here are some of the best:

➤ ✪ **Faulkner House Books.** 624 Pirates Alley (☎ 504/524-2940). This shop is on a lot of walking tours of the French Quarter, because it's the place Nobel Prize–winner William Faulkner lived while he was writing his early works *Pylon* and *Soldiers' Pay.* Every bit of shelf space inside is occupied by books that are both highly collectible and highly literary, including a large collection of first-edition Faulkners and rare and first-edition classics by many other authors.

➤ **George Herget Books.** 3109 Magazine St. (☎ 504/891-5595). More than 20,000 rare and used books covering absolutely every subject are available for your browsing and collecting pleasure.

➤ **Old Children's Books.** 734 Royal St. (☎ 504/525-3655). You can find thousands of antique and rare children's books here, from the 19th century through the 1970s. The proprietor is a frequent traveler, so call before heading over. Otherwise, ring the buzzer to get in.

➤ **Beckham's Bookshop.** 228 Decatur St. (☎ 504/522-9875). Beckham's stocks old editions, rare secondhand books, and thousands of classical LPs.

Candies & Pralines

When the sweet tooth speaks, you must listen. (And of course, a box of pralines makes a fine gift for the folks back home.) Here's a few good places to get your fix:

➤ **Aunt Sally's Praline Shops.** 810 Decatur St. (☎ **800/642-7257** or 504/524-5107). You can watch the Creole pecan pralines being cooked here, so you'll know they're fresh. The large store also has a big selection of regional cookbooks; New Orleans history books; Creole and Cajun foods; folk and souvenir dolls; local memorabilia; and a selection of zydeco, Cajun, R&B, and jazz CDs and cassettes.

➤ **Laura's Candies.** 600 Conti St. (☎ **800/992-9699** or 504/525-3880). Established in 1913, Laura's is said to be New Orleans' oldest candy store. Seven varieties of pralines are on sale here, plus hand-dipped chocolates, rum-flavored pecans, and praline sauce.

➤ ✪ **Leah's Candy Kitchen.** 714 St. Louis St. (☎ **504/523-5662**). Leah's tops the list of New Orleans' Creole candy shops. Everything here, from the candy fillings to the chocolate-covered pecan brittle, is made fresh by second- and third-generation members of Leah Johnson's praline family.

Costumes & Masks

Costumery is big business in New Orleans, and not just during Carnival. Here's some of the best shops in the city for Mardi Gras and Halloween costumes and masks for any other occasion that demands them:

Dollars & Sense

New Orleanians often sell their **costumes** back to the costume shops after Ash Wednesday, and you can sometimes pick up an almost new outfit at a small fraction of its original cost.

➤ ✪ **Little Shop of Fantasy.** 523 Dumaine St. (☎ **504/529-4243**). This shop sells the work of local artists and more than 20 mask makers. Some of the creations are just fun and fanciful, but there are many fashionable ones, too.

➤ **Mardi Gras Center.** 831 Chartres St. (☎ **504/524-4384**). Mardi Gras Center carries sizes 2 to 50 and has a wide selection of new, ready-made costumes as well as used outfits. It also carries accessories such as beads, doubloons, wigs, masks, hats, makeup, jewelry, and Mardi Gras decorations.

➤ **Uptown Costume & Dance Company.** 5533 Magazine St. (☎ **504/895-7969**). The walls of this small store are covered with spooky monster masks, goofy arrow-through-the-head-type tricks, hats, wigs, makeup, and all other manner of playful stuff. It draws a good business year-round, but at Mardi Gras things really get cooking.

Food & Drink

For Creole and Cajun specialties to go (all the way home), check out these places:

➤ **Creole Delicacies Gourmet Shop.** 533 St. Ann St. (☎ 504/ 523-6425). Cajun and Creole packaged foods and mixes are what you'll find here. Fill your shopping basket with everything from jambalaya and gumbo mix to remoulade and hot sauces. (There is a second branch at the Riverwalk Marketplace, too.)

➤ **Martin Wine Cellar.** 3827 Baronne St. (☎ 504/899-7411). The Wine Cellar carries an eye-popping selection of wines, spirits, and champagnes at prices that are surprisingly reasonable and also stocks preserves, coffees, teas, crackers, biscotti, cookies, and cheeses.

➤ **Orleans Coffee Exchange.** 712 Orleans Ave. (☎ 504/522-5710). Java junkies will burst their beans over this place, which stocks 500 varieties of coffee beans from all over the world, plus more than 350 flavored coffees and scores of exotic teas.

Jewelry & Gifts

You know your cousin Bob or your friend Cindy expects a gift from you when you get home, and if you plan to be more generous than a Bourbon Street baseball cap, here's a few interesting options:

➤ **Hempstead Company Store.** 607 Chartres St. (☎ 504/529-HEMP). The operative word here is "hemp," which is what everything the store sells is made from—even the soap (from hemp oil). Because hemp growing is problematic in the United States, the raw materials here come from China and Hungary. The store hours are a bit loose around the edges, so you might want to call before visiting.

➤ **Importicos.** 736 Royal St. (☎ 504/523-3100). This place carries a selection of hand-crafted silver jewelry; pottery; textiles; leather, wood, stone, and metal items; teak, mahogany, and wrought-iron furniture; and reproductions of 17th- and 18th-century mirrors. The goods come from Central America, Indonesia, and all over the world. There are branches of the store at 517 St. Louis St. (☎ 504/523-0306) and 5523 Magazine St. (☎ 504/891-6141).

➤ **Latin's Hand.** 1025 N. Peters St. (☎ 504/529-5254). You'll find goods here from Brazil, El Salvador, Guatemala, Bolivia, and Mexico, including hammocks, dresses, jackets, sandals, and leather goods.

> **Extra! Extra!**
>
> If you're looking for **jazz recordings,** don't forget to check out the selection while you're touring the jazz collection at the **Old U.S. Mint.** Also look for the **GHB Jazz Foundation** outlet (☎ 504/525-1776) at the French Market.

➤ **Mignon Faget Ltd.** Canal Place, Level One (☎ 504/524-2973). This is the place for pendants, bracelets, rings, earrings, shirt studs, and cufflinks by this noted New Orleans native designer. A second branch is located at 710 Dublin St. (☎ 504/865-7361), uptown in the Riverbend area.

Men's & Women's Fashions

Aside from the big-name stores I already talked about at the beginning of the chapter, check out these specialty shops:

➤ **Body Hangings.** 835 Decatur St. (☎ 504/524-9856). How many cities can boast that they have a caps and cloak store? New Orleans does, and when the Sherlock Holmes look comes back in style, it'll be right on the cutting edge of fashion. Cloaks are available for men and women in wool, cotton, corduroy, and velveteen, and you can get scarves to go with 'em.

➤ **Kruz.** 432 Barracks St. (☎ 504/524-7370). Kruz has a wide selection of ethnic fashions, with clothing and accessories from around the world.

➤ **Yvonne La Fleur–New Orleans.** 8131 Hampson St. in the Riverbend district (☎ 504/866-9666). This is the place for romantic silk dresses, evening gowns, lingerie, and sportswear, and it's all surprisingly affordable.

Music

You'll be a rare visitor if you don't want to bring some New Orleans music home with you. In addition to the giant **Tower Records** at 408 N. Peters (☎ 504/529-4411), there are a few other places around town you should check out:

➤ **Louisiana Music Factory.** 210 Decatur St. (☎ 504/586-1094). This popular music store carries a large selection of regional music, including Cajun, zydeco, R&B, jazz, blues, and gospel. It also sells books, posters, and T-shirts and is an occasional venue for live music.

➤ **Record Ron's.** 239 Chartres St. (☎ 504/522-2239). At Record Ron's, you'll find thousands of CDs, cassettes, 45s, and LPs covering classic rock, jazz, Cajun, zydeco, R&B, and blues. T-shirts, posters, sheet music, music memorabilia, and jewelry are also available.

Pipes & Tobacco

If you're a pipe-lover, stop into **Ye Olde Pipe Shoppe** at 306 Chartres St. (☎ 504/522-1484). This place is run by Mr. Edwin Jansen, grandson of the shop's founder, August (who opened the place in 1868 and at one time repaired Jefferson Davis's pipes). Jansen hand-makes briar pipes, repairs broken pipes, and sells tobacco and pipe accessories. While you're there, take a look at the collection of antique pipes put together by his father and grandfather.

If you're a longtime cigar aficionado or have been caught up in the mid-1990s cigar craze, stop in **Dos Jefes Uptown Cigar Shop** at 5700 Magazine St. (☎ **504/899-3030**) for a great selection of cigars and plenty of paraphernalia, including personal humidors. There's a smoking lounge on the premises, and the shop has recently opened a cigar bar at 5535 Tchoupitoulas (☎ **504/891-8500**), which is open in the evenings.

The Spooky Stuff

At the following stores, you can find voodoo dolls, mojos, crystals, and tarot cards—everything you need to conjure up your memories of New Orleans (or at least, the darker side of New Orleans) once you get home:

➤ **The Bottom of the Cup Tearoom.** 732 Royal St. (☎ **504/523-1204**). The Bottom of the Cup Tearoom has been open since 1929 and bills itself as the "oldest tearoom in the United States." In addition to having tea and getting your palm, your tarot, or tea leaves read; your crystals gazed into; and your astrological chart done, you can also purchase books, jewelry, crystal balls, tarot cards, crystals, and healing wands.

Extra! Extra!

At the **Second Skin Leather Shop** (521 St. Philip, ☎ **504/561-8167**) you'll find some very *unique* personal leather items (leave the kids at home).

➤ **Marie Laveau's House of Voodoo.** 739 Bourbon St. (☎ **888/ 4VOODOO** or 504/581-3751). A popular attraction in the French Quarter, this is also a good place to find a voodoo doll or mojo to take home to friends. You can also get a consultation with the resident psychic and palm reader.

➤ **Westgate—The Original Necrotorium.** 5219 Magazine St. (☎ **504/899-3077**). This store is headquarters for everything to do with death. For example, there's death jewelry and a selection of books on death and the undead.

Toys

For kids and for adults who are kids at heart, **Le Petit Soldier Shop,** 528 Royal St. (☎ **504/523-7741**), sells miniatures that depict soldiers from ancient Greece up to Desert Storm, made by local artists and often crafted to resemble major figures in military history, such as Eisenhower, Grant, Lee, Hitler, and Napoleon. There's also a large collection of medals and decorations.

If you're looking for some really beautiful dolls, look no further than **The Little Toy Shoppe** at 900 Decatur St. (☎ **504/522-6588**). This shop also stocks wooden toys from Germany, cuddly stuffed animals, tea sets, toy soldiers, and miniature cars and trucks.

Chapter 17

Battle Plans for Seeing the Sights: Six Great Itineraries

In This Chapter

➤ Six itineraries that will show you New Orleans' hot spots and cool strips

➤ Historical, hedonistic, and spooky highlights of the French Quarter

➤ What to look for while riding the St. Charles Streetcar

➤ Exploring City Park

Everybody needs somebody sometime, and if you're planning your trips around the city, I'd say you need me *now*. You want to organize yourself, so you don't go ping-ponging from the Garden District up to Metairie and then down to Algiers, instead of laying your trip out logically to save yourself some serious hoofing and a heck of a lot of time.

In this chapter, I'll give you six itineraries you can follow on your own with no need for a tour guide. I'll tell you where to go, what to look for, and how much time to budget for each stop and tip you off to some good places to eat and take breaks along the way. I'm not going to give you a lot of history about each place—you can get that in elsewhere in this book or along the way, with tours and literature available at a lot of the stops. Instead, I just want to help you plan your strategy, give you a feel for the area you're visiting, and then let you experience it on your own.

Itinerary #1: Down by the River

After breakfast at your hotel or somewhere in the vicinity, head for the
Presbytere in the center of the Quarter for a look at some New Orleans history before heading to the **Aquarium of the Americas** for a look at some
fish. After your visit, head over to the foot of Canal Street and take the free
ferry to Algiers, where you'll be met by a van that'll take you to **Blaine
Kern's Mardi Gras World.** When you return to the Quarter after your
trip, those of you with kids might opt to visit the nearby **Louisiana
Children's Museum;** those without might prefer a stroll through
Woldenberg Riverfront Park and a tour of the **Cabildo.** This itinerary
is good for any day of the week except Monday, when the Presbytere and the
Children's Museum are closed.

1. **The Presbytere.** Head for Jackson Square, where at 751 Chartres St.
   (at the corner of St. Ann), you'll find this branch of the Louisiana State
   Museum. Plan to arrive around opening time (9am) and remember that
   the museum is closed Mondays. A tour of the art and history exhibits
   should take about an hour. (See chapter 14.)

2. **Aquarium of the Americas.** When you leave the Presbytere, head
   down along the riverfront to the aquarium and its million-gallon display of sea life. You'll probably spend at least an hour or two just on
   the main displays, but if you want to stretch your visit a bit, you can
   take in one of the hourly shows in the IMAX theater. If you do, you'll
   probably be finishing up your visit around 1pm, which is when they
   feed the penguins, and if you stay for that, you'll probably have to skip
   stop 4 on this itinerary. (See chapter 14.)

   Lunch. So, did your visit with the fishes make you hungry for seafood
   or will you never eat your fishy brothers and sisters again? Whichever
   the answer, you'll probably be ready for lunch at about this point. A
   few good (and relatively inexpensive) bets right in the neighborhood
   are **Mother's** (401 Poydras at the intersection with Tchoupitoulas
   Street), **Café Maspero** (601 Decatur St. at the intersection with
   Toulouse Street), and **Ralph & Kacoo's** (519 Toulouse St. between
   Decatur and Chartres). Or you could just opt for a lucky dog from one
   of the street vendors. (See chapters 10 and 11.)

3. **Blaine Kern's Mardi Gras World.** After you've eaten, head directly
   to the foot of Canal Street and hop the free ferry across the river to
   Algiers. You'll be met there by a van that'll take you to Mardi Gras
   World. Allow about two hours to get here, take the tour, and get back
   to the Quarter. (See chapter 14.)

4a. **Louisiana Children's Museum.** If you're traveling with kids, head
   southward along the river after getting off the ferry, turn right onto
   Julia Street, and walk the four blocks to the children's museum at no.
   420. Allow about an hour for your visit and remember that the museum is closed Mondays except June through August. (See chapter 14.)

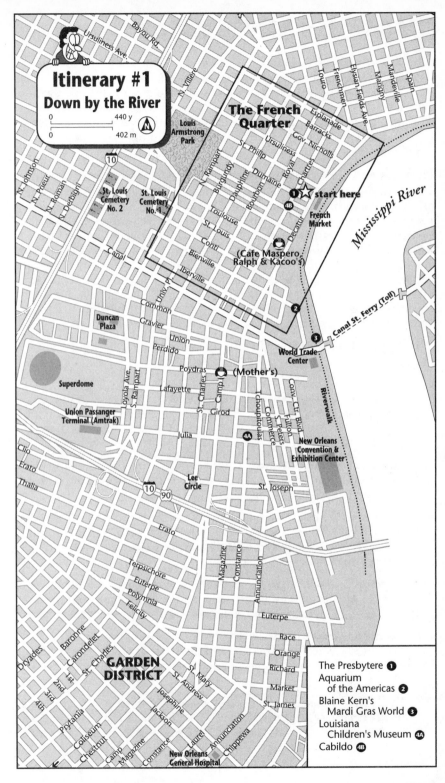

Itinerary #1
Down by the River

The French Quarter

Louis Armstrong Park

St. Louis Cemetery No. 2

St. Louis Cemetery No. 1

Louis Armstrong Park

☆ start here

French Market

(Café Maspero, Ralph & Kacoo's)

Mississippi River

Canal St. Ferry (Toll)

World Trade Center

Riverwalk

Duncan Plaza

Superdome

Union Passanger Terminal (Amtrak)

(Mother's)

New Orleans Convention & Exhibition Center

Lee Circle

GARDEN DISTRICT

New Orleans General Hospital

The Presbytere ❶
Aquarium
    of the Americas ❷
Blaine Kern's
    Mardi Gras World ❸
Louisiana
    Children's Museum ❹Ⓐ
Cabildo ❹Ⓑ

4b. **A walk to the Cabildo.** No kids along? Then you might consider taking a stroll (romantic or otherwise—it's up to you) through Woldenberg Riverfront Park on the way to a short tour of the historic Cabildo (701 Chartres St. at the corner of St. Ann on Jackson Square). Allow about one hour to see the place, but remember that it closes at 5pm and time the length of your walk there accordingly. (See chapter 14.)

Itinerary #2: French Quarter Time Machine Tour

This itinerary will cover many of the French Quarter's historical houses and give you an idea of how people lived way back when. In the morning, you'll visit the **Gallier House** museum, the **Old Ursuline Convent,** and the **Beauregard-Keyes House,** and afternoon will see you at the **Pontalba Apartments, St. Louis Cathedral, Historic New Orleans Collection,** and the **Original Old Absinthe House.** Take this tour any day but Sunday and Monday, when some of the attractions are closed. Note that none of the first sights on this tour opens earlier than 10am, so you can have a leisurely breakfast, either at your hotel or elsewhere in the Quarter, before making your way to Royal and Ursulines streets for stop number 1.

1. **Gallier House.** First stop on this itinerary is this 1857 home, where you'll get a feeling for mid-19th century New Orleans life. Allow one hour. (See chapter 14.)

2. **Old Ursuline Convent.** One block closer to the river (at 1114 Chartres St. at Ursulines) you'll find the oldest surviving building in the Mississippi Valley. Once the country's first girls' school, it now makes for a fascinating look back. Allow one hour. (See chapter 15.)

3. **Beauregard-Keyes House.** Right across the street at no. 1113 you'll find this historic home, where Frances Parkinson Keyes wrote *Dinner at Antoine's.* Allow about 45 minutes. (See chapter 14.)

   Lunch. You're right in the middle of the Quarter, so you've got about a zillion options, any one of which would be a good bet. The closest places? **G & E Courtyard Grill, Maximo's Italian Grill,** and the **Palm Court Cafe.** (See chapter 11.)

4. **Jackson Square.** Shake off that after-lunch lethargy and head over to Jackson Square. If you want to hang out for a while, rest, and watch the world go by, be my guest. I'll meet you at stop number 5.

5. **Pontalba Apartments.** Right on the east side of the square (at 523 St. Ann St.), you'll find these beautifully restored buildings with their period furniture and private courtyard. Allow about one hour. (See chapter 15.)

6. **St. Louis Cathedral.** The next stop is on the north side of the square, at 721 Chartres. The current church building dates from 1794 and features lovely stained glass windows. This stop is a short one: Allow 15 minutes. (See chapter 15.)

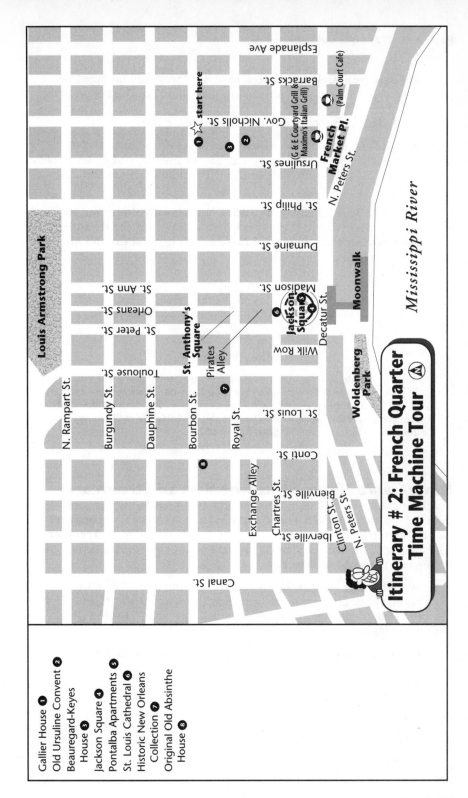

Itinerary # 2: French Quarter
Time Machine Tour

Mississippi River

Esplanade Ave

Barracks St.

(Palm Court Cafe)

Gov. Nicholls St.   start here

(G & E Courtyard Grill &
Maximo's Italian Grill)

Ursulines St.   French
Market Pl.

N. Peters St.

St. Philip St.

Dumaine St.

Madison St.

St. Ann St.

Orleans St.   Jackson
Square

St. Peter St.   Decatur St.

St. Anthony's
Square   Wilk Row

Pirates
Alley   Moonwalk

Toulouse St.

St. Louis St.

Bourbon St.

Royal St.

Conti St.

Exchange Alley

Bienville St.

Chartres St.

Iberville St.

Clinton St.

N. Peters St.

Canal St.

N. Rampart St.

Burgundy St.

Dauphine St.

Louis Armstrong Park

Woldenberg
Park

Gallier House ❶
Old Ursuline Convent ❷
Beauregard-Keyes
  House ❸
Jackson Square ❹
Pontalba Apartments ❺
St. Louis Cathedral ❻
Historic New Orleans
  Collection ❼
Original Old Absinthe
  House ❽

237

7. **Historic New Orleans Collection.** Head westward on Royal Street to no. 533, just past the intersection with Toulouse. The historical displays here will give you a nice wrap-up of the history you've been seeing all day. Allow about one hour. (See chapter 14.)

8. **Original Old Absinthe House.** Head over three blocks to 240 Bourbon St. Take in the atmosphere, sip an anisette, and pretend you're in 1806, plotting against the British with Andrew Jackson and Jean Lafitte.

9. **The End.** You're done—now reward yourself with dinner and some nightlife. Here's a tip: If you don't want to travel far, the restaurants **Tony Moran's** and **Pasta E Vino** are both right on the Old Absinthe House premises.

Dollars & Sense

The fare for the streetcar is $1 for each ride—if you get off along the way, you'll have to pay another fare when you hop back on. However, you can get unlimited bus and streetcar rides by buying a one-day ($4) or three-day ($8) VisiTour pass, available at many hotels or at the **Historic New Orleans Collection,** 533 Royal St. (☎ **504/523-4662**).

Itinerary #3: From Sternwheelers to Streetcars

You'll get around on this tour, which begins after breakfast with a long view from the top of the **World Trade Center,** takes you on a **riverboat trip to Chalmette Battlefield National Park,** and then hops a **streetcar** for a leisurely trip through the Garden District and the Uptown/University area on the way to the **Audubon Zoo.**

1. **World Trade Center.** Begin your day around 9 or 9:30am with a photo opportunity by taking the outside elevator to the 31st floor of the Trade Center and then taking in the view of the city and river. Allow about 30 minutes. (See chapter 14.)

2. **Riverboat Cruise.** The *Creole Queen* paddlewheeler (☎ **504/529-4567**) departs from the Riverwalk Marketplace at 10:30am, traveling seven miles downriver to the Chalmette Battlefield National Park, site of Andrew Jackson's victory over the British regulars in 1815. Enjoy a walking tour of the area and then get back aboard for the trip back to the Riverwalk. You can eat lunch on board or wait until you get back to town for something fancier. The boat will dock at around 1pm. (See chapter 14.)

Lunch. If you didn't eat on the boat, enjoy lunch nearby. **Mother's** is close, as is **Praline Connection No. 2.** (See chapter 11.)

3. **Streetcar Tour.** After lunch, make your way to St. Charles and hop the streetcar headed west. Take in the sights along the way. (See the "Streetcar Highlights" box in this chapter for tips on what you'll see.)

4. **Audubon Zoo.** Hop off the streetcar at the entrance to Audubon Park (6500 St. Charles) and take the free shuttle that runs to the zoo every 20 minutes. Enjoy the 2,000 animals that call the zoo home, and then head back to the Quarter by bus or streetcar. Allow at least two to four hours, including transportation time.

Streetcar Highlights

Taking the St. Charles Streetcar? Watch for these sights along the way. (When traveling from the French Quarter through the Garden District toward Audubon Park, please note that all odd-numbered addresses are on the right and all even-numbered addresses are on the left.)

➤ After passing Julia and St. Joseph streets you'll go around **Lee Circle.** That's General Robert E. Lee atop the massive column. You'll notice he's facing north so his back won't be to the Yankees. The statue was erected in 1884.

➤ At **2040 St. Charles** is **Catering de la Tour Eiffel.** If it looks like the Eiffel Tower in Paris, that's because it actually *was* a part of the tower, built in Paris as an upper-level restaurant, and then moved to New Orleans and reassembled in 1936. It now houses the Red Room, an upscale supper club/cabaret with live jazz.

➤ The **Columns Hotel** (1883), located at 3811 St. Charles, was used in the filming of the movie *Pretty Baby.*

➤ Does the **Palmer House** at **5705 St. Charles** look familiar? If you've ever seen *Gone With the Wind*, it should: It was built as a replica of Tara.

➤ **Audubon Park** (extending all the way from St. Charles to the Mississippi River) was the site of the 1884 World's Industrial and Cotton Centennial Exposition. The renowned Audubon Zoo is on the far side of the park.

➤ After passing **Tulane University** and the old **St. Mary's Dominican College** (now Loyola's Broadway Campus), you'll enter what used to be the town of **Carrollton,** named for General William Carroll, a commander at the Battle of New Orleans. Carrollton was founded in 1833 and incorporated in 1845 and was connected to New Orleans by the New Orleans and Carrollton Railroad in 1835. New Orleans annexed the city in 1874.

➤ After the streetcar turns right onto Carondelet, look ahead and a little to the left. The tall building with the cupola at the top is the **Hibernia Bank Building** (1921) at **325 Carondelet,** which was the tallest building in the city until 1962. The cupola is lit at night in colors that change with the seasons. It took years of drainage and the engineering advances of the 1960s to allow really tall buildings to be constructed on New Orleans' soggy soil.

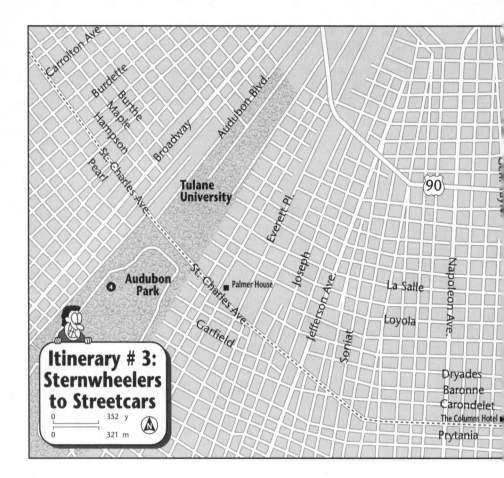

Itinerary #4: Spooky & Supernatural New Orleans

Toss on your black cape and get ready to hit the boneyards. This tour begins late, because you'll probably want to take an organized tour of the first major stop: **St. Louis Cemetery No. 1.** After that, you visit the **New Orleans Pharmacy Museum** to see the kind of medical practices that probably landed a lot of people in the graves you just saw, and then, after lunch, visit the **New Orleans Historic Voodoo Museum** and **Marie Laveau's House of Voodoo.** A quick palm reading at the **Bottom of the Cup Tearoom** will get you ready for a trip to your final stop, **Lafayette Cemetery No. 1.** (Note that the Pharmacy Museum is closed on Mondays and the Bottom of the Cup Tearoom is closed on Sundays.)

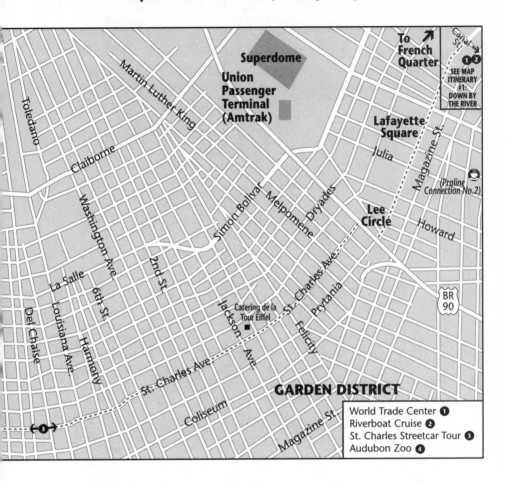

World Trade Center ❶
Riverboat Cruise ❷
St. Charles Streetcar Tour ❸
Audubon Zoo ❹

1. **Our Lady of Guadalupe Church and International Shrine of St. Jude.** After breakfast, head north to N. Rampart Street and this old church, built to make the processing of yellow fever victims into the cemetery easier. Say a quick prayer to St. Expedite before you start off on your ghostly expedition. Allow 15 minutes. See chapter 15. (Note: Time your visit so you can meet up with a cemetery tour group when you're done.)

2. **St. Louis Cemetery No. 1.** Join a guided tour of this 18th-century necropolis and dig the bones (but not literally, of course). You'll probably find a tour leaving at around 10 or 10:30am. Call **Save Our Cemeteries** (☎ 504/588-9357), **Historic New Orleans Walking Tours** (☎ 504/947-2120), **Haunted History Tours** (☎ 504/897-2030), **Magic Walking Tours** (☎ 504/588-9693), or **Hidden Treasures Tours** (☎ 504/529-4507) for information and schedules. (See chapter 15.)

241

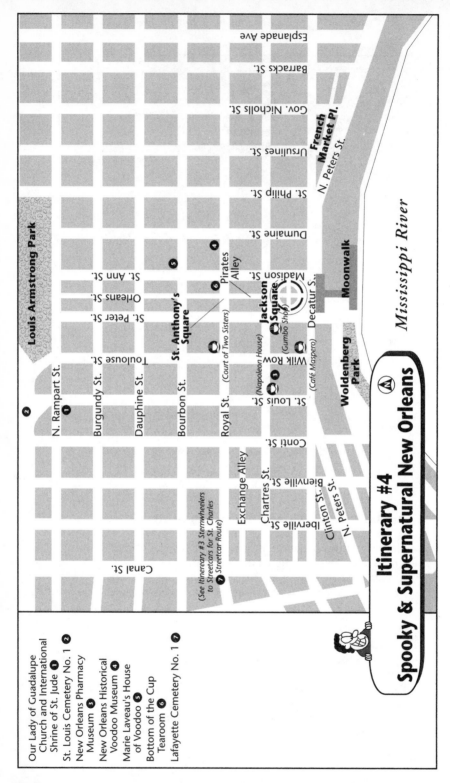

Itinerary #4
Spooky & Supernatural New Orleans

Mississippi River

Louis Armstrong Park

French Market Pl.

Esplanade Ave
Barracks St.
Gov. Nicholls St.
Ursulines St.
St. Philip St.
Dumaine St.
N. Peters St.

N. Rampart St.
Burgundy St.
Dauphine St.
Bourbon St.
Royal St.
Chartres St.
N. Peters St.

Canal St.
Iberville St.
Bienville St.
Conti St.
St. Louis St.
Toulouse St.
St. Peter St.
Orleans St.
St. Ann St.
Madison St.

Clinton St.
Exchange Alley

St. Anthony's Square

Jackson Square

Pirates Alley

(Court of Two Sisters)
(Napoleon House)
Wilk Row
(Gumbo Shop)
(Café Maspero)
Decatur S...

Moonwalk

Woldenberg Park

(See Itinerary #3 Sternwheelers to Streetcars for St. Charles Streetcar Route) 7

Our Lady of Guadalupe Church and International Shrine of St. Jude 1
St. Louis Cemetery No. 1 2
New Orleans Pharmacy Museum 3
New Orleans Historical Voodoo Museum 4
Marie Laveau's House of Voodoo 5
Bottom of the Cup Tearoom 6
Lafayette Cemetery No. 1 7

242

3. **New Orleans Pharmacy Museum.** After your cemetery tour, visit this place at 514 Chartres St., between St. Louis and Toulouse streets. If you don't think pharmacy can be spooky and supernatural, take a look at the leeches and the drill they used to bore into people's skulls to relieve headaches. Allow 15 to 30 minutes. (See chapter 14.)

   Lunch. With all that morbidity, you've probably built up a good appetite, right? If so, there's more restaurants in the area than you can shake a stick at, including **Napoleon House,** the **Gumbo Shop, Café Maspero,** and the **Court of Two Sisters.** Order red wine with lunch and pretend it's blood. (See chapter 11.)

4. **New Orleans Historic Voodoo Museum.** At 724 Dumaine, between Bourbon and Royal streets, you'll find the one and only voodoo museum. Say a spell, scope the artifacts, tip your hat to the resident snakes, and spend about 30 minutes before heading to 739 Bourbon St. at St. Ann, where you'll find stop number 5.

5. **Marie Laveau's House of Voodoo.** Need a voodoo doll or other charm to take care of—I mean give to—a friend? This is the place to find it.

6. **Bottom of the Cup Tearoom.** Head one block riverward to 732 Royal St., between Pere Antoine's Alley and St. Ann St., and step into a tearoom with a difference: You can get your fortune told here. Have a cup of tea and rest up for the final leg of your tour.

7. **Lafayette Cemetery No. 1.** Take a taxi or walk down Royal Street to Canal Street and hop the streetcar. Get off at Washington Street and go one block south to the cemetery. This cemetery is generally safe, so if you're with a few people, you shouldn't avoid walking around. If you want to tour with a group, though, contact the organizations listed in the **St. Louis Cemetery No. 1** stop and adjust this itinerary accordingly.

Itinerary #5: Hedonism & Revelry Day

You know that old saying, "Eat, drink, shop, and be merry"? This itinerary is where it comes true. Your day begins with one venerable New Orleans tradition, **breakfast at Brennan's,** and ends with another: **dinner at Antoine's.** In between, you'll visit the jazz and Mardi Gras displays at the **Old U.S. Mint,** shop at all the best places in **Jackson Square** and the **French Market,** see the costumes displayed at the **Germaine Wells Mardi Gras Museum,** and look into the **Hermann-Grima House's** crystal ball and see the ghost of kitchens past. (Remember to make reservations way ahead for Brennan's and Antoine's, and note that the Old U.S. Mint is closed on Mondays, and the Hermann-Grima House is closed on Sundays.)

1. **Breakfast at Brennan's.** How many breakfasts are landmarks in their own right? This one is. Make reservations, sip an early morning drink, and be decadent. (Brennan's in located at 417 Royal St.; see chapter 11.)

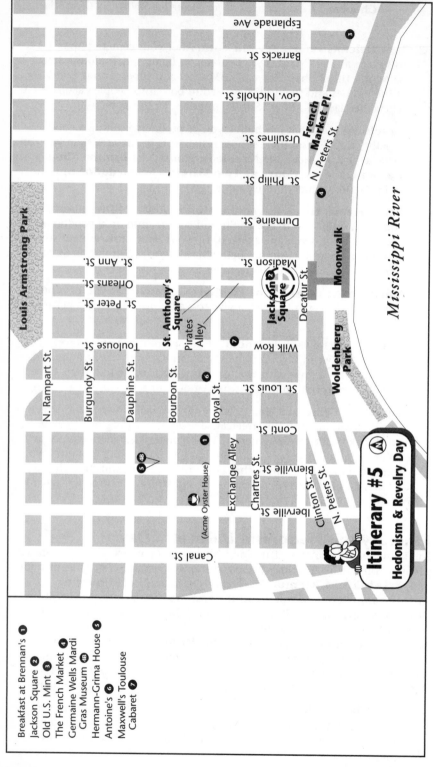

Louis Armstrong Park

N. Rampart St.

Burgundy St.

Dauphine St.

Bourbon St.

Royal St.

St. Ann St.
Orleans St.
St. Peter St.
Toulouse St.

St. Anthony's Square

Pirates Alley

Wilk Row

St. Louis St.

Conti St.

Exchange Alley

Chartres St.

Bienville St.

Iberville St.

Clinton St.
N. Peters St.

Canal St.

(Acme Oyster House)

Esplanade Ave

Barracks St.

Gov. Nicholls St.

Ursulines St.

St. Philip St.

Dumaine St.

Madison St.

Jackson Square

Decatur St.

Moonwalk

Woldenberg Park

French Market Pl.

N. Peters St.

Mississippi River

Itinerary #5
Hedonism & Revelry Day

Breakfast at Brennan's ❶
Jackson Square ❷
Old U.S. Mint ❸
The French Market ❹
Germaine Wells Mardi
Gras Museum ❹ᴮ
Hermann-Grima House ❺
Antoine's ❻
Maxwell's Toulouse
Cabaret ❼

244

2. **Jackson Square.** Take a leisurely walk through the Square and window-shop or for-real shop (whichever your budget allows). Keep heading generally southeast toward the river, where you'll find your next stop.

3. **The Old U.S. Mint.** If this place was open late, I'd have you come here after Antoine's, so it would be an after-dinner mint. (Yuk, yuk.) But seriously, despite its austere name, this place is fun, with major displays on jazz and Mardi Gras history. Both are great, and the Mardi Gras one is *wild*. The Mint is located near the corner of Decatur and Barracks streets. Allow one hour.

4a. **The French Market.** From the Mint, it's only a couple blocks west to the Market and its shops, flea market, and farmer's market. Grab some beignets from Café du Monde while you're there, just 'cause it's hedonism day—and what's hedonism without a sack of beignets?

   Lunch. Unbridled oyster-eating is one of the more decadent things I can think of, so head to the **Acme Oyster House** at 724 Iberville St. between Royal and Bourbon streets. You can get 'em raw, fried, or in a po boy, and wash 'em all down with beer. Acme is loud and crowded a lot of the time; you can think of it as your slumming meal between Brennan's and Antoine's. (See chapter 11.)

4b. **Collapse.** Head back to your hotel. Why? One of two reasons: (a) to unload your shopping finds, digest, and rally yourself for the next round; or (b) because it's true what they say about oysters being an aphrodisiac. Skip numbers 4c and 5 and rest up for dinner and nightlife.

4c. **Germaine Wells Mardi Gras Museum.** If you're still moving, walk about a block and a half from the Acme Oyster House to 813 Bienville St., between Dauphine and Bourbon, and climb to the second floor of Arnaud's restaurant for the display of Mardi Gras costumes and memorabilia. It's only open until 2:30pm (and reopens at 6pm), so if you went back to your hotel you can figure on skipping it. Allow 15 minutes. (See chapter 14.)

5. **Hermann-Grima House.** The last stop before dinner for you intrepid souls should get you in the mood as you watch its operational 1832 kitchen in action. It's located at 820 St. Louis St., a half-block above Bourbon Street, and is open Monday through Saturday until 3:30pm. Allow 30 to 60 minutes. (See chapter 14.) When you're through, head back to your hotel to rest up and get changed for dinner.

6. **Dinner at Antoine's.** The flipside of Brennan's breakfast is another polestar of New Orleans' culinary universe. Enjoy it like there's no tomorrow. (Antoine's is at 713 St. Louis St., right off Royal Street.)

7. **Jazz in the Evening.** To round out your day so it matches your belly, head over to **Maxwell's Toulouse Cabaret** (at 615 Toulouse, between Chartres and Royal streets; reservations recommended) or

Fritzel's European Jazz Club (at 733 Bourbon St., between Orleans and St. Ann) for some cool sounds. (Fritzel's is especially known for its frequent late-night jam sessions.)

Itinerary #6: A Whole Day Half a Town Away from the Quarter

It's time to get out of the Quarter on an itinerary that's especially good if you're traveling with kids. After breakfast, pick up some picnic fixins for later and hop the Esplanade bus from the Quarter. Get off right in front of the **New Orleans Museum of Art.** After checking out the exhibits, have your picnic lunch in the park before checking out **Storyland**—where your kids can climb Little Miss Muffet's spiderweb or climb aboard Captain Hook's pirate ship—and **Carousel Gardens** for a ride on the flying horses. After your kids have had their fill, tour the **Botanical Garden** before getting back on the Esplanade bus and heading back to the Quarter. End the day with dinner and a dose of glitz at **Planet Hollywood.**

Take this tour on a Saturday or Sunday (some attractions are closed weekdays during some months) and begin getting ready to go around 9am to get to the museum around opening time (10am). All of the attractions in this itinerary (except Planet Hollywood) are in close proximity within the park.

1. **Preparation.** Pack the fixins for a picnic lunch, and then hop the Esplanade bus. Get off at the Museum stop.

2. **New Orleans Museum of Art.** There are always displays geared toward kids at the museum, so don't worry about the munchkins getting bored. There are also, of course, displays for adults. Allow about two hours.

   Lunch. You're right in City Park at this point, so pick a shady spot and chow down.

3. **Storyland.** Once you've digested, head down Victory Avenue to Storyland, where your kids can lose themselves in the different fantasy themes.

4. **Carousel Gardens.** When the younguns have almost exhausted themselves, drag them away with the promise of a carousel ride. The "Flying Horses," as they're known, date from 1906 and are among the few remaining wooden carousels in the country.

5. **Botanical Garden.** The garden is close by and makes a nice wrap-up of your trip to the park. WPA workers built this garden in the 1930s, and it's full of beautiful pools, Art Deco fountains, sculptures, and, of course, flowers.

6. **Heading home.** Take the Esplanade bus back to the Quarter to rest up a bit. This may be the ideal time for a dip in the hotel pool.

7. **Planet Hollywood.** After you're all refreshed, head on over to the Jackson Brewery complex (at 620 Decatur St., on the western side of Jackson Square) and its branch of the famous theme restaurant.

Itinerary #6
A Whole Day Half a Town Away

0 ——————— 220 y

0 ——————— 201 m

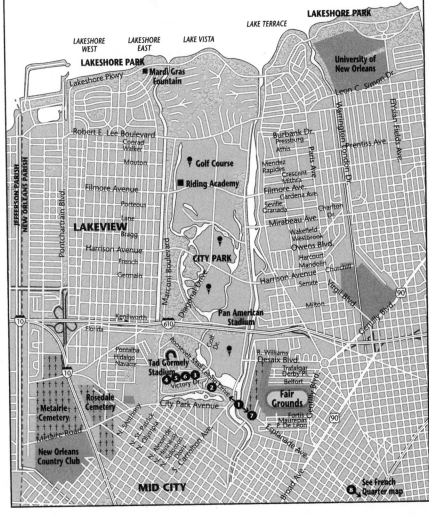

Lake Pontchartrain

LAKESHORE PARK

LAKE TERRACE

LAKESHORE WEST   LAKESHORE EAST   LAKE VISTA

LAKESHORE PARK

University of New Orleans

Lakeshore Pkwy

■ Mardi Gras Fountain

Leon C. Simon Dr.

Warrington Tondon Dr.

Elysian Fields Ave.

Robert E. Lee Boulevard

Burbank Dr.

Pressburg

Conrad Walker

Athis

Prentiss Ave.

Mouton

♀ Golf Course

Mendez

Rapides

Paris Ave.

Crescent

Mithra

Filmore Avenue

■ Riding Academy

Filmore Ave.

Gardena Ave.

Porteous

Seville

Granada

Charlton Dr.

Lane

Mirabeau Ave.

Pontchartrain Blvd.

Bragg

Wakefield

Westbrook

LAKEVIEW

Harrison Avenue

Owens Blvd.

French

Harcourt

Mandolin

Churchill

Germain

CITY PARK

Harrison Avenue

Senate

Marconi Boulevard

Virgil Blvd.

Milton

90

JEFFERSON PARISH

NEW ORLEANS PARISH

Kenilworth

Pan American Stadium

10

Florida

610

Diagonal Drive

Golf Dr.

Pontalba

Hidalgo

Navarre

R. Williams

Desaix Blvd.

Roosevelt Mall

Lelong Drive

Tad Gormely Stadium

4 5 6 3

2

Trafalgar

Derby Pl.

Belfort

Gentilly Blvd.

10

Victory Dr.

City Park Avenue

1

7

Fair Grounds

90

Metairie Cemetery

Rosedale Cemetery

N. Anthony

N. St. Patrick

N. Olympia

N. Alexander

N. Johnson

N. Rennes

N. Davis

S. Carrollton Ave.

Fortis

Maurepas

De Leon

Esplanade Ave.

Metairie Road

New Orleans Country Club

MID CITY

Broad Ave.

8 See French Quarter map

Chapter 18

Designing Your Own Itinerary

> ### In This Chapter
> ➤ Budgeting your time
> ➤ Pacing yourself
> ➤ Making tough choices

There comes a time in planning every trip when you sit down and say "I want to see that and that and that..." and realize there just isn't enough time. Of course, you can see more if you organize your days efficiently; disorganized travelers waste a lot of time, show up at the museum on the day it's closed, and end up having breakfast at Antoine's and dinner at Brennan's. The worksheets in this chapter are designed to help you decide what to see and organize your trip so you can fit it all in.

Back to the Drawing Board: Your Top Attractions

The first step is to go back to chapter 14, where you rated the top attractions from 1 to 5. Using this list, break down the sights by number. For example, write in all the #1s, all the #2s, and so on.

#1 Picks

➤ _____
➤ _____
➤ _____
➤ _____
➤ _____
➤ _____
➤ _____
➤ _____
➤ _____
➤ _____

#2 Picks

➤ _____
➤ _____
➤ _____
➤ _____
➤ _____
➤ _____
➤ _____
➤ _____
➤ _____

#3 Picks

➤ _____
➤ _____
➤ _____
➤ _____
➤ _____
➤ _____
➤ _____
➤ _____
➤ _____

#4 Picks

➤ _____
➤ _____
➤ _____
➤ _____
➤ _____
➤ _____
➤ _____
➤ _____
➤ _____

Once you've filled in the sights, go back to chapter 15 and pick up the "other fun stuff" that fit your particular interests. Assign each of these activities a number and put them into the above lists, too. You're probably wondering why there are no spaces for the #5s. That's because, if you're a typical visitor, there are so many #1s, #2s, and #3s in your list that you won't need the #5s and may not even be able to visit the #4s.

What if your #1 list says "Bourbon Street, Mardi Gras World, Lafayette Cemetery #1, the Museum of Art, Metairie Cemetery, the Voodoo Museum, the Pharmacy Museum, and the Aquarium of the Americas"? That list would easily fill two days by itself. You could have your "creepy and spooky" itinerary on day 1—visiting the Voodoo Museum, the Pharmacy Museum, and the cemeteries during the day and then heading to Bourbon Street to liven yourself up at night. On day 2, you could take the ferry to Algiers and visit Mardi Gras World in the morning, go to the aquarium when you get back, and then head up to the museum in City Park for the afternoon and maybe end the day with dinner and a jazz show in the Quarter.

Budgeting Your Time

On average, sights take about two hours to visit. Some take less, and some take more—as you saw from my notes in the individual sight listings—but figure in time for travel and time to eat, sit down for a breather, and look in the occasional shop window, and you come out to about two hours. Therefore, you can "do" about four sights in a day.

Add up the number of #1s and #2s in your list, and then divide by the number of full days in your trip. If the result is a number larger than four and the sights are all large and time-consuming, then you may have a problem, because you can't see six or eight major sights in a day except superficially. How do you get that sights-per-day number down?

➤ **Lengthen your visit.** This may or may not be easy for you to do.

➤ **Split up.** If you're a couple or group, make individual lists, and then see whether splitting up for a half day or two will provide enough time for everyone to see all their favorites.

➤ **Axe the #3s.** It's better to see less and see it well than to spend 20 minutes at the Aquarium, sprint through Bourbon Street, take a picture of the Cabildo from your speeding cab...you get the idea.

Time-Savers

Don't forget the season. If you're in New Orleans when it's particularly hot, you won't be doing as much walking around in the sun as you may think. At the very least, you'll need more breaks for shade and water; at worst, you may think about skipping a walk around the cemeteries in favor of visiting an air-conditioned sight.

Getting All Your Ducks in a Row

Making your plan concrete may also help make your ideal trip doable. Take a map and mark the locations of all the sights you've listed so far, and then mark your hotel. Now try to find clusters of activities that naturally group together. Avoid the Ricochet Rabbit approach to sightseeing, where you're bouncing from north to south to east to west like a Ping-Pong ball. For instance, you don't want to set up an itinerary that reads "Metairie Cemetery to Jackson Barracks to Audubon Park to the Confederate Museum"—you'd spend your whole day in transit. What you want to do is try to line up your visits in a logical progression, so you can travel in a more or less straight line from one event to another and avoid doubling back where possible. Think strategically.

Fill-Ins

Fill-ins are things you do on the way to someplace else. Shopping is a natural; go back to chapter 16 and pick out the specific stores and neighborhoods you want to spend time in. List them here:

Shopping

➤ _____
➤ _____
➤ _____
➤ _____
➤ _____
➤ _____
➤ _____
➤ _____
➤ _____

Locate these places on the map and figure out what sights they lie in between. Allow different amounts of time depending on whether you're just window shopping or really planning to graze these places. If you intend to buy a suit at Saks or get all your holiday shopping done at a major department store, shopping may become an attraction-length process.

Dining is another fill-in. Leave the question of dinner aside for now. If there are specific places where you want to lunch, locate them on the map in terms of your clusters of sights. If you have no "musts," use the listings in chapters 11 and 12 to pick out some lunchtime options for each of the clusters so you won't go hungry. List the lunch restaurants using the space provided:

Lunch

➤ _____
➤ _____
➤ _____
➤ _____
➤ _____
➤ _____
➤ _____
➤ _____
➤ _____

Sketching Out Your Itineraries

Now you're ready to plot some itineraries. A basic itinerary should be something like this:

"Breakfast at *[hotel/place/neighborhood]*. See *[attraction]* in the morning. Lunch at *[place/neighborhood]* or *[alternate]*. Walk or take the streetcar to *[attraction]* in the afternoon."

Of course, you can fit another attraction into the morning and/or afternoon ("Check out the Riverwalk on the way to the Aquarium of the Americas") and leave room for shopping ("browse like crazy on Magazine Street on the way to Lafayette Cemetery #1").

Time-Savers

If making itineraries seems like a real drag to you, you can always cannibalize the recommended itineraries in chapter 17. You can mix-and-match my morning and afternoon activities or substitute activities from the same neighborhoods and keep the basic structure.

Itinerary #1

➤ _____
➤ _____
➤ _____
➤ _____
➤ _____

Itinerary #2

➤ _____
➤ _____
➤ _____
➤ _____
➤ _____

Itinerary #3

➤ _____
➤ _____
➤ _____
➤ _____
➤ _____

Itinerary #4

➤ _____
➤ _____

➤ _____

➤ _____

➤ _____

Planning Your Nighttime Right

Like Elvis said, "The world is more alive at night—it's like God ain't looking." My advice is this: Don't schedule yourself so tightly that you miss out on the fun. You could arrange it so that when your last sightseeing stop closes you come out the door and stand facing that great restaurant you wanted to try, but that would be just a little bit *too* organized—and also exhausting. You'll probably want a little downtime between the end of your sightseeing day and the beginning of your evening's activities, so I suggest you head back to your hotel to curl up with a glass of wine and a novel for an hour or maybe catch a quick snooze to recharge your batteries. This plan also allows you to think about your nightlife plans as a separate mini-itinerary. Instead of planning your nightlife by where you end your sightseeing, you can plan a separate sortie from your hotel and hit the town refreshed, duded up in your evening best (or funkiest), and ready for action.

Spontaneity rules the night, so check out the nightlife recommendations in the following chapters and do what comes naturally—but don't forget to keep track of any dinner reservations you've booked in advance. Write them in the spaces provided. For the nights that are blank, you might want to write in tentative options, such as "dinner in *[neighborhood]*; go to *[club/bar]* afterward?"

Night #1

➤ _____

➤ _____

Night #2

➤ _____

➤ _____

Night #3

➤ _____

➤ _____

Night #4

➤ _____

➤ _____

Lastly, keep geography in mind enough so that you don't find yourself finishing up your day way up by Lake Pontchartrain only an hour before you have dinner reservations at Arnaud's. Remember to leave time not only for resting, showering, changing, and dressing, but for just slowing down, leaning against a lightpost, listening to the musicians tuning up from the club down the street, and breathing in all that sweet New Orleans atmosphere.

Part 6

On the Town: Nightlife & Entertainment

Laissez les bon temps roulez! ("Let the good times roll" for you French-impaired.) And they certainly will, unless you retreat to your hotel room and pull the covers over your head. And if that's what you want, you came to the wrong city. Eat, dance, listen to music—that's what you do in New Orleans. All other time is wasted.

Walk down Bourbon Street—yes, it's full of strip joints and T-shirt shops, and you have to dodge drunken tourists (if you aren't one yourself)—but listen to that music: traditional jazz here, bar-band rock there, zydeco over yonder. And that's without trying. If you hit some of the specific clubs in this section, you might hear some of the finest jazz, blues, Cajun, and zydeco there is. In between, bars dispense drinks from streetside windows just in case you get thirsty before you hit the next one. Clubs go all night, giving you the chance to bop till you drop—or at least work off some of that cream sauce from dinner. Stagger home near dawn, try to sleep, and then get up and do it all over again. Sounds like utter hedonism? It is. Got a problem with that? If so, you came to the wrong city.

Chapter 19

Hitting the Clubs & Bars

In This Chapter

➤ The lowdown on the Bourbon and Decatur street scenes

➤ Where to find the bar that's right for you

➤ Where to go to gamble

➤ Where to find the extremes—from high tea to lowdown strip clubs

Maybe everything goes, and maybe it doesn't—there's got to be a line drawn somewhere, but New Orleanians haven't seen it in a long, long time. Choose your poison: Do you want to spend your evenings trolling from bar to bar along Bourbon Street, or do you want to plunk yourself down in a cozy jazz club and bop your head along with the music? New Orleans has it all—and mostly within a few square blocks.

In this chapter, I'll run down your extra-musical options. Just remember this: It's sometimes hard to distinguish the bars from the music hot spots in New Orleans. In fact, for better or worse, it's almost impossible to separate music and alcohol in this city. The clubs and bars listed in this chapter may have live music occasionally, but they are not places in which you can always *expect* to find bands. Instead, what you'll find are rowdy saloons, upscale bars (suitable for a business meeting or a quiet drink before or after dinner), dance clubs, strip joints, and other allegedly sinful entertainments. Chapter 20 is the place to turn if you're looking for music clubs.

Entering the Party Zone

Like most other things in New Orleans, most tourist nightlife is centered in the French Quarter. Narrowing it down even further, nightlife ground zero is Bourbon and Decatur streets. Here's the scoop on both of 'em.

A Moon over Bourbon Street

You can't visit New Orleans without spending at least one night exploring world-famous Bourbon Street. Music of every sort, jazz, rock and roll, rhythm and blues, country, Cajun, and alternative, flows through windows and doors, and people from all walks of life gather on the street and in the various music halls and watering holes. It's a cacophony of sights, sounds, and smells, where T-shirt shops, souvenir shops, and restaurants compete with the bars for your attention. Buggy drivers are hollering "Buggy ride?" Scam artists, people selling time shares, and people soliciting for local charities are trying to get your attention while scantily dressed women (and men dressed like women) stand in doorways displaying their wares, and barkers entice you with vague promises of thrills beyond imagination.

Although every place on Bourbon Street isn't open 24 hours a day, many are. The ones that aren't usually open late in the afternoon. Nighttime is when Bourbon Street wakes up. After 8pm, the street is blocked off to traffic, and the streets and sidewalks are filled with people strolling from bar to bar, drinks in hand, listening to different performers.

The Rules of the Game

The **legal drinking age** in Louisiana was 18 for much of its history, but it's now 21. Although it's legal to walk along the street with a drink in your hand, the drink must be in a plastic cup. It's illegal, however, to drink in a vehicle, even if you're just a passenger. The law is seldom enforced in the French Quarter (or most places in the city, for that matter), but it could be. Don't take the risk.

If you walk along Bourbon Street from Canal Street, you'll notice a change when you reach St. Ann Street (about eight blocks from Canal). St. Ann is sort of an unofficial boundary between the straight and gay sections of Bourbon Street. That doesn't mean every bar or person after St. Ann is gay, nor that every bar or person before it is straight, but there is a marked difference. The further you go away from the river or the farther you continue down Bourbon Street (away from Canal), the fewer people will be around. These areas aren't particularly safe, and anytime you're away from the herd, you're more likely to get in trouble. Stay alert.

The bars and clubs on Bourbon Street are in such close proximity to one another, and the acts change so often that there's little need to tell you about each and every one. Instead, I've highlighted the best jazz spots in chapter 20 and the best bars in the section titled "The Bar Scene," later in this chapter.

French Quarter Nightlife

Mississippi River

Louis Armstrong Park

Jackson Square

St. Anthony's Square

Pirates Alley

Moonwalk

Woldenberg Park

French Market Pl.

Streets:
Esplanade Ave.
Barracks St.
Gov. Nicholls St.
Ursulines St.
St. Philip St.
Dumaine St.
St. Ann St.
Orleans St.
St. Peter St.
Toulouse St.
Madison St.
Wilk Row
St. Louis St.
Conti St.
Exchange Alley
Bienville St.
Iberville St.
Clinton St.
Canal St.
N. Rampart St.
Burgundy St.
Dauphine St.
Bourbon St.
Royal St.
Chartres St.
N. Peters St.
Decatur St.

258

De Action on Decatur Street

Decatur Street is alive and well both day and night. It's home to souvenir shops, praline and candy stores, daiquiri shops, many restaurants and sandwich shops, Planet Hollywood, House of Blues, the Hard Rock Cafe, and the Jax Brewery Shopping Center. This street is also where you'll find Jackson Square and St. Louis Cathedral, the Cabildo, the Presbytere and the Pontalba buildings, and the French Market. The area between the river and Decatur is where the Moonwalk and Woldenberg Parks are located. Artists display their wares along the iron fence of Jackson Square, while tarot readers and psychics tell fortunes; buggy drivers hawk their rides; and street musicians, mimes, and clowns entertain you while you take a break, look at the old buildings, shop in the small boutiques, or grab a bite to eat.

As Decatur heads farther away from the Quarter toward the Faubourg Marigny, it turns into alternative heaven, with thrift stores and punk kids galore. When it crosses Esplanade, it becomes the Frenchman section, with a marvelous assortment of clubs, bars, and gay- and alternative-themed stores. It's an increasingly happening scene at night.

The Royal Street Alternative

Royal Street is the exact opposite of Bourbon. During the day, when Bourbon is so dead you can almost see tumbleweeds blowing through, Royal Street (one block away) is closed to traffic and bustling with life. It's home to museums, art galleries, antique shops, and restaurants. Tourists stroll along and shop; admire the ironwork and architecture of the 18th- and 19th-century buildings; watch musicians, mimes, and other performers in the middle of the street; or pause on a corner to get a hot dog, ice cream, or soft drink from a street vendor.

The Bar Scene

A non-drinker might be forgiven for thinking that Bourbon Street is just one big open-air bar. In some ways, it is. Open containers of liquor are legal, and everywhere you look folks are sporting "Go" (or "Geaux") cups, usually full of the famous hurricane drink (a rum concoction that packs a wallop). You can stroll from bar to bar, hearing an incredible mix of music from blues to Cajun to jazz to bar-band rock to Celtic. It's not so much the quality but the variety, and it's all audible from the street. Not only can you enjoy music from outside the bars, you can refill that cup of yours at one of the many walk-up windows. Bourbon Street is a scene, and that's for sure. Some will find it heaven, but others may consider it the eleventh circle of hell.

Consequently, just about any bar on Bourbon will do (and all will seem much the same), but here's a few standouts in the Quarter that you shouldn't miss:

➤ The **Cat's Meow** (701 Bourbon St., ☎ **504/523-2788**) plays popular rock songs all night long (karaoke is also popular here).

➤ **The Gold Mine** (701 Dauphine St., ☎ **504/586-0745**) is a good place to dance your feet off to the latest hot songs—unless you can't stand a college-age crowd, that is.

➤ **Pat O'Brien's** (718 St. Peter, ☎ **504/525-4823**) is the home of the hurricane, the world-famous gigantic rum drink served in hurricane lamp-style glasses—some of which are nearly hurricane size themselves. The patio and interior rooms are almost always crowded.

➤ Dating from 1772, **Lafitte's Blacksmith Shop** (941 Bourbon St. ☎ **504/523-0066**) is the oldest building in the Quarter and was reportedly the headquarters of the notorious pirate Jean Lafitte. It looks like it hasn't been touched since. Agreeably dark (barely candlelit at night), it's a good place to hatch your nefarious plots.

➤ Another dark and historic place that seems full of schemes—or maybe it's just the low-key lighting—is the **Napoleon House** (500 Chartres St., ☎ **504/524-9752**). If you're the imperial type, have a drink and muse over what the place would've been like if Napoleon had moved in here, as certain New Orleanians hoped he would. (See chapter 15 for more on the joint's history.)

Experiences Fit for a Queen

To prove that there's more to do in New Orleans than listen to music and celebrate, here's a couple of royal experiences (of course, there's more than one kind of queen...):

➤ **For the British monarchy kind,** I suggest you have afternoon tea at **Le Salon** in the Windsor Court Hotel (300 Gravier, ☎ **504/523-6000;** reservations required).

➤ **For the drag kind,** visit **Lucky Cheng's** (720 St. Louis, ☎ **504/ 529-2045**), where your dinner and drinks will be served by drag queen waitresses.

➤ If you're looking for a bit o' the green in New Orleans, try **Kerry Irish Pub** (331 Decatur St., ☎ **504/527-5954**), which has a variety of beers and other spirits, but is most proud of its properly poured pints of Guinness and hard cider. The pub is a good bet for live Irish and alternative folk music, and it's also a good place to throw darts and shoot pool.

Escaping the Tourist Zone

Sometimes you just may want to slip the clutches of the tourism industry, strike off on your own, and pretend to be a local for a while. If you get in that mood and want to find a comfortable local watering hole, I know a few good places that should fit the bill. If you're looking for a real down-and-dirty experience, it's hard to tell the genuine barflies from the slumming celebs at the **Saturn Bar** (3067 St. Claude Ave, ☎ **504/949-7532**), whose crumbling (and I mean crumbling) booths and pack rat decor hide a multitude of sins and sinners. This place must be seen to be believed. See page 268 in chapter 20 for a map which locates these happening hot spots.

At the other end of the spectrum are **Feelings** (2600 Chartres St. at Franklin Ave., ☎ **504/945-2222**) and the **Apple Barrel** (609 Frenchmen St., ☎ **504/949-9399**). Feelings is a sweet and simple, low-key neighborhood restaurant and hangout set around a classic New Orleans courtyard—which is where most people drink unless they're hanging out with the fabulous piano player, singing the night away. The Apple Barrel is a small, dusty, wooden-floored watering hole where locals, refugees from the craziness elsewhere in town, and runaway diners from Alberto's restaurant (upstairs) sit listening to the jukebox, gabbing at the bar, or playing darts.

Somewhat in the same league is **Snake & Jake's Xmas Club Lounge** (7612 Oak St., ☎ **504/861-2802**). Owned by local musicians, this petite, dimly lit establishment is the kind of local joint folks bring their dogs to. Be prepared to make friends and be surprised. Jose the bartender was voted best in the city by the readers of *Gambit* magazine. Lastly, **St. Joe's Bar** (5535 Magazine St., ☎ **504/899-3744**) is an agreeably dark corner bar. It's very typical New Orleans—a friendly, unpretentious place with a well-stocked jukebox and a nice patio out back.

Gay Nightlife in the Big Easy

In this section, you'll find listings of New Orleans' most popular gay nightspots. For more information, you can check *Ambush* magazine, which is a great source for the gay community in New Orleans and for those visiting. The magazine's Web site, **www.ambushmag.com**, has links to other sites of gay interest and includes info on local gay bars (**www.gaybars.com/states/louisian.htm**). Once you're in New Orleans, you can pick up a copy of the magazine at Tower Records (408 N. Peters, in the French Quarter) or Lenny's News (5420 Magazine St., Uptown).

Hot Gay Bars & Clubs

The **Bourbon Pub and Parade Disco** (801 Bourbon St., ☎ **504/529-2107**) is reputed to be one the largest gay nightclubs in the country. The 24-hour pub is downstairs, offers a video bar, and is the calmer of the two places—at least until around 8pm, an hour before the upstairs disco opens.

Café Lafitte in Exile (901 Bourbon St., ☎ **504/522-8397**) is a legendary spot in the gay community, having been opened by Tom Caplinger, who used to run Lafitte's Blacksmith Shop. Friends say that it broke his heart to leave the original place behind, so he opened this newer place and brought friends and patrons like Tennessee Williams with him. The place is open 24 hours daily and is almost always crowded.

If you're looking for rampant diversity, visit **LeRoundup** (819 St. Louis St., ☎ **504/561-8340**), which attracts the most diverse crowd around. You'll find transsexuals lining up at the bar with drag queens and well-groomed men in khakis and Levi's. The atmosphere is friendly, and it's open 24 hours.

If you want a more homey experience, **Good Friends Bar & Queens Head Pub** (740 Dauphine St., ☎ **504/566-7191**) fits the bill. Downstairs is a mahogany bar and a pool table, and upstairs is the quiet Queens Head Pub, decorated in the style of a Victorian bar.

Despite being out on the edge of the Quarter, **The Mint** (504 Esplanade Ave., ☎ **504/525-2000**) is nearly always full, though it comes off as less of a scene than Café Lafitte (perhaps thanks to the non–Bourbon Street location). There's live entertainment all the time (including impersonations), so ask around or look in *Ambush* to find out what's happening during your visit.

Extra! Extra!

In addition to the gay nightspots I've listed, you might also try **The Golden Lantern** (1239 Royal St., ☎ **504/529-2860**), a nice neighborhood spot where the bartender knows the patrons by name. If Levi's and leather are your scene, **The Rawhide** (740 Burgundy St., ☎ **504/525-8106**) is your best bet; during Mardi Gras, this place hosts a costume contest that's not to be missed.

Best Lesbian Bar in Town

Actually, it may be the only lesbian bar in town (unless you count Rubyfruit Jungle, which is also a disco), but **Charlene's** (940 Elysian Fields, ☎ **504/945-9328**) is definitely the place to go. It's a little out of the way if you're staying in the Quarter, but there's dancing and live entertainment, so it might be worth the trip. Take a cab.

Gay Dance Clubs

Hot spots for gyration include **Oz** (800 Bourbon St., ☎ **504/593-9491**), which has become the place to see and be seen. It was ranked as the city's number-one dance club by *Gambit* magazine, and *Details* magazine ranked it as one of the top 50 clubs in the country.

Wolfendale's (834 N. Rampart St., ☎ **504/523-7764**) is a popular dance spot with the city's gay African-American population. It has a courtyard, a raised dance floor, and a pool table, but the courtyard and pool table don't get much use—people come here to dance. Take a cab if you visit.

Rubyfruit Jungle (640 Frenchmen St., ☎ **504/947-4000**) is another of the city's hottest gay and lesbian dance clubs. Some nights offer techno; others bring country and western, and still others feature comedy and other local gay talent. Everyone is welcome here—it's a very friendly, attitude-free establishment.

Hey There, Big Boy

The strip clubs along Bourbon Street are an inseparable part of the street's ambiance, but beware: The "no cover charge" policy just means you have to buy overpriced, watered down drinks if you want to stay for the show. And though the signs often advertise "live love acts," they're generally simulated and utterly tame (kinda like nude aerobics). **Rick's Cabaret** (315 Bourbon St., ☎ **504/524-4222**) is the classiest joint, an attempt at an upscale gentleman's club. Unlike at some other places, you won't be scared to touch the plush furnishings here with your bare hands. You get the feeling that businessmen and conventioneers are probably Rick's target audience, but couples can come here too because women aren't made to feel uncomfortable. Afterward, you can shop at the many Bourbon Street shops featuring, er, marital aids.

Casino Royale

Gambling as a tourist attraction just has not gone over very well in New Orleans. The Harrah's casino got a lot of press when it was announced and when construction began, but it's never been finished and probably never will be. At this time, there are three riverboat casinos left in the metro area, but only one of those is in the New Orleans city limits: **Bally's Casino** (1 Stars and Stripes Blvd., about nine miles northeast of the French Quarter, ☎ **800/57-BALLY** or 504/248-3200). Take a taxi; it'll cost you about $15.

Bet You Didn't Know

The Faubourg Marigny neighborhood, just downriver from the French Quarter, is where the Kowalskis lived in Tennessee Williams' *A Streetcar Named Desire*, so if you feel a need to yell "Ste-LAAHHHH!!!" out a window, this is the place for it. (If you want to yell it and not have someone call the cops, go to Bourbon Street, where no one will give you a second glance—they're too busy yelling a lot weirder stuff.)

In Harvey, you'll find the **Boomtown Belle Casino** (4132 Peters Rd., located about 15 miles due south of the French Quarter, ☎ **504/366-7711**). In Kenner, you'll find the **Treasure Chest Casino** (5050 Williams Blvd., 15 miles northwest of the French Quarter, ☎ **504/443-8000**). A taxi to either of these casinos from the Quarter will cost you about $21.

Chapter 20

The Music Scene

HELP ME BECOME PRESIDENT

In This Chapter

➤ The lowdown on the New Orleans music scene

➤ The best places to hear jazz and blues

➤ Where to go for Cajun and zydeco music

➤ Where to go for rock and R&B

➤ Where to go for high culture

Music runs deep through life in New Orleans. It goes out to the nightclubs on weekends and into church on Sunday mornings; it celebrates Mardi Gras and St. Patrick's Day and funerals, too. Music here is subject to spontaneous outbursts: As school lets out for the day, you're likely to see a few students playing their band instruments at the bus stop. It's also spawned during carefully planned annual outbursts, such as the Jazz and Heritage Festival. In this chapter, I'll run you through some of the best spots to hear all the different kinds of sounds offered in the Big Easy.

Where the Action Is

Most of the clubs I've listed in this chapter are in the French Quarter, either in the areas around Bourbon and Decatur streets or up on Rampart Street, at the top edge of the Quarter. You'll also notice that some places are on Frenchman Street in Faubourg Marigny, which is a blossoming entertainment street just across Esplanade Avenue from the Quarter. Aside from these two primary areas, the selections are spread out from St. Charles Street in the Warehouse District (another good neighborhood for the arts) all the way out to Carrollton. *Note:* For safety reasons, it's best to take a cab to and from any and all of the nightspots outside the French Quarter.

Because many clubs change performers more often than some people change their socks, finding your kind of music isn't always the easiest task. One night a club will have jazz, the next rock and roll, and the next it's something else. For up-to-date information on what's happening around town when you're there, look for current editions of *Where, Gambit,* and *OffBeat,* all of which are free and are distributed in most hotels. You can also check out *OffBeat* magazine on the Internet (**www.nola.com**—once you get to the nola home page, go to the music and entertainment section).

Other sources include the *Times-Picayune's* daily entertainment calendar as well as Friday's "Lagniappe" section of the newspaper. Additionally, **WWOZ** (90.7 FM) broadcasts the local music schedule several times throughout the day. If you miss the broadcasts, call ☎ **504/840-4040,** WWOZ's "Tower Records's Second Line," for the same information.

The venues listed in this chapter are hot spots at the time this guide was written; however, the notoriously fickle fortunes of the nightclub business mean that your best bet may be to walk down Bourbon Street and follow the sounds of your favorite type of music or follow the loudest (or quietest) crowd to a spot you might like to try. Most places open for happy hour (around noon in most cases) and stay open until the wee hours.

All That Jazz

Legend has it that jazz was born in the brothels of the old Storyville neighborhood (New Orleans' legendary red-light district), and while that's not precisely true, it's such a good story that it's hard to give up. It is true that young musicians from around town were hired by the madams to entertain their clients, and through this exposure, word of the new music got out to a lot of people who wouldn't otherwise have heard it.

From the moment Buddy Bolden blew the first notes of jazz from his cornet near the end of the last century, New Orleans has had a reputation as a music city, and since then, jazz greats such as Louis Armstrong, Jelly Roll Morton, Sidney Bechet, and later Harry Connick, Jr. and the Marsalises have honed their skills in French Quarter clubs. In the past several decades, musicians such as the Neville brothers and Dr. John have broadened the New Orleans music scene beyond its original jazz roots.

You'll still find uninhibited dancers performing in the streets outside jazz spots (sometimes passing the hat to onlookers); jazz funerals for departed musicians (the trip to that final resting place accompanied by sorrowful dirges and "second liners" who shuffle and clap their hands to a mournful beat); the return (a joyful, swinging celebration of the deceased's "liberation"); and occasionally a street parade (even when it isn't Carnival), complete with a brass band. As jazz legend and native New Orleanian Louis Armstrong once said about jazz, "If you got to ask what it is, you'll never get to know." You've already taken one giant step toward understanding by deciding to visit New Orleans, now all you have to do to complete your education is dive into a good club. The following sections list the good ones.

I Wish I Were in Dixie

Kids If you want to hear traditional New Orleans Dixieland jazz, head to **Preservation Hall** (726 St. Peter St., ☎ 504/523-8939), where you'll find some of the oldest jazz musicians still tootin' their own horns. Run by a non-profit group dedicated to the preservation of jazz, the Hall is around the corner from Bourbon Street and next door to Pat O'Brien's. The show starts at 8pm and ends around midnight, with 45-minute sets and about a 10-minute break after each set. People begin lining up as early as 6pm, but I recommend coming later in the evening (say around 10pm)—the early crowd will have left by then, and you can often get in with little or no wait. Admission is only $4, but there are drawbacks such as minimal seating, no air-conditioning, no food, and no drinks. Still, you'll almost certainly enjoy yourself, and the kids will love it, too. There's a selection of tapes and CDs for sale if you want to take home some sounds of New Orleans.

In the same vein as Preservation Hall but not quite as historic is **Maison Bourbon** (641 Bourbon St., ☎ 504/522-8818), whose sign proclaims, "Dedicated to the Preservation of Jazz," which means that Dixieland jazz is the order of the day. There's a one drink minimum, and no children are allowed, but if you don't want to go in, you can easily stand outside the bar and hear and see everything just fine. You can purchase records and CDs here, too.

Another alternative for old-style jazz is the *Kids* **Palm Court Jazz Café** (1204 Decatur, ☎ 504/525-0200), which has a cast of performers similar to that at Preservation Hall, but the Palm Court also has air-conditioning, food, and drinks. The cover charge is $4, and kids under 12 get in for free.

Contemporary Jazz

In comparison with Preservation Hall and the Palm Court, *Kids* **Snug Harbor** (626 Frenchmen St., ☎ 504/949-0696) is more in line with the times. Located in Faubourg Marigny, just outside the French Quarter, the acts change nightly, but you'll often find the likes of **Charmaine Neville** or **Ellis Marsalis** here. Drinks, sandwiches, and a full dinner service are all available. The cover charge varies according to the performer, but it is usually between $8 and $20. Shows begin nightly at 9pm and 11pm.

Born to be Blue

If you want to mix some blues into your jazz diet, visit the **Funky Pirate** (727 Bourbon St., ☎ **504/523-1960**), where Big Al Carson, one of the "biggest" men in blues (and at what he once told me is 433 pounds, I mean *big*) belts out the blues nightly. His schedule varies; call to see when he's playing.

How can you not love a place called **Funky Butt** (714 N. Rampart St., ☎ **504/558-0872**)? Named after one of the liveliest clubs in the early days of jazz (and for a famous tune associated with legendary coronet player Buddy Boudin), it's a typical dive bar downstairs and a performance space upstairs. Owner Richard Rochester brings in a varied assortment of performers, from eclectic jazz to an amazing Billie Holiday "tribute" artist to the New Orleans Klezmer All Stars. Like Donna's (see following section), it's located on North Rampart Street but is worth the walk or taxi ride. Creole food and vegetarian cuisine are served. Few people take their children here (it's a bit gloomy for young 'uns), but if you do, ask for Richard and tell him "Big Ray the Buggy Driver" sent you. He'll probably waive the cover if the kids are under 12.

What's the difference between the Superdome and the "Original Superdome"? Well, one's a football stadium, and the other is the great jazz musician Pete Fountain. (The "dome" refers to his bald head.) If you want to hear sweet jazz clarinet melodies, check him out Tuesday through Saturday at 10pm at **Pete Fountain's** (2 Poydras St., in the Hilton Hotel, ☎ **504/523-4374**). The $19 cover charge includes one drink. Children are not allowed.

You may not be able to catch **Harry Connick, Jr.** playing around town, but the apple doesn't fall far from the tree. His father, Harry Connick, Sr. (the city's District Attorney for more than 20 years), performs with the Jimmy Maxwell Orchestra on Mondays and Thursdays at 〈Kids〉 **Maxwell's Toulouse Cabaret** (615 Toulouse, one and a half blocks from Bourbon, ☎ **504/523-4207**). The rest of the week, you can enjoy the likes of Steamboat Willie or the new Dukes of Dixieland. It's a nice space with tables and chairs, but they bus tourists in here, which should tell you something. As we go to press, Maxwell's is transforming itself into a dinner club, and in order to listen to the music, you must buy something to eat.

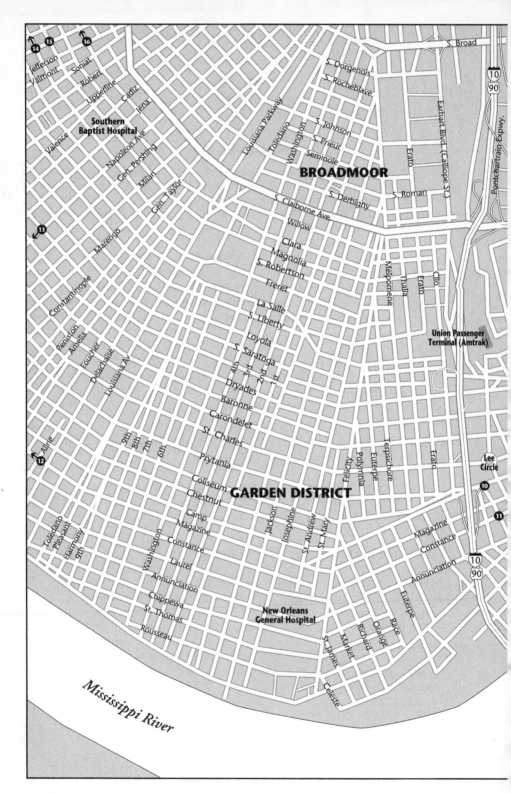

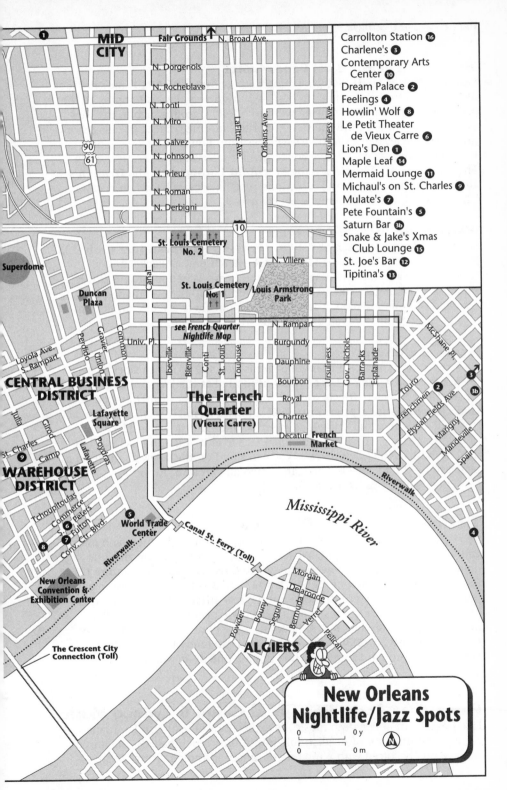

Carrollton Station 16
Charlene's 3
Contemporary Arts
  Center 10
Dream Palace 2
Feelings 4
Howlin' Wolf 8
Le Petit Theater
  de Vieux Carre 6
Lion's Den 1
Maple Leaf 14
Mermaid Lounge 11
Michaul's on St. Charles 9
Mulate's 7
Pete Fountain's 5
Saturn Bar 3b
Snake & Jake's Xmas
  Club Lounge 15
St. Joe's Bar 12
Tipitina's 13

**New Orleans
Nightlife/Jazz Spots**

Where Have All the Brass Bands Gone?

Donna's Bar & Grill (800 N. Rampart St., ☎ **504/596-6914**) may not look like much—a funky dive joint at best—but it's nearly always hopping to the best brass bands in town. The crowds often follow groups such as the New Birth Brass Band out onto the street for a second-line parade. The neighborhood's not great, but it's only three blocks from Bourbon Street at North Rampart and St. Ann. If you're concerned for safety, take a taxi. It's worth it. The **Maple Leaf, Tipitina's,** the **Mermaid Lounge,** and the **Dragon's Den** (all reviewed in following sections) also have brass bands on occasion. Check their schedules when you get to town.

Where to Go for Late-Night Jazz

For jazz with a little different slant, try **Fritzel's European Jazz Club** (733 Bourbon St., ☎ **504/561-0432**). Go here after 10pm, sit back, enjoy a German beer, and feel the beat within your heart. When musicians finish their gigs at other jazz spots, they come over here to have a late-night or early morning jam session. There's no cover, but there is a one drink minimum per set. Children are not allowed.

Jazz on the Cheap

One my favorite places to hear good jazz is also one of the cheapest: The ⁂**Market Cafe** (☎ **504/527-5000**) is located at the French Market where Decatur and N. Peters streets split off from one another near Dumaine. Joe Gun's Jazz Band usually performs Dixieland jazz from 10:30am to 10pm daily (the schedule changes during inclement weather and slow periods). On top of the great music, you'll love the price—it's free! If you don't feel like buying anything at the sidewalk cafe, you can stand on the sidewalk or sit on a bench in the small adjacent park and listen all you want for nothing. The band does solicit tips, which is only fair.

Tickling the Ivories: Piano Bars

According to Billy Joel, if you're in the mood for a melody, the piano man will have you feeling all right. Well, the people in New Orleans must be doing fine—piano bars are everywhere. The **Carousel Bar & Lounge** (214 Royal St., in the Montelone Hotel, ☎ **504/523-3341**) features great piano music Tuesdays through Saturdays, but the real attraction is the bar itself. Aptly named, the bar is a real working, revolving carousel. Beware: You might get dizzy even before you have anything to drink. At the **Bombay Club** (830 Conti St., ☎**504/586-0972**), you can enjoy live piano jazz Wednesdays through Saturdays while sipping one of its world-famous martinis.

Pump That Accordion, Jack! Cajun & Zydeco Music

Like jazz, Cajun and zydeco music are expressions of southern Louisiana's cultural history. Born of Acadian folk music and French ballads, the music was eventually spiced with a mixture of American Indian, Scotch-Irish,

Spanish, Afro-Caribbean, and German influences that reflected the popula-tion of the bayous and swamps around Lafayette. The accordion is the com-mon bond between these two native Louisiana music styles, though Cajun music largely remains rural and rustic, with button accordions and scratchy fiddles playing lively two-steps and sorrowful waltzes and zydeco has evolved into a more urbanized sound.

Traditionally played on accordions, violins, triangles, and rub-boards (or frottoir), **Cajun dance music** is upbeat and somewhat reminiscent of blue-grass and country music, though its elaborate accordion styles set it apart. Many Cajun songs are still sung in the Acadian dialect of French or with such thick accents that you probably won't understand much of it, but that doesn't matter—it's really music to dance to, anyway. You can listen with your feet.

Zydeco developed over 150 years by mixing Acadian sounds and the African, blues, and R&B traditions favored by rural black Creoles. It took the Cajuns' melodious music and sped it up, emphasized syncopation, added Afro-Caribbean folk music and rhythms, and wrapped it in funkier rhythms that kicked it into hyper-energetic, overpowering, high-stepping overdrive. Older generation zydeco performers relied only on the accordion, drums, and trademark rub board to produce their sound, but recent decades have seen electric guitars and basses, saxophones, and trumpets getting into the mix to create a hard-rockin', foot-stompin' sound.

If you're looking for true Cajun culture and music, you aren't going to find it in New Orleans. The real McCoy remains where it originated, out in the coun-try, so unless one of the better Cajun bands (BeauSoleil, Savoy-Doucet Band, Steve Riley and the Mamou Playboys, or Balfa Toujours) are in town at one of the following clubs, what you'll most likely hear is a watered-down version. At **Michaul's on St. Charles** (840 St. Charles Ave., ☎ **504/522-5517**) and **Mulate's** (201 Julia St., ☎ **504/522-1492**) you're going to get the Cajun-for-the-tourists experience. Mulate's at least is a branch of an authentic (though these days creeping to the tourist-trade side of things) venue in Cajun country. Expect "atmos-pheric" wood floors and walls, kitsch, and crawfish galore. However, there's a chance on any night that you might hear a really good band that's in town for a day. If nothing else, both of these are fine places to learn to Cajun dance (Michaul's offers free lessons).

Bet You Didn't Know

There's only one right way to make the tee fer (pro-nounced *tea*-fare) or *bas-trinque*, which is the musical triangle that provides the rhythm in most traditional Cajun music. You've got to get your hands on a tine from an old horse–drawn hay rake, and then bend it till it's triangle-shaped, with its ends curled into the tradi-tional fiddlehead curl.

As for zydeco, who'd ever guess that a bowling alley would be one of the hottest places in town to hear the stuff? But in New Orleans, anything goes, and on Wednesdays and Thursdays at **Mid-City Lanes Rock 'N' Bowl** (4133 S. Carrollton Ave., ☎504/482-3133), it's zydeco party time! Over the past few years, almost every zydeco artist of note has played at one of the weekly shows. A couple times a year this place has zydeco wars, where groups such as Beau Jaques and Nathan and the Zydeco Cha Cha's duke it out for the title of Zydeco King. Bowl if you must, but don't expect to lower your score: The lanes are warped. The **Maple Leaf Bar** (reviewed in the following section) is sometimes another good option for Cajun and zydeco tunes, though it also books R&B, blues, and brass band acts. Call ahead to find out what's playing.

A Great Big Musical Stew

If you've eaten any jambalaya in town, you know that it can be made with just about any mix of ingredients, usually cooked together in one pot. The same rule applies pretty well to a lot of the bars and music clubs in New Orleans: They're a spicy stew, where the kind of music you'll hear one night probably won't be anything but a distant cousin to the kind you'll hear the next night. The following sections review some of the choice spots—just remember to call ahead. Or be adventurous and just show up; I'm sure you'll enjoy yourself.

In the French Quarter

I almost hate to send people to **House of Blues** (225 Decatur, ☎ 504/529-2583). It's a prefab place that's stolen acts away from the venerable (and immeasurably more authentic) **Tipitina's,** but I've gotta admit that the walls cluttered with primitive art and folk art are endlessly fascinating, and most of the big acts who come through town do play here.

I'm going to heave another sigh here and send you to **Jimmy Buffet's Margaritaville** (1104 Decatur, ☎ 504/592-2565). This place used to be the Storyville jazz club (though this is *not* where Storyville used to be), but now it's a mecca for Buffet's Parrothead fans. Still, you can find decent blues and R&B acts here, and yes, Mr. Buffet sometimes plays here, when he's in town.

In the Frenchman Area

As you cross Esplanade and edge from the Quarter into Faubourg Marigny, there are several clubs all bunched up together in a little sliver of an area that's usually referred to as the Frenchman area. Each of these clubs is probably dingier than the last—no House of Blues hyper-decorating here!—and bouncing from one to another, or just standing on the street outside listening to whoever's playing inside, is an increasingly popular New Orleans pastime.

Check Point Charlie (501 Esplanade, ☎ 504/947-0979) comes up first on the corner of Esplanade and Decatur. It plays mostly rock and R&B and feels like something between a biker bar and a college hangout. As a bonus, you can do your laundry here while you listen to a band.

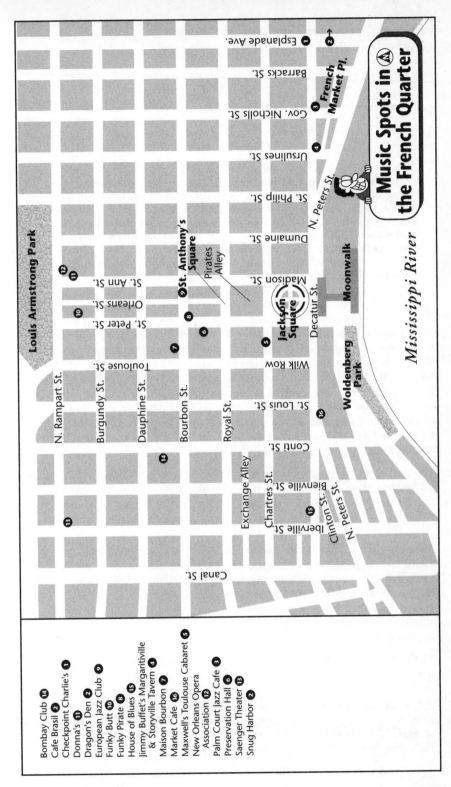

Music Spots in the French Quarter Ⓐ

Mississippi River

Louis Armstrong Park

French Market Pl.

Esplanade Ave. ❶
❷ →
Barracks St.
Gov. Nicholis St. ❸
❹
Ursulines St.
St. Philip St.
N. Peters St.
Dumaine St.
Moonwalk
❾ St. Anthony's Square
Pirates Alley
Madison St.
Decatur St.
❺ Jackson Square
❽
❻
Wilk Row
❼
St. Ann St. ❷ ❶
Orleans St. ❿
St. Peter St.
Toulouse St.
N. Rampart St.
Burgundy St.
Dauphine St.
Bourbon St.
Royal St.
St. Louis St.
❶❻ Woldenberg Park
Conti St.
❶❹
Exchange Alley
Chartres St.
Bienville St.
Iberville St.
❶❺
Clinton St.
N. Peters St.
❶❸
Canal St.

Bombay Club ❶❹
Cafe Brasil ❷
Checkpoint Charlie's ❶
Donna's ❶❶
Dragon's Den ❷
European Jazz Club ❾
Funky Butt ❿
Funky Pirate ❽
House of Blues ❶❺
Jimmy Buffet's Margaritiville
  & Storyville Tavern ❹
Maison Bourbon ❼
Market Cafe ❶❻
Maxwell's Toulouse Cabaret ❺
New Orleans Opera
  Association ❶❷
Palm Court Jazz Cafe ❸
Preservation Hall ❻
Saenger Theater ❶❸
Snug Harbor ❷

Neville Alert

On any given night, somewhere in New Orleans, a Neville is playing (or so it seems). Most often, you can find them at Tipitina's, House of Blues, Snug Harbor, and Margaritaville. The singing Neville Brothers—Charles, Art, Cyrille, and the angel-voiced Aaron (whose rendition of "Ave Maria" in the Gospel tent at Jazz Fest is not to be missed)—have been a New Orleans institution since the mid-'50s, and lately they've been reproducing. Charmine Neville does a soul act like a voodoo queen, and Ivan Neville has played with Keith Richards and also has his own group, Diversity. Makes you wonder if someday *everybody* in New Orleans will be a Neville.

The **Dragon's Den** (435 Esplanade, ☎ **504/949-1750**) is a cozy, vaguely mysterious, Oriental-type place that gets mighty hot and sweaty when the ReBirth Brass Band is playing. **Dream Palace** (534 Frenchmen, ☎ **504/945-2040**) doesn't look like much, but the music's range (anything from Latin to rock and New Orleans' own Continental Drifters) makes up for it. **Snug Harbor** (626 Frenchmen St., ☎ **504/897-1825**) is a sit-down performance space filled with tables. The order of the day is usually R&B, and Charmine Neville plays here quite often. It is one of New Orleans' best known and best jazz rooms.

The center of the Frenchman scene is **Cafe Brasil** (2100 Chartres St., ☎ **504/947-9386**), where Romanian poet-turned-New-Orleans-resident Andrei Codrescu gets his coffee during the day. Cafe Brasil salutes the diversity of New Orleans music at night with a mix of Latin/Caribbean, jazz, and the blues.

Music's Just a Taxi Ride Away

There's some great music venues outside the Quarter and the Faubourg Marigny—it's best to take a taxi to them. The original **Tipitina's** (501 Napoleon St., ☎ **504/897-3943**) is a sweaty and joyous, two-story club that opened as a showcase for Professor Longhair. Until the House of Blues came along, all the best touring acts played here. If you get lucky and see the Neville Brothers here, you'll never stop talking about it.

Tip's Big Room (No. 2) (310 Howard St., ☎ **504-568-1702**) is the new space owned by Tip's and boy does it ever live up to its name. It's a former disco and unfortunately that means it's pretty grim—a glitzy upscale joint that seems antithetical to the real Tip's gestalt. Tip's can expect some serious competition for touring acts now that **Howlin' Wolf** (828 S. Peters, ☎ **504/523-2551**) has completed a massive remodeling job that's made it Tip's rival in size. This is a place for the indie/alternative crowd.

Carrollton Station (8140 Willow, ☎ **504/865-9190**) is a long, narrow space, so if you get stuck in back, you won't see much of what's on stage. That position puts you closer to the bar, though. You can catch both classic New Orleans acts and established or up-and-coming local and touring blues acts.

The Lion's Den (2655 Gravier St., ☎ **504/821-3745**), with serious R&B leanings, is especially worth a visit if owner Irma Thomas, one of the great R&B/soul singers around, is playing. She often is and occasionally even cooks up some specialties in the kitchen.

Then there's the **Maple Leaf** (8316 Oak, ☎ **504/866-5323**), what a New Orleans club is all about. Small, with a hammered tin ceiling, patio out back, and a good bar, it's always crowded, so the spillover crowd is often standing in the aisles or dancing outside on the street. Outside is sometimes even more fun than inside: The stage is conveniently set in the front, with only a window separating you from the performers' butts. If BeauSoliel or the ReBirth Brass Band is playing, go and dance till you drop.

Dancing the Night Away

Basically, if you want to dance, just walk down the street. There are no places specifically for dancing, but there's dancing almost every place there's music—and there's music practically everywhere. The best places—the Maple Leaf, the original Tip's, the Mermaid Lounge, the clubs grouped in the Frenchman—often see serious dancers skipping the club itself and hitting the sidewalk instead. You should see the two-stepping that goes on in the street outside the Maple Leaf when BeauSoliel is playing. Mid-City Lanes is where serious local dancers go, but space can be a problem if it's a popular night. For Cajun dancing, hit Michaul's on St. Charles or Mulate's on most nights. Dancing is intense for the brass bands at Donna's and anywhere the ReBirth or New Birth Brass Bands are playing, and you should see the combination folk dancing/Deadhead–like hippie twirling that erupts when the New Orleans Klezmer All-Stars are playing. Find these bands, and you can work off any meal.

The **Mermaid Lounge** (1100 Constance Ave. in the Central Business District, ☎ **504/524-4747**) books everything from the Hackberry Ramblers (a Cajun band that's been playing together for nearly 70 years!) to hard-core grunge on any given night. It's all worth it to see the pierced, blue-haired kids come to dance to the Cajun bands. The place has one of the coolest vibes in town, but a series of one-way streets and a cul-de-sac location under an interstate ramp make it very hard to find. Everyone *knows* it's the hardest club in town to find, though, so all the cabbies should have its location down.

New Orleans A to Z: Facts at Your Fingertips

AAA   Road service ☎ 800/222-4357; other services ☎ 800/926-4222.

American Express   The American Express Office (☎ **504/586-8201**) is located at 201 St. Charles St. in the Central Business District. It's open Monday to Friday from 9am to 5pm. For cardholder services, call ☎ **800/528-4800;** for lost or stolen traveler's checks, call ☎ 800/221-7282.

Baby-sitters   Ask your hotel or call the following agencies for sitting services: **Accents on Children's Arrangements,** ☎ **504/524-1227; Dependable Kid Care,** ☎ **504/486-4001; Kinder Friend,** ☎ **504/469-5059.**

Camera repair   Try **AAA Camera Repair,** 1631 St. Charles (☎ **504/561-5822**).

Doctors   If you're in need of a doctor, call one of the following: **Orleans Parish Medical Society,** ☎ **504/523-2474; Tulane Medical Clinic,** ☎ **504/588-5800; Children's Hospital,** ☎ **504/899-9511.**

Emergencies   For fire, police, and ambulance call ☎ **911.** For the **Poison Control Center,** call ☎ **800/256-9822.**

Hospitals   Should you become ill during your visit, most major hospitals have in-house staff doctors on call 24 hours a day. If there's not a doctor available in your hotel or guest house, call or go to the emergency room at **Ochsner Medical Institutions,** 1516 Jefferson Highway (☎ **504/842-3460**), or the **Tulane University Medical Center,** 1415 Tulane Ave. (☎ **504/588-5800**).

Hotlines   **Sex Crimes Investigation** (Rape) is ☎ **504/826-1523; YWCA Rape Crisis** is ☎ **504/483-8888; Travelers Aid Society** is ☎ **504/525-8726; Gamblers Anonymous** is ☎ **504/836-4543; Narcotics Anonymous** is ☎ **504/899-6262; Alcoholics Anonymous** is ☎ **504/525-1178.**

Liquor laws   The legal drinking age in New Orleans is 21. You can buy liquor most anywhere 24 hours a day, 7 days a week, 365 days a year. All drinks carried on the street must be in plastic cups. Bars will often provide a plastic "to-go" cup, so you can transfer your drink as you leave.

Maps   You can obtain maps at any of the information centers listed throughout the book and at most hotels.

Newspapers and magazines   To find out what's going on around town, you might want to pick up a copy of the *Times-Picayune*. The *Gambit Weekly* is the city's free alternative paper and has a good mix of news and entertainment information. The paper conducts an annual "Best of New Orleans" readers' poll, and if you have access to the Internet, you can find the results at **www.gambit-no.com**. *OffBeat* is a monthly guide—probably the most extensive one available—to the city's evening entertainment, art galleries, and special events. You can find it in most hotels, though it's often hard to find toward the end of the month. *Where* magazine and *Arrive* magazine, also published monthly, are some other good resources for visitors.

Pharmacies   There's a Walgreen's with 24-hour prescription service two miles from the French Quarter at 3311 Canal St. The number for store information is ☎ **504/822-8070**. The number for prescriptions only is ☎ **504/ 822-8073**. I wouldn't travel by foot here in the middle of the night, and I'd be a little apprehensive even if I were in a car. Many of the hotels call the prescriptions in and have a taxi pick them up.

Police   For non-emergency situations, call ☎ **504/821-2222**.

Rest rooms   There are public rest rooms located at Jax Brewery Shopping Center, Riverwalk Shopping Center, One Canal Place Shopping Center, Washington Artillery Park, and any of the major hotels.

Safety   In general in New Orleans, you have to be careful everywhere, all the time. Always use caution when walking through an unlit area at night. Avoid the Iberville Housing Project located between Basin, N. Claiborne, Iberville, and St. Louis streets, just outside of the French Quarter; you should also avoid St. Louis Cemetery No. 2 near Claiborne on the lakeside of the Iberville Housing Project unless you're traveling with a large tour group. Also stay away from the area behind (lakeside and downtown of) Armstrong Park. Beware: The city looks deceptively safe, and neighborhoods change very quickly.

Taxes   Louisiana's sales tax is very confusing. In addition to the state and federal taxes, each parish may have additional taxes. To make things more confusing, some things like un-prepared food and some types of drugs are partially exempt, while prescriptions are totally exempt. In general, the total sales tax in New Orleans is 9%; it's 8.75% in Jefferson Parish.

Taxis   In most tourist areas, you can usually hail a taxi or get one at a taxi stand. If you can't find a taxi, call **United Cab** at ☎ **504/522-9771**. If you have any complaints or left something in a taxi, call the **Taxicab Bureau** at ☎ **504/565-6272**.

Time zone   New Orleans is on Central time.

Tourist information   The **Tourist Information Center** is located at 529 St. Ann St. (☎ **504/568-5661** or 504/566-5031).

Transit information   For information about streetcars and buses, call ☎ **504/248-3900**.

Toll-Free Numbers & Web Sites for Airlines, Car Rental Agencies, Hotel Chains & Cruise Ships

Airlines

Air Canada
☎ 800/776-3000
www.aircanada.ca

AirTran Airways
☎ 800/247-8726

America West Airlines
☎ 800/235-9292
www.americawest.com

American Airlines
☎ 800/433-7300
www.americanair.com

Canadian Arlines International
☎ 800/426-7000
www.cdair.ca

Carnival Airlines
☎ 800/824-7386
www.carnivalair.com

Continental Airlines
☎ 800/525-0280
www.flycontinental.com

Delta Airlines
☎ 800/221-1212
www.delta-air.com

Kiwi International Airlines
☎ 800/538-5494
www.jetkiwi.com

Midway Airlines
☎ 800/446-4392

Northwest Airlines
☎ 800/225-2525
www.nwa.com

Southwest Airlines
☎ 800/435-9792
www.iflyswa.com

Tower Air
☎ 800/34-TOWER (800/348-6937)
www.towerair.com

Trans World Airlines (TWA)
☎ 800/221-2000
www.twa.com

United Airlines
☎ 800/241-6522
www.ual.com

USAirways
☎ 800/428-4322
www.usair.com

Car Rental Agencies

Advantage
☎ 800/777-5500
www.arac.com

Alamo
☎ 800/327-9633
www.goalamo.com

Avis
☎ 800/331-1212 in the continental
United States
☎ 800/TRY-AVIS in Canada
www.avis.com

Budget
☎ 800/527-0700
www.budgetrentacar.com

Dollar
☎ 800/800-4000

Enterprise
☎ 800/325-8007

Hertz
☎ 800/654-3131
www.hertz.com

National
☎ 800/CAR-RENT
www.nationalcar.com

Payless
☎ 800/PAYLESS
www.paylesscar.com

Rent-A-Wreck
☎ 800/535-1391
www.rent-a-wreck.com

Thrifty
☎ 800/367-2277
www.thrifty.com

Value
☎ 800/327-2501
www.go-value.com

Major Hotel & Motel Chains

Best Western International
☎ 800/528-1234
www.bestwestern.com

Clarion Hotels
☎ 800/CLARION
www.hotelchoice.com/cgi-bin/
res/webres?clarion.html

Comfort Inns
☎ 800/228-5150
www.hotelchoice.com/cgi-bin/
res/webres?comfort.html

Crowne Plaza Hotels
☎ 800/227-6963
www.crowneplaza.com

Days Inn
☎ 800/325-2525
www.daysinn.com

Doubletree Hotels
☎ 800/222-TREE
www.doubletreehotels.com

Econo Lodges
☎ 800/55-ECONO
www.hotelchoice.com/cgi-bin/
res/webres?econo.html

Fairfield Inn by Marriott
☎ 800/228-2800
www.fairfieldinn.com

Hampton Inn
☎ 800/HAMPTON
www.hampton-inn.com

Hilton Hotels
☎ 800/HILTONS
www.hilton.com

Holiday Inn
☎ 800/HOLIDAY
www.holiday-inn.com

Howard Johnson's
☎ 800/654-2000
www.hojo.com/hojo.html

Hyatt Hotels and Resorts
☎ 800/228-9000
www.hyatt.com

ITT Sheraton
☎ 800/325-3535
www.sheraton.com

Marriott Hotels
☎ 800/228-9290
www.marriott.com

Motel 6
☎ 800/4-MOTEL6 (800/466-8536)

Quality Inns
☎ 800/228-5151
www.hotelchoice.com/cgi-bin/
res/webres?quality.html

Radisson Hotels International
☎ 800/333-3333
www.radisson.com

Ramada Inns
☎ 800/2-RAMADA
www.ramada.com

Red Roof Inns
☎ 800/843-7663
www.redroof.com

Residence Inn by Marriott
☎ 800/331-3131
www.residenceinn.com

Rodeway Inns
☎ 800/228-2000
www.hotelchoice.com/cgi-bin/
res/webres?rodeway.html

Super 8 Motels
☎ 800/800-8000
www.super8motels.com

Travelodge
☎ 800/255-3050

Cruise Lines Sailing from New Orleans

Carnival Cruise Lines
☎ 800/438-6744
www.carnival.com

Commodore Cruise Line
☎ 800/237-5361
www.commodorecruises.com

Crystal Cruises
☎ 800/446-6620

Index

oyster bars, 166
price categories,
    132-35, 137-39
romantic, 143
sales tax and tips, 133
twenty-four-hour, 150
vegetarian, 166-67
with live entertain-
    ment, 155
Rex (King of Carnival), 45
Rex krewe, 48
Rice, Anne, 206-7, 209-11
Riddle, Macon, 177
Riverboat cruises, 177, 238
Riverside, meaning of, 114
Rivertown, 196
Rivertown Saints Hall of
  Fame Museum (Kenner),
  196
Riverwalk Marketplace,
  225
Rodrigue, George, 226
Royal Street, 207, 259
    shopping, 225

S
Safety, 277
    Mardi Gras and, 54
St. Alphonsus Church, 209
St. Ann Street, 257
St. Bernard Parish, Mardi
  Gras parades in, 50-53
St. Charles Streetcar, 120,
  196, 239
St. Elizabeth's Orphanage,
  209, 211
St. Joseph's Day, 8, 59
St. Jude, International
  Shrine of, 200
St. Louis Cathedral, 200-1,
  236
St. Louis Cemetery No. 1,
  205-6, 241
St. Patrick's Day, 8, 59
Sales tax, 223
Save Our Cemeteries, 176
Scams, 20
Science Center, Freeport
  McMoRan Daily Living
  (Kenner), 196

Seeing-eye dogs, traveling
  with, 13
Senior citizens
    accommodations, 90
    travel tips, 11-12
Shopping, 217-32
    bookstores, 227
    budgeting, 21
    costumes and masks,
      228
    department stores,
      220
    fashions, 230
    for children, 231-32
    French Market, 223
    Magazine Street, 224
    music, 230
    New Orleans Centre,
      225
    pipes and tobacco,
      230-31
    Riverwalk Marketplace,
      225
Sights and attractions, 21,
  178-98
    Anne Rice–related,
      206-7, 209-11
    Cajun country, 211-14
    for children, 182, 184
    free (or practically
      free), 191
    historical, 199-201
    sports, 201
Softball center, at City
  Park, 188
Soniat House, 103-4
Southern Decadence
  Festival, 9, 60
Souvenirs, 25, 221, 223
Special events. *See* Festivals
  and special events
Spring Fiesta, 8, 60
Stolen wallet or purse, 19
Storyland, 188, 246
Streetcars, 20, 24, 120-21,
  238
    St. Charles Streetcar,
      120, 196, 239
Sugar Bowl, 59
Superdome, 201
Swamp tours, 176-77

T
Taxis, 123-24, 277
    for disabled travelers,
      13
    from Union Passenger
      Terminal, 36
    to/from airport,
      110-11
Tennessee Williams
  Literary Festival, 8, 60
Tennis courts, City Park,
  188
Tipping, 23, 133
Tobacco and pipes, shop-
  ping for, 230-31
Tolliver, William, 226
Toole, John Kennedy,
  206
Tourist information, 2-3,
  119
Tours. *See also* Guided
  tours
    Anne Rice–related,
      210-11
    carriage, 174-75
    for disabled travelers,
      13
    for gays and lesbians,
      14
    for senior citizens,
      12
    package, 24, 29-32
    riverboat cruises,
      177
    St. Charles Streetcar,
      239
    walking, 173-74
Toys, 231-32
Train travel, 36
Transportation, 120-25
    VisiTour pass, 20, 45
Travel insurance, 66-67
Traveler's checks, 15-16,
  18-19

U–V
Union Passenger Terminal,
  36
United Cab, 111, 124

285